JAPANESE COOKING

Susan Fuller Slack

Acknowledgements:

I would like to thank the following individuals and companies who have helped make this book possible: Richard and Jan Kilpatrick, Irvine, California; Lily Hataye, Orange, California; J. Denise Wilson, R.D., Rochester, Minnesota; William Shurtleff, Lafayette, California; Ria Kendal, translator, Dana Point, California; Betty Boza, Home Economist, *Sentinal Star*, Orlando, Florida; Hinode Tofu Co., Los Angeles, California; Miyako Oriental Foods, Inc., Baldwin Park, California; Mitsuo Someya, Manager, International Trade Dept., Kikkoman Corporation, Tokyo, Japan; Takayasu Akiyama, Manager, Tadashi Momotori, Executive Chef, and Tomonori Miura, Fujiya Hotel, Miyanoshita, Japan; Aya Yoshikawa, Nagoya, Japan; Yukari Oya, Tokyo, Japan; Terumi Oya, translator, Udawara, Japan; Nobuo Komatsu, Akabori Nutrition College, Tokyo, Japan; Hideo Ebime, Central Miso Research Institute, Tokyo, Japan.

Haiku poems reprinted by permission from *Japanese Haiku* (copyright 1955-56) and *Haiku Harvest*, translated by Peter Beilenson (copyright 1962), both published by The Peter Pauper Press, Inc.

The author also wishes to thank the following companies for providing equipment and accessories for use in the photography: Ichi Corporation (Ichi grill); Iwatani & Company (Casset Feu grill and burner unit); Mutual Trading Company Inc. (Saladacco vegetable slicer); The Learning Tree (tofu-making kit); and Warren Imports, Laguna Beach (antique lacquer-ware).

ANOTHER BEST-SELLING VOLUME FROM HPBooks®
Publisher: Rick Bailey; Editorial Director: Elaine R. Woodard; Editor: Veronica Durie
Art Director: Don Burton; Book Design: Paul Fitzgerald
Typography: Cindy Coatsworth, Michelle Carter; Director of Manufacturing: Anthony B. Narducci
Food Stylists: Carol Flood Peterson, Susan Slack; Assistants: Susan Draudt, Lily Hataye
Photography: George de Gennaro Studios

NOTICE: The information contained in this book is true and complete to the best of our knowledge. All recommendations are made without any guarantees on the part of the author or HPBooks. The author and publisher disclaim all liability in connection with the use of this information.

Published by HPBooks, Inc.
P.O. Box 5367, Tucson, AZ 85703   602/888-2150
ISBN 0-89586-327-8
Library of Congress Catalog Card Number 85-80113
© 1985 HPBooks, Inc.   Printed in the U.S.A.
1st Printing

Cover Photo: Top left corner: Pinwheel-Shrimp Consommé, page 46. Shown in a shokado bento box for a cherry-blossom-viewing party (hanami): Scalloped Lotus-Root Flowers, page 32; Blanched edible pea pods; Scored Shiitake Mushrooms, page 29; Simmered Carrot Flowers, page 92; Simmered Devil's-Tongue-Jelly Braids, page 93, Box-Lunch Rice, page 142, decorated with sweet chestnuts and a pickled ginger shoot, Lacy Batter-Fried Foods, page 116, using Fan-Shaped Shrimp, page 122, and Japanese-Eggplant Fans, page 32; and a Sashimi Rose, page 53.

Contents

Susan Slack

Before writing this book, Susan Slack lived in Japan for a total of four years during which time she fell in love with the beautiful country and its courteous people. By traveling extensively all over Japan, Susan has gained a tremendous amount of knowledge about Japanese culture and cooking in particular. While in Japan, Susan studied with many famous chefs and has since taught classes on Japanese and Chinese cooking in Japan itself. As a military wife, Susan has lived all over the United States and is well-known in food circles for her expertise in French and Asian cooking, food-processor techniques, food sculpting and children's cooking. She has written many articles for magazines and newspapers and made numerous media appearances with demonstrations in her areas of interest. Until the next move, Susan, son Todd and her husband Richard, a lieutenant colonel in the Marine Corps, are based in Rhode Island. In between all her other family- and food-related projects, Susan runs a successful cooking school and food-consulting business called *Culinary Bouquets* from her home.

Japan — An Oriental Wonderland

My first visit to Japan filled me with tremendous excitement. Never before had I encountered such an incredible array of foodstuffs like the ones I was discovering in the food markets, department-store food emporiums, restaurants and at the street festivals throughout Japan. On every street corner, vendors were selling mouthwatering snacks, like warm and tender sweet-bean-paste-filled pancakes and tasty mixed fried golden noodles. Small food carts appeared early in the evenings selling roasted sweet potatoes or chestnuts, boiled corn and savory fish stews. Tokyo's famous Tsukiji Central Market came to life at dawn when auctioneers began to sell off thousands of pounds of fresh fish, caught only hours before.

In the markets, I purchased flavorful miniature seasonal vegetables, baskets of tiny edible flowers, exquisite fruits wrapped separately in tissue with ribbons and attractive Western-style breads shaped like sea creatures and filled with sweet red-bean paste. Long counters were filled with dazzling displays of impeccably fresh fish and shellfish. Hand-crafted wooden tubs held mounds of fragrant miso (fermented soybean paste), colorful pickled vegetables, nutritious sea vegetables and even crisp rice crackers.

When I was a guest at a traditional Japanese inn in the seaside resort of Atami, close to a dozen small delicious dishes were served to each guest during dinner. Our serving maid kept the rice bowls and teacups filled while we feasted upon fresh chilled raw fish (sashimi), tempura and a steamed pork and rice dish. Dessert was fresh mandarin oranges picked from the trees around the inn.

Dinner another evening was at Petit Pois, a charming French restaurant overlooking the scenic Izu Peninsula. The owners, Mr. and Mrs. Oya, prepared the festive dish, steamed red beans and rice to celebrate my arrival.

On another occasion, high in the snowy mountains of Kyoto, I dined equally well in the more humble surroundings of a family-style public lodging (minshuku). The most memorable dish was an incredibly tasty chicken hot pot. Along with my companions, I cooked a succession of vegetables and some chicken in a communal pot of miso-based simmering broth. Fortunately, my friend, Aya Yoshikawa, helped me persuade the chef to share his secret recipe so now you too can cook and enjoy this dish with a group of friends.

During my time in Japan, I wanted to experience as many of the ancient customs as possible. At the country home of the Kaiede family in Gifu Prefecture, my son and I were lucky enough to take part in the ceremonial ritual (mochi-tsuki) of pounding cooked sweet glutinous rice to make dough for rice cakes (mochi). If you don't have a strong arm to pound the rice into dough, make my easy instant version, Sweet Glutinous-Rice Cakes, page 144. They are just as delicious and much easier to make.

The Japanese influence has given the Western world a fresh look at many familiar ingredients and introduced us to many healthful and delicious new ones. I have based this book solidly on Japanese tradition but the recipes have been developed with an awareness of changing trends and practicality for the Western kitchen. Within the framework of each recipe, feel free to experiment with the subtle seasonings and to reduce salt and sugar if health reasons dictate. Traditional Japanese foods, such as tofu, sea vegetables, fresh fish and low-salt miso, could certainly replace a portion of the high-calorie high-cholesterol foods which often make up most of our diet. We might also supplement our diets with more fresh seasonal fruits and vegetables, in the Japanese style.

A growing movement in the direction of lighter foods and better health has brought this age-old cuisine ever-increasing popularity. Time-honored tradition will still have its place in the Western kitchen, but the Japanese cook's healthful outlook and creative approach toward food preparation is a welcome and necessary change.

The simple elegance of Japanese cuisine sets it apart from other cuisines. The early teachings of Zen Buddhism instilled a deep respect for nature within the people, and encouraged them to make good use of the limited land and generous sea. Simply prepared foods presented within their season retain their natural textures and flavors. Appropriate seasonal garnishings further enhance foods. Through his classic haiku verse quoted below, the 17th century poet Basho gently hints to us that foods should be in harmony with the cycles of nature.

Under cherry trees
Soup, the salad,
Fish and all . . .
Seasoned with petals   *Basho*

A Brief Visit to Japan

The emphasis on fresh and natural food and presentation is apparent in all cooking throughout the four major islands of the Japanese archipelago. But partly due to mountainous terrain and other natural divisions, regional foods and cooking techniques are diversified.

The sparsely populated northern island of Hokkaido produces top-quality dairy products, delicious Sapporo ramen, and Hokkaido salmon which is famous throughout the country. Hearty stews and one-pot dishes are often served with the onset of the freezing winter winds.

The main island of Honshu boasts two main culinary areas. Tokyo lies in the eastern Kanto plains region and Osaka and Kyoto lie in the western Kansai plains region. It has been said that Tokyo is the embodiment of the new and modern Japan. It has some of the finest international restaurants in the world. One of the latest trends among these restaurants is the nouvelle Franco-Japanese cuisine and it promises to become an important and distinctive style of cooking in the future. By contrast, Kyoto, formerly the ancient capital Heian-Kyo, offers a glimpse of the elegance and refinement of the old Japan.

South beyond Shikoku, the smallest of the four major islands, is the island of Kyushu. This was Japan's first contact point with the West when Portuguese settlers arrived in the 16th century. Later, the Dutch also settled on this island in the Nagasaki area. These foreign influences brought to Japan the style of cooking known as *agemono* or deep-frying which you can enjoy in recipes, such as Lacy Batter-Fried Foods, page 116. Because of the strong Chinese influence throughout Kyushu, pork is very popular. This influence extends southward into the Ryukuan Islands. A style of cuisine has developed throughout this southern area known as *shippoku ryori,* a unique blend of Chinese and Japanese cooking. Mixed Fried Tofu & Vegetables, page 111, is an example of shippoku-style cuisine found on Okinawa, the largest island in the Ryukuans.

Korean foods, especially spicy meat dishes, are popular in the Kyushu area, because of the closeness of Korea. Flavorful Marinated Grilled Meat, page 81, has origins in both Japan and Korea. Some of the finest seafood and the best shiitake mushrooms come from Kyushu.

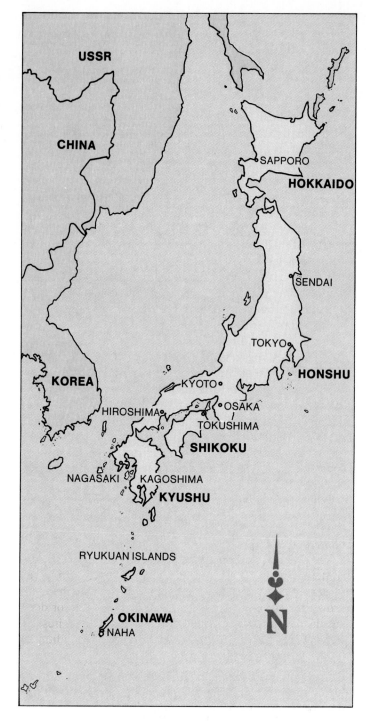

Japanese Festivals & Celebrations

Festivals and celebrations are an important part of Japanese life. Countless numbers of festivals are celebrated yearly in shrines and temples throughout the country. Originally, all these festivals centered around agricultural observances. Now these festive occasions remind people of their heritage and the traditions of their ancient culture.

The most important celebration is for New Year (Shogatsu). For weeks before, preparations are in full swing. Special New Year dishes (osechi ryori), often symbolic, are prepared ahead so the entire family can enjoy the festivities. The photograph on pages 106 and 107 shows a typically lavish New Year's feast. The handsome stacked lacquered box at the back of the display is called a *jubako*. A tempting assortment of food is layered in the box and served at room temperature.

Girls' Day (Hina Matsuri) on March 3rd is also known as the *Peach-Blossom Festival* because, to the Japanese, peach blossoms represent the virtues of gentleness, beauty and grace. During this special celebration of womanhood, beautiful highly valued ceremonial dolls are displayed on specially constructed shelves. On the top shelf, a pair of dolls representing the Imperial couple holds court. The dolls are greatly admired by friends at special tea parties. I attended my first Girls' Day at the home of Yukari Oya in Odawara. We admired the splendid doll collection belonging to Yukari and her sister Terumi, then enjoyed tea-party foods, including cups of fragrant sweet rice saké and exquisitely formed cherry-blossom rice cakes.

The Japanese celebrate Boys' Day (Tango No Sekku), sometimes called Children's Day, on May 5th with hopes of good health for their sons and prayers that they will grow up to be strong and courageous men. Warrior dolls are displayed at home and colorful carp-shaped kites are flown from poles and rooftops. One of the traditional foods is steamed sweet glutinous rice, stuffed with various fillings and formed into cone shapes, then wrapped in bamboo or oak leaves. The boys you know and their friends would probably prefer to munch on my Sweet Peanut Rice Cakes, page 162. Boys' Day falls during a time known in Japan as *Golden Week* when both the Emperor's birthday and Constitution Day are celebrated.

The Japanese believe that the full moon of August is of such great beauty that it deserves its own celebration. Once a year, people gather, often in large groups, for moon-viewing parties (tsukumi) on hilltops, in parks or at other moon-viewing sites. Alternatively, for a moon-viewing in a traditional Japanese home, the paper-covered sliding doors are opened wide to the outside so observers can gaze upon the magnificence of the rising full moon. A special supper, such as the one shown on page 121, is served during which many toasts of saké are made. Frequently, haiku poetry is created in honor of the spectacular full moon.

For the children's celebration called *Shichi Go San* on November 15th, parents dress children aged seven, five and three in their finest traditional clothing. Then the children are taken to the shrines to pray for good health, happiness and future success.

Throughout Japan, there are many charming regional festivals less well-known than the ones mentioned above. In all these events, food plays an important part. Whatever the occasion, vendors are on the street corners selling everything from grilled meat and dumplings to sushi and rice cakes.

Eating out in Japan

Specialty restaurants in Japan are named after the type of food they serve, combined with the suffix *ya* which means *shop*. Popular specialty restaurants include the *Tempura-ya, Soba-ya, Sushi-ya, Okonomiyaki-ya* and the *Yakitori-ya*. The *Robatayaki-ya* specializes in grilled foods and resembles a country farm house with a hearthside grill.

The term *o'bento* covers a large variety of box lunches served daily throughout Japan. They are prepared in the early morning hours in grocery stores and food shops, to be sold to hungry customers for their lunch. Housewives prepare bento lunches in their homes and set up small roadside stands to sell their wares. The bento lunch is based upon a large serving of rice accompanied by a protein food, vegetable dishes, perhaps a piece of egg omelet and pickles. *Eki-bento* are sold at train stations throughout Japan. Passengers can lean from train windows to purchase eki-bento for lunch or snacks. Bento vendors also sweep up and down aisles of trains during station stops.

Food carts (yatai mise) are part of the nostalgic traditions of Japan's street life. The carts appear early in the evening selling their specialties, such as roasted sweet potatoes, little fish-shaped pancakes filled with bean paste (tai yaki), boiled corn, skewered fish stew (oden) and meat and vegetable pancakes (okonomiyaki).

Kissaten are the enormously popular small shops where people can relax, enjoy snacks and drink coffee and other refreshing beverages. These coffee shops play an important role in Japanese life by providing a meeting place where people can go to read, listen to music and visit with friends. Japanese-style kissaten serve green tea and traditional sweets, such as ice cream and bean paste sundaes, rice crackers, fruit and custards.

Beer halls and beer gardens are also very popular places for the Japanese to meet and enjoy good company along with some eating and drinking. Over the years, the Japanese have become master beer makers and now consumption of their mellow-tasting brew far exceeds that of saké.

Glossary of Japanese Ingredients

Shop for these items in Oriental or gourmet grocery stores and health-food stores.

Agar-agar (kanten): Freeze-dried gelatin made from a blend of several red sea algae. Comes in stick form and in flakes. See page 170 for more information.

Amazu shoga: Thinly sliced or shredded, young, pickled, pink ginger. Refrigerate in its vinegar marinade in an airtight container. Traditional accompaniment to sushi, known as *gari* by sushi chefs.

Aonoriko: Nutty-tasting, dried, crushed nori (laver). Use as a seasoning for rice, noodles and other foods. Store at room temperature away from moisture.

Ao togarashi: Small sweet green peppers resembling hot green peppers in appearance. Bell-pepper strips can be substituted. *Togarashi* are small, dried, hot, red peppers; use whole or ground as a seasoning.

Arame: See Hijiki, opposite.

Azuke: Small dried red beans, high in protein and vitamins B-1 and B-2. Served steamed with sweet rice for special occasions. Also pureed into a paste called *an*, a popular sweet filling for traditional sweets. Sweetened red-bean paste can be made at home or purchased in cans.

Beni shoga: Peeled gingerroot knobs, dyed red and pickled in vinegar; also available shredded or sliced. Refrigerate in its vinegar marinade in an airtight container.

Burdock root (gobo): Long thin roots of burdock plant. Rich in minerals, burdock adds crunchiness and a sweet subtle flavor to foods. Wrap burdock root in damp newspaper or paper towels, then in plastic and refrigerate until needed. Before using, rinse and scrub off brown earthy covering. If desired, you can scrape root lightly or thinly peel it with a vegetable peeler. Immerse cut pieces in vinegar water to help prevent discoloration. If your skin becomes sensitive while scraping burdock root, it may be helpful to wear rubber gloves.

Chikuwa: Mild white-fish paste bound by a starch, shaped on metal rods, then steamed and grilled. Rolls can be stuffed with a number of ingredients for further cooking. Add to salads, soups and noodle dishes or serve plain with soy sauce and prepared Japanese horseradish.

Cloud ear or tree ear mushrooms (kikurage): Dried mushrooms, highly regarded for their chewy texture after rehydration. Soak in hot water 30 minutes. Rinse well; trim off tough thick parts. Small mushrooms are the most desirable and expand to many times their dried size after soaking.

Cornstarch: An excellent substitute for traditional kuzu starch and potato starch thickeners used in Japan. Cornstarch produces satiny-smooth clear sauces. In marinades, it helps to keep meat moist. In deep-frying, it helps to seal in natural juices of foods. To dissolve cornstarch in a mixture, stir thoroughly over medium-high heat 1 full minute after it comes to a boil. This removes the raw starch taste and fully expands the starch molecules for maximum thickening. It also helps to prevent weeping. Too much acid, fat or sugar can interfere with the thickening capabilities of cornstarch. Always stir a cornstarch mixture before cooking.

Cucumber, European: Ten- to twelve-inch-long cucumber, identical in taste to regular cucumber.

Cucumber, Japanese: Short, thin seedless cucumber.

Daikon radish: Sweet-tasting, juicy, giant, white radish. Some varieties are long and thin; others are as fat and round as a football. Peel daikon and slice for pickling, cut into chunks for stewing or grate in small portions for use as a condiment. Stems and leaves are rich in vitamin C and are excellent in pickles and braised dishes. Purchase firm unwrinkled fresh daikon and store in the refrigerator. *Kiriboshi daikon* are shredded naturally dried radish strips which are sweet and rich in flavor. They are delicious pickled, braised and sautéed. *Kaiwari daikon* are the crisp flavorful radish sprouts. Daikon is often used in sushi making and is thought to be an important aid in the digestion of fats.

Dashi: Japan's basic soup stock and seasoning ingredient is made from dried bonito (katsuo-bushi) and good-quality dried kelp (dashi konbu). Instant stock (dashi-no-moto) comes in granular form, premeasured powdered form, in liquid concentrate (memmi) and in tea-bag form. Dilute concentrate with water to taste or use a few drops in cooking for added flavor.

Denbu or soboro: Pink and green dried-fish flakes, sweetened with sugar.

Eggplant, Japanese: Small elongated eggplant, starting at finger-size.

Enokitake (enoki or snow puff mushrooms): Clusters of long thin white stems and tiny round caps characterize these delicate crunchy mushrooms. Before using, rinse mushrooms and trim off stem base. Use fresh mushrooms rather than canned whenever possible.

Ginger (shoga): Pungent-tasting gingerroot is indispensable to Japanese cuisine. Widely available mature ginger has a thin brown covering and should be moist and firm when purchased. Spring ginger has a thin pinkish skin which does not need to be peeled. Store gingerroot in a cool place in the kitchen, or in a paper bag wrapped in plastic in the refrigerator. Peeled gingerroot can be stored in a jar of dry sherry or vegetable oil. To obtain gingerroot juice, freeze old gingerroot until solid, then thaw to a spongy consistency and squeeze out juice. Frozen gingerroot is too fibrous and tough for most other uses. Fresh young ginger can be potted in sandy soil and grown in a sunny spot. Uncover roots where new shoots appear and break off a tender piece for use. Smash gingerroot slices before use to release maximum flavors. Do not substitute powdered ginger for the fresh.

Gingko nuts (ginnan): Mild-flavored white nuts. To shell, crack hard white shells with a nutcracker. Soak nuts in hot water to help loosen inner skins. Nuts turn light green when cooked. Use fresh nuts if possible.

Harusame: Also known as *spring rain,* these wiry noodle-like vegetable strands are made from mung beans and sometimes sweet potatoes. If shorter lengths are needed, snip with scissors before soaking. Pour boiling water over noodles and let stand about 30 minutes. Reduce soaking time if noodles are to be cooked any more. Strands will plump up, becoming jelly-like and translucent. Drain well before adding to salads or other dishes.

Hijiki: A brown sea grass, preboiled and wind dried after harvesting. Hijiki is high in calcium, low in calories and rich in iron, iodine, protein and vitamin A. Its sweet flavor is brought out by sautéing. Store in an airtight container in a dark dry place. Another variety of sea grass is called *arame.* It has a milder flavor than hijiki and can be used interchangeably.

Hiyamugi: Smooth, thin, white, wheat noodles similar to *somen,* below and page 12. Noodles are cooked, then usually eaten cold with a dipping sauce and condiments. Sometimes characterized by several pink and green noodles tucked into each package.

Horseradish, Japanese (wasabi): Spicy green root grows wild in Japan. Purchase in powdered and paste form. Reconstitute powder with water or saké. Use sparingly as a spicy hot seasoning for sashimi, sushi and other foods. Delicious pickled-horseradish condiment (wasabi-zuke) is made with saké lees, a saké-making byproduct; serve as an excellent accompaniment to sushi. Wasabi is known in sushi bars as *sabi* or *namida (tears).*

Kamaboko: Fish paste bound by starch, formed into loaves, steamed and sometimes grilled. Sizes can vary from 6 to 8 ounces. Some loaves are coated with pink, green or blue coloring. They are often shaped onto cypress boards before steaming. Slice loaves and serve with soy sauce and prepared Japanese horseradish. Or, add to stews, noodle dishes and soups. When different colors are added to the fish paste, it is called *narutomaki.* When

Japanese Ingredients

1	Dried Chinese noodles (chukamen)
2	White wheat noodles (somen)
3	Fresh yaki soba noodles
4	Fresh white wheat noodles (udon)
5	Flat white wheat noodles (kishimen)
6	Thin white wheat noodles (hiyamugi)
7	Buckwheat noodles (soba)
8	Plum-flavored wheat noodles
9	Bean-thread noodles
10	Sweet glutinous-rice flour
11	Instant sea-vegetable and fish stock
12	Granular rice koji starter
13	Dried kelp
14	Azuke beans
15	Panko bread crumbs
16	Dried-gourd strips
17	Dried shredded daikon radish
18	Dried tree ear mushrooms
19	Dried shiitake mushrooms
20	Agar-agar
21	Nori sheets
22	Shredded nori
23	Hijiki
24	Shredded dried kelp
25	Powdered seaweed
26	Dry-roasted white sesame seeds
27	Dry-roasted black sesame seeds
28	Thin, pale-green, dried-kelp strip (tororo)
29	Dried-bonito shavings
30	Dried-bonito sheets
31	Wheat gluten

sliced, the pieces are swirled with colors, such as pink and white, creating a pinwheel effect. Use like kamaboko.

Kampyo: White sun-dried strips of calabash or bottle gourd. Soften fibers in salted water 15 minutes, rinse and simmer in a seasoned liquid. A delicious edible string for decoratively tying foods.

Katsuo-bushi: Dried bonito fillet; a primary ingredient for making sea-vegetable and fish stock. Fresh bonito fillets are boiled, smoked and sun-dried into hard pieces. For the best flavor, fillets are cut into shavings as needed. Shavings can be purchased in packages. If possible, purchase from a reliable store so shavings will be no older than 1 year. Thread shavings are used to garnish foods. *Teimaki katsuo* are sheets of dried bonito. Pale pink sheets come in several flavors including plum. Use like nori in making sushi. Store shavings and sheets in an air-tight container.

Kelp (konbu): A brown algae of the genus *Laminaria*. It is a primary ingredient for making sea-vegetable and fish stock. Blades of kelp are harvested, sun-dried and folded into smooth sheets. Kelp is rich in minerals and vitamins, and contains glutamic acid, a natural amino-acid flavoring compound found in monosodium glutamate. Do not wash off the natural white-powder covering, instead wipe kelp lightly. Place a piece of kelp in the bottom of the pan when cooking vegetables and other foods to enhance flavors. Shredded kelp is excellent for pickling, braising, sautéing and deep-frying for snacks. *Tororo konbu* are delicate pale-green strips which are shaved from blades of dried kelp. A similar product is called *oboro;* use interchangeably as a flavoring for broth and in other dishes. Mild-flavored oboro can be used in place of nori in sushi or for wrapping rice balls.

Kinako (roasted-soybean powder): Nutty-tasting powder used for making traditional Japanese sweets. Powder is perishable; refrigerate several weeks or freeze several months.

Kinome: Delicate leaves from the prickly ash tree. Mint-

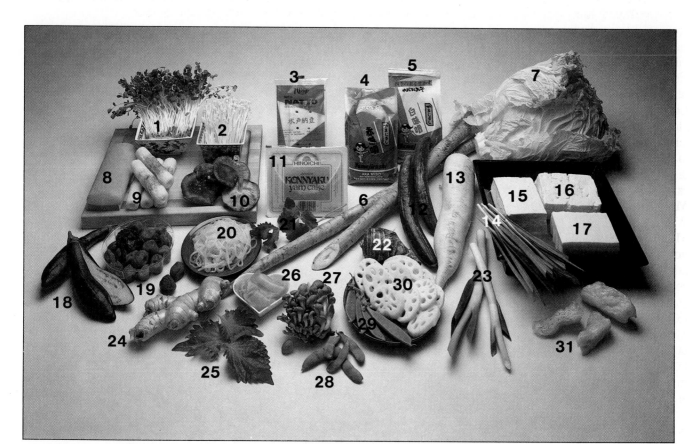

Japanese Ingredients

1	Radish sprouts	10	Fresh shiitake mushrooms	21	Trefoil leaves
2	Enokitake mushrooms	11	Devil's-tongue jelly	22	Taro root
3	Steamed fermented soybeans	12	Japanese cucumber	23	Long Japanese green onions
4	Red miso	13	Daikon radish	24	Fresh gingerroot
5	Yellow miso	14	Japanese chives	25	Shiso leaves
6	Burdock root	15	Regular tofu	26	Pickled pink-ginger slices
7	Napa cabbage	16	Firm Chinese-style tofu	27	Tree oyster mushrooms
8	Steamed fish loaf	17	Silken Japanese-style tofu	28	Fresh soybeans
9	Hollow fish rolls	18	Japanese eggplant	29	Edible pea pods
		19	Pickled plums	30	Sliced lotus root
		20	Devil's-tongue-jelly noodles	31	Fried tofu pouches

like peppery taste compliments sushi and sashimi. Although no taste substitute is readily available, parsley, watercress or fresh mint leaves can be used instead.

Kishimen: A flat wide wheat noodle similar to *udon,* page 13. Often added to one-pot dishes as final course.

Koji: Short-grain steamed rice innoculated with the mold *Aspergillus Oryzae.* Used for making sweet rice saké (amasaké), miso and koji pickles. Soybean koji is used to make saké.

Konnyaku or konjac: A jellied vegetable paste made from a tuber called *devil's tongue.* It comes in pure white form and in a dark unrefined form and is available in bars, slices and noodle-like strands (shirataki). Devil's-tongue jelly is high in water, low in calories and contains calcium. It has no taste of its own but readily absorbs flavors of other foods. Before using, blanch devil's-tongue jelly in boiling water to firm the texture and remove the smell of milk of lime used in processing.

Lobe leaf (wakame): This sun-dried sea vegetable of the genus *Undaria* is one of Japan's most delicious and sweet-tasting sea algaes. Highly nutritious with few calories, fresh packaged lobe leaf is salted in the preservation process. Remove salt by soaking in cool water. Dried lobe leaf must be plumped by soaking it in warm water 30 minutes. Cut away any tough parts. Cut into smaller pieces before use. Crumbled pieces of toasted lobe leaf can be sprinkled over soups and other foods.

Lotus root (renkon or hasu): Root of the aquatic lotus plant. When sliced and peeled, hollow canals running length of root form an attractive pattern. Soak cut pieces in a lemon or vinegar and water solution to prevent discoloration. It can be pickled, stir-fried, braised and candied.

Matsutake: Highly prized large autumn mushrooms. Wipe clean and sauté quickly for maximum enjoyment.

Mirin: Slightly syrupy rice wine made from sweet glutinous rice, a mold (koji) and a fiery distilled 90 proof liquor (shochu). Mirin is indispensable in Japanese cooking, adding sweetness to foods and an attractive glaze. It contributes to luster of sushi rice. If you cannot locate mirin, slightly increase amount of sugar in a recipe.

Miso: Fermented soybean paste; one of Japan's most important foods since antiquity. Miso resembles peanut butter in consistency. This Japanese wonder food is made in a large variety of colors and textures, each with its own aroma and flavor. The three basic categories of miso are: rice miso, soybean miso and barley miso. Miso is high in protein and B vitamins.

Miso came to Japan from China by way of Korea. For centuries, it was produced in Japanese farmhouses by hanging balls of mashed cooked soybeans in the open air to develop a natural mold covering. Modern miso is made by innoculating cooked soybeans with a *koji* starter of rice, barley or soybeans. Color, flavor, aroma, texture and saltiness of each type varies according to proportion of soybeans, koji and salt. Salt is an important preserva-

tive used to prevent growth of undesirable bacteria.

Miso is selected for cooking by color, taste and area of production. One popular type is sweet, white, low-salt, rice miso, popular in the Kyoto area. Less-sweet mellow white miso is a variation from Hawaii. Add a little honey to increase the sweetness or a pinch of salt for a more savory seasoning. Golden or yellow Shinshu miso (chu miso) is a mellow, high-salt, all-purpose blend. Fragrant Sendai miso (aka miso) is a delicious reddish-brown miso popular in Northern Japan. It has the highest salt content. Fudgy brown *hatcho miso* is popular in the Nagoya area around central Japan. *Moromo miso* is a whole-bean miso, used as a condiment. An indispensable source of protein in the Japanese diet, the digestibility of miso is increased through the fermentation process.

Use miso as an instant seasoning for soups, salads, marinades, dips and as a pickling agent. Different kinds of miso are usually interchangeable in cooking, but you should consider the salt content of each variety in relation to your recipe. Low-salt miso is available. Refrigerate miso in an airtight container, especially natural miso with no preservatives, and low-salt white miso.

Mochi gome: Short-grain sweet glutinous rice. It has the highest starch content of any rice, causing grains to lose shape and become very sticky when cooked. Used for making rice cakes, confections, and red beans and rice.

Mochiko: Rice flour made from finely ground cooked sweet glutinous rice. Used for making instant rice cakes and traditional confections.

Mountain yam (yamo-imo): Several types of this long slender tuber exist. Interior white flesh becomes gummy and adhesive when grated. Often eaten with soy sauce as a delicacy or used as a binding agent for uncooked foods. Wear rubber gloves if mountain yam becomes irritating to your skin.

Mustard cabbage: Growing 12 to 18 inches in length, this tonic-tasting cabbage resembles a bok choy in shape. Substitute spinach, kale or Swiss chard.

Nananegi: Mild-flavored large green onions. Substitute regular green onions.

Napa or Chinese cabbage (hakusai): This popular, elongated, crinkly leaf cabbage has a mild but distinctive taste. Leaves require little cooking and are tasty eaten raw or pickled. Refrigerate in an airtight plastic bag.

Natto: Steamed fermented soybeans with a sticky texture and flavor similar to strong cheese. This native Japanese food is a popular breakfast food over rice. Try it mixed with mustard, chopped green onions and soy sauce. Some forms of natto come dried and well-salted.

Nira: Flat green chives with a pleasant garlic-onion taste.

Nori: Often translated as *laver,* this prized algae of the genus *Porphyra Tenera* is extremely rich in protein, calcium, iron, minerals and vitamins. Fronds are washed, chopped, soaked and spread out on screens to sun-dry into paper-thin sheets. Quality is rated on number of tiny pieces per square inch. When dried, it is cut into sheets, strips and other shapes. Rich black nori with a shiny surface is the best. The better the color, the higher the vitamin content. Used in sushi rolls. Store nori in an airtight container in a cool dark place. It also freezes well.

Panko: Pressed coarse dry bread crumbs used for coating foods for deep-frying.

Pear-apple (nashi): Same size as a pear but rounder. Juicy like a pear and crisp like an apple. Ripe fruit can be refrigerated several months.

Pickled plums (umeboshi): One of the most popular condiments in Japan. Pickled in brine with red shiso leaves. Plums also come in paste form.

Potato starch (katakuriko): Potato starch is a popular inexpensive starch in Japan. Similar in use to cornstarch but used in smaller amounts for thickening. Potato starch thickens at a slightly lower temperature, so do not cook beyond thickening or it will break down. Excellent for extra-crisp coatings on foods.

Rice vinegar (su): Naturally fermented clear rice vinegar distilled from white rice. It has a mild flavor and natural sweetness. Among other uses, it can reduce discoloration of certain vegetables and soften fibers of vegetables during cooking.

Saké (Nihon shu): Japanese wine brewed from steamed rice, a special mold (koji) and spring water. Alcoholic content ranges from 12 to 15 percent. Amino acids in saké act as a tenderizer on meats. Saké dispels fish odors and acts as a balancing agent for other salty seasonings, such as soy sauce. Store saké in a cool dark place. Opened saké should be recapped tightly and refrigerated after each use; it will keep this way for several weeks or can be used for cooking. See page 123 for more information.

Sansho: Greenish aromatic pods of the prickly ash tree. Ground sansho lends a peppery spicy taste to foods. Especially popular on grilled foods, it also adds zest to noodle dishes, soups and one-pot dishes. Related to Szechwan peppercorns.

Sesame oil (goma abura): Aromatic pressed oil of toasted sesame seeds. Rarely used alone as cooking oil but sometimes added to other vegetable oils for frying tempura. Use sparingly to add fragrance and flavor.

Sesame seeds (goma): Introduced into Japan in the Nara period (A.D. 645-798), sesame seeds are abundant in protein, vitamins, calcium and phosphorous. White and black seeds are available.

Shiitake: Flavorful, earthy-tasting, black, forest mushrooms. Available fresh or dried. Purchase thick dried caps. Rehydrate in warm water before use. Add soaking liquid to soups, sauce.

Shiso: Bright-green leaf of the beefsteak plant (perilla). It has a pleasant minty taste and makes an excellent addition to a herb garden. Refrigerate in an airtight plastic bag 1 to 2 days.

Soba: Buckwheat noodles are one of the oldest and favorite noodles of Japan. This beige-colored firm-textured round noodle is enjoyed cold with dipping sauce or in a bowl of hot broth. Other categories of buckwheat noodles include green soba made with green tea and mushroom-flavored soba. *Chuka-soba* is a Chinese-style thin noodle used for soups and cold dishes. *Ramen,* a similar crinkly Chinese-style noodle, is used in dry-packaged instant cup-style noodle snacks. *Yaki-soba* is a Chinese-style yellow noodle used for making stir-fried noodles.

Somen: Thin white wheat noodles made from a dough to which sesame oil has been added. Available in a variety of colored flavors, such as pink plum and green tea. Noodles are usually cooked, then served cold with a dipping sauce and condiments.

Soy sauce (shoyu): Japan's most important seasoning ingredient. Top-quality soy sauce is naturally fermented from soybeans, wheat, a mold (koji) and water. Two main types of soy sauce are available. *Koikuchi shoyu* is a medium-dark soy sauce and the most widely used kind in Japan. *Usukuchi shoyu* is a slightly saltier lighter-colored thin soy sauce. It is used as a dipping sauce and when the flavor of soy sauce is desired but not the dark color. In sushi bars, soy sauce is known as *murasaki* (purple).

Tamari, the original soy sauce, is brewed with 100 percent soybeans with no wheat products added. It is a by-product of the production of dark miso. Tamari has a strong soybean taste and is mostly used in Japan in commercial food preparation. It makes an excellent dipping sauce for sushi.

Don't limit the use of soy sauce to Oriental cooking; it will add flavor to many of your favorite foods. Be sure to buy only soy sauce imported from Japan. A low-sodium soy sauce is available.

Takuan: Distinctive-tasting pickled daikon radish is rich in vitamins and minerals, and is believed to be an excellent aid to digestion. Fresh whole daikon are sun-dried then packed into crocks of salt and rice bran for pickling. It is the most well-known pickle in Japan.

Taro or Japanese field potatoes (sato-imo): Tubers have hairy dark exteriors and greyish interiors. Sizes range from tiny to the large Okinawan tubers ranging from 1 to 2 pounds. They can be steamed, boiled, deep-fried and candied like sweet potatoes.

Tempura-ko: Low-gluten wheat flour primarily used for making tempura batter. Cake flour can be substituted.

Tofu: Formerly known as *bean curd,* tofu is a white custard-like food substance made from soy milk processed from soybeans. See page 100 for more information.

Tosakanori: An attractive, dried, red, sea algae sold in its natural red color, bleached white, or treated with lime ash to turn it bright green. Rehydrate in warm water.

Tree oyster mushrooms (shimeji): Clumps of beige mushrooms with caps vaguely resembling oysters. Also said to resemble oysters in rich deep flavor. Another variety, *hon shimeji,* have small brownish-grey caps. Use only the freshest available for the best flavor. Quickly rinse mushrooms just before use; pat dry and cut into smaller pieces for cooking.

Trefoil (mitsuba): Long-stemmed herb with three flat leaves; has a distinctive fragrance. Add to soups and

Japanese Ingredients

1	Saké	6	Plum wine	12	Sweetened bean paste
2	Soy sauce	7	Soup flavoring	13	Tonkatsu sauce
3	Mirin	8	Gingko nuts	14	Pickled vegetables
4	Rice vinegar	9	Powdered Japanese horseradish	15	Black soybeans
5	Sesame oil	10	Sansho pepper	16	Shredded red pickled ginger
		11	Pickled ginger shoots	17	Sweet chestnuts in syrup

other hot foods during final minutes of cooking to avoid bitterness. To store fresh leaves, rinse and shake dry, then refrigerate in an airtight plastic bag. Substitute parsley or watercress.

Tuna (maguro): Sweet-tasting rich tuna is sliced raw and served as one of the most popular toppings for hand-pressed sushi. Fat-bellied yellowfin tuna (hon-maguro) is considered the finest. Pale-colored albacore tuna is also popular and is the top grade of canned tuna. Quality of various types of tuna depends on the season. Buy only top-quality fresh seasonal fish. Tuna is one of the few fish which freezes well enough to be used for sashimi.

Udon: Thick white wheat noodles, usually served in hot broth with other ingredients. Season with Seven-Spice Mixture, page 147.

Wheat gluten (fu): High-protein, low-starch substance with a chewy texture made from gluten flour, used in many stir-fried and braised dishes. Sweet, doughy, fresh wheat gluten (namafu) is difficult to obtain. Crisp dried wheat gluten (yakifu) is readily available and often shaped like coins, flowers, wheels and croutons. Soak dried wheat gluten in water a few minutes until spongy; squeeze out excess water. Use as directed in recipe.

Japanese Cooking Equipment

Bamboo baskets (zaru): Woven bamboo baskets are used in Japan for rinsing, cooking and serving food. Round baskets are used in place of a colander for rinsing foods, such as rice, shellfish and vegetables. Baskets are excellent for holding arranged foods for tabletop cooking or for serving individual portions of noodles. Cooking baskets (seiro) are used for dipping foods into boiling water, for soaking and for steaming doughs and grains.

Bamboo mat (sudare): Mats of various sizes are used for rolling foods, such as sushi rolls, omelet rolls and spinach rolls. Slats are lashed together with string. Rinse mat well under cool water after each use; dry thoroughly. Many sushi chefs line their mats with plastic wrap before making sushi rolls, especially for those where rice is rolled on the outside. If a bamboo mat is unavailable, substitute a piece of heavy foil, a folded kitchen towel or a bamboo placemat with tied wooden slats. Bamboo mats are called *maki-su* in sushi bars.

Benriner cutter: Rectangular plastic box with a lid fitted with several interchangeable blades for thin-slicing, shredding and grating. Substitute a mandoline or a large sharp knife. A food processor cannot duplicate the long thin vegetable shreds and slices. Finely shredded daikon radish and carrot are traditional garnishes for sashimi.

Domburi: Large deep pottery or porcelain bowl with matching lid, used for rice-based one-bowl meals which are also known as *domburi*. Buckwheat and white wheat noodles are also served in dombuo bowls covered with hot appetizing broth and various other ingredients. Bowl can be used for serving many other foods including stews, noodle dishes and even chili.

Donabe: Heatproof earthenware casserole, traditionally used for cooking one-pot dishes, such as chicken hot pot. Soak donabe in water 1 hour to prevent cracking during cooking. It is best to raise temperature of cooking liquid in pot slowly to prevent breakage. Hot cooking broth is poured into donabe, then it is placed over a portable tabletop burner. Substitute an electric wok or electric skillet.

Drop lid (otoshi-buta): Cypress or cedar lid which can be dropped into a slightly larger straight-sided cooking pot to rest directly on simmering foods. Lid holds food in place in simmering sauce, keeping it moist. Lid also helps to prevent boiling, which in turn helps retain shape of vegetables. Excess moisture is allowed to escape between edge of lid and side of pot preventing sauce from becoming diluted. Soak lid in water before use; pat dry. Do not put in the dishwasher. You can make a drop lid by cutting appropriate-sized circles from thin sheets of cypress or cedar. Or, use circles of waxed paper, slightly larger than diameter of pan, for cooking times up to 15 minutes and parchment paper for times up to 30 minutes. Both waxed

paper and parchment are likely to disintegrate during longer cooking. You can also use a flat lightweight cover, such as a metal lid or pie plate.

Fan (uchiwa): Flat round fan used frequently in Japanese cooking but most often for cooling sushi rice as it is tossed with vinegar dressing. Substitute a folded newspaper, cardboard or use a small electric fan.

Fine strainer (uragoshi): Traditional strainer made of a fine-mesh horsehair net stretched over a round wooden frame; fine metal strainers are also widely available. To puree foods, press food through strainer using a rice paddle or wooden spatula. After use, rinse strainer under hot water; then, if necessary, soak in hot soapy water to remove pieces of food.

Fish scaler (uroko-fuki): Handy item to own if you clean your own catch. Grasp fish by the tail, using a kitchen towel to get a good hold, then run scaler down fish toward head. Continue scraping all around fish until scales are removed. Rinse fish and fish scaler. The back of a knife can also be used.

Graters (oroshi gane): Flat aluminum or stainless-steel graters vary in size and purpose. Graters with widely set ridges are used for grating daikon radish. Closely set ridges are for finely grating horseradish root and gingerroot. For best results, grate in a circular motion. Well at bottom of each grater is designed to catch grated pulp with its juices. Tilt grater while holding grated gingerroot in place with your fingers. Pour off ginger juice for cooking purposes.

Grinding bowl and pestle (suribachi and surikogi): Earthenware bowl, usually coated on outside with a dark-brown glaze. Unglazed interior is patterned with raised ridges to made an abrasive surface for grinding foods in the bowl. Pestle is made from unfinished cedar wood. Use bowl for grinding seeds and spices, and for pounding and blending foods. Set bowl on a damp cloth to keep it from sliding around during use. Grinding bowls come in a variety of sizes ranging from a few inches wide up to 12 inches wide. They are excellent for grinding small amounts of spices which would be difficult to do in a blender or food processor.

Hand-pressed-sushi molds: Use for quickly forming sushi rice into a variety of traditional shapes. Molds come in a variety of whimsical shapes, such as flowers and butterflies. They come in stainless steel, wood or plastic. Before use, soak wooden molds in vinegar water or quickly dip metal or plastic molds in vinegar water.

Hangiri: Handsome shallow cypress-wood tub bound with copper hoops, used for mixing warm sushi rice with vinegar dressing. Wood does not react with vinegar and effect taste of rice. It also helps rice to cool evenly and absorbs excess moisture, adding to luster of rice. Some tubs come with lids and make excellent serving containers for rice dishes. Do not store onions, garlic or other aromatic vegetables in your sushi tub or your rice will have an unintended flavor! Before use, wet inside of tub with vinegar water. Substitute an unseasoned wooden salad bowl or a glass or plastic bowl.

Kim-chee pot: Stainless-steel pot, sold in a variety of sizes. Clamps on the side hold lid tightly shut. Usually available in Korean markets.

Nagashi-bako: Stainless-steel metal mold with removable inner-lining tray for easy removal of foods. Used for steaming egg dishes and custards, and molding jellied desserts. To remove food, simply lift out inner tray and if necessary, loosen edges with a small knife.

Oshiwaku: Three-piece cypress pressing box for making pressed sushi. Soak frame in vinegar water before use, then pat dry. Fit wooden frame over bottom section of mold. Pack rice and other ingredients inside lined mold; put pressing lid into place. Press rice firmly. Remove lid and frame, leaving molded rice resting on bottom of mold. Turn molded rice off frame. Substitute a loaf pan,

cake pan or small springform pan.

Pickling jar (tsukemono-ki): Plastic container for pickling vegetables. Lid contains a built-in screw-top for pressing salted vegetables. As vegetables exude their liquid, lid is tightened several times. Substitute a bowl, crock or plastic tub and use a plate or flat pan of the appropriate size to fit into container on top of vegetables. Set a heavy object on top for pressing. See page 151.

Saladacco cutting box: Cutting tool which looks like a round plastic box with a handle in the top. Two stainless-steel cutting blades are safely fitted into middle portion of box. To slice vegetables, fit them inside dome-shaped lid and rotate handle while applying pressure. An adjustment allows you to switch blades to cut long thin shreds traditionally used to garnish sashimi. An excellent tool for those not proficient with knives.

Wooden rice paddle (shamoji): Flat round paddle. Dampen and use to scoop cooked rice from cooking pot, to toss sushi rice with vinegar dressing and for pressing ingredients through a fine strainer. Substitute a regular wooden spatula.

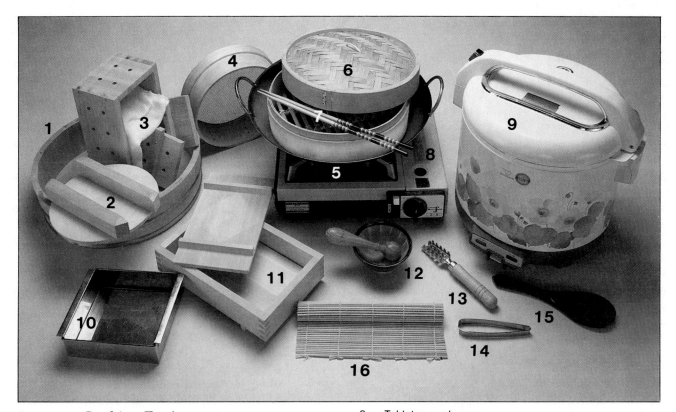

Japanese Cooking Equipment

1	Sushi-rice tub
2	Lid for small rice tub
3	Tofu-pressing box with cheesecloth
4	Fine strainer
5	Wok
6	Bamboo steamer
7	Cooking chopsticks
8	Tabletop gas burner
9	Electric rice cooker
10	Mold with removable tray
11	Three-piece cypress pressing box for molding sushi
12	Grinding bowl and pestle
13	Fish scaler
14	Fish-boning tweezers
15	Rice paddle
16	Bamboo sushi mat

Japanese Knives

The skill of the professional Japanese chef (itamae) is judged by his ability to cut and arrange food artistically for cooking and serving. This is especially important in Japan where cooking is often a secondary consideration, the primary concern being the preservation of natural tastes and textures. The Japanese feel that the understanding and mastery of cooking cannot come about without first understanding the tools. To achieve success in the kitchen, the proper use of top-quality knives is the first step.

The Japanese chef is the samurai warrior of the kitchen, and treasures his kitchen knife (hocho) as much as the ancient samurai once treasured his sword. A kitchen knife is a treasured personal possession, almost an extension of the chef's arm. Special prayers of thanks are offered to the spirit of the knives each year on January 28th during the Hocho-Shiki festival. At this time, the most skillful chefs are allowed to display their carving talents at a special performance at the Imperial Palace.

Top-quality knives (hon-yaki) are forged from hard steel using methods perfected by the Japanese for producing some of the world's finest swords. Hon-yaki blades are hand-fashioned for professional chefs and can cost hundreds of dollars each. Ordinary good-quality kitchen knives (hon-gasumi) are made from layered iron and steel. They are forged with a single cutting edge, usually located on the right side of the blade. This type of knife, used in Japan for over a thousand years, cuts quickly and cleanly. Double-edged Western blades are not as popular in Japan. High-carbon steel knives are preferred because it is not difficult to maintain their cutting edge and they are stain-resistant.

Selection of Japanese Tableware

1	Serving tub for sushi
2	Miso-soup bowl
3	Serving tub for hot steamed rice
4	Bowl for noodle dishes
5	Domburi for serving one-dish meals
6	Teapot for green tea
7	Tempura basket and absorbent paper
8	Bowl for clear soup or dessert miso soup
9	Picnic box (bento)
10	Place-serving tray
11	Sashimi bowl and dipping-sauce bowl
12	Bowl for braised and simmered dishes
13	Bowl for dressed foods and vinegared salads
14, 15	Saké cups
16	Teacup
17	Teacup to accompany sashimi
18	Tea-ceremony bowl
19	Lacquer-ware dessert plate
20	Dipping-sauce bowl
21, 22	Chopsticks with rest
23	Dish for grilled foods
24	Chopstick rest
25	Saké pot
26	Teacup
27	Soy-sauce dish for fish dishes
28	Pickle dish
29	Basket for fried foods or appetizers
30	Covered rice dish
31	Soy-sauce pot

Japanese knives are designed for specific purposes. Although a variety of types and shapes exist, they all fall into the following basic catagories:

Vegetable knives (nakiri-bocho, usuba-bocho): The *nakiri-bocho* has a thin blade with a dark-colored, straight, double cutting edge. It resembles a small lightweight cleaver. It is used for paring, chopping, slicing and mincing. It is an indispensable knife for the Japanese home kitchen. The *usuba-bocho* is a professional-quality vegetable knife with a single cutting edge. It is excellent for cutting paper-thin vegetable slices and shreds. To slice raw vegetables properly, use a forward thrusting cut (tsuki-giri). The bent fingers of the opposite hand should guide the knife and hold the food securely in place. When cutting, you should establish a smooth, rhythmic, continuous cutting motion. You can substitute a lightweight Chinese cleaver, although cutting will be harder work.

Fish-cutting knife (deba-bocho): A versatile, thick, heavy, triangular-blade knife used for filleting or cutting fish and for cutting meats and chicken. Cutting and slicing are done with the front portion of this knife; chopping requires the use of the thick base. A top-quality Western boning knife and a chef's knife are good substitutes.

Fish-slicing knife (sashimi-bocho): This long narrow thin knife is used for slicing fresh fish for sashimi and for cutting some cooked foods. The willow-leaf-blade knife (yanagi-ba sashimi bocho) has a pointed end and is favored in the Osaka/Kyoto area. The octopus knife (tako-biki bocho) has a blunt end and is popular in the Tokyo area. Sashimi knives are used with a long drawing cut called *hiki-giri*. Place the knife blade on the fillet of fish and draw it the full length of the blade toward you as the food is cut. A vertical cut, called *oshi-giri,* is used for making swift clean cuts. The center of the blade is pushed straight down into the food. This cut is perfect for slicing rolled sushi. Wipe the blade with a damp cloth between cuts. It is important that the knife be well-rinsed after sharpening to avoid a metallic taste on the fish. A top-quality Western slicing knife is a good substitute.

If you keep your knives sharp, they will serve you well and reduce much of the effort usually associated with cutting chores. Ideally, good knives should be honed on a whetstone before each use. To sharpen a knife, wet the knife and the whetstone with water. Place the stone vertically on a damp kitchen towel to hold it in place. Hold the knife in your right hand and place the cutting edge of the blade facing left on the stone. With your fingertips on the blade, push the entire length of the blade-edge up into a curved motion over the stone. Bring the knife back to the starting point and repeat the sharpening process several more times. Turn the knife over and run it over the stone a few times. Rinse the knife well before use.

Carbon-steel knives have a tendency to rust and discolor. Carefully dry the blades after washing and wipe them with a lightly oiled paper towel. If knives do rust, scour the blades lightly with a mild abrasive cleanser. A damp cork will help "erase" any rust spots from the blade. Never put your knives in the dishwasher. For storing, place in a knife rack or wrap each blade in a soft kitchen towel.

Styles of Cuisine in Japan

Cha kaiseki is the grand cuisine of Japan, served before the formal tea ceremony. The word *kaiseki* comes from the ancient practice of Zen priests who put warm stones into their robes during periods of meditation to warm their stomachs and take the edge off their hunger. A simple exquisite meal is served on precious porcelain, lacquer or pottery dishes, according to prescribed rules.

Kyo ryori is a lighter and more delicate variation of kaiseki popular in Kyoto.

Kaiseki ryori features Japanese-style party dishes which are served to guests while they are enjoying cups of warm saké. This type of kaiseki began over 300 years ago as light snacks served at poetry-party gatherings. Kaiseki ryori is available in tranquil garden restaurants called *ryotei.*

Chuka ryori is Chinese-style food which is served in inexpensive neighborhood restaurants. Fried-rice and noodle dishes are the most common.

Kaitei ryori is the nutritious and delicious everyday family cooking of Japan. The recipes are handed down through families from generation to generation.

Kappo ryori is the cordon bleu cuisine of Japan, prepared by highly skilled chefs and served a la carte in the prestigious (kappo) restaurants.

Kyodo ryori is the regional cuisine of Japan and is served in quaint rustic restaurants.

Nihon ryori offers a tremendous variety of simple Japanese-style foods served in family-style restaurants called *Nihon ryori ya.* Often found on the top floor of department stores, the restaurants display colorful plastic models of their food in the front windows so diners will have a glimpse of the tempting selections offered within.

Shojin ryori is the delicious and incredibly varied cuisine of the Zen Buddhist monks who were forbidden to eat animal protein for centuries. Tofu is an important protein substitute and is prepared in dozens of ways.

Shokudo ryori is a mixture of Western-, Japanese- and Chinese-style foods. This style of food is served in small inexpensive restaurants with plastic models of the foods displayed at the entrances.

Yushiki ryori is the ancient cooking of the Imperial Court. It is only served at very special occasions.

Japanese Knife Cuts

A large number of knife cuts are used in Japanese cooking; here are some of the most frequently used:

Sen-giri (matchstick strips): Cut desired food into 1-1/2- to 2-inch lengths. Make thin slices along the grain using a straight vertical cut. Stack several slices, then cut into matchstick strips. Fineness of strips can be varied according to personal preference.

Katsura-muki (wide strips and shreds): With a gentle sawing motion, cut carrot, daikon radish and cucumber into a paper-thin continuous sheet. Cut requires skill and is easier if vegetable is soaked in a strong salt-water solution several hours before cutting. For easier handling, cut vegetable pieces into 2- to 3-inch lengths. Stack sheets and cut into fine shreds. Soak shreds in iced water. Use as a garnish for sashimi and other dishes. Sheets can be rolled and cut into curly thin shreds called *kaminari*.

Hangetsu-giri (half-moon cut): Cut cylindrical vegetables in half lengthwise, then crosswise into half-moon shapes. A popular cut for pickled daikon radish (takuan).

Namami-giri (diagonal cut): Cut vegetables diagonally. Vegetables cut on the diagonal are more attractive, absorb more flavors in cooking and cook more evenly because more surface is exposed.

Tazuna (braids): Cut food into thin rectangular pieces. Make a slit in the middle of each piece. Stick 1 end through slit, pulling it gently through to form a braided shape. This attractive cut can be used for devil's-tongue-jelly noodles (konnyaku) or steamed fish loaf (kamaboko). Braids make an excellent addition to braised and one-pot dishes.

Kika-kabu (chrysanthemum cut): See Marinated Radish Mums, page 36.

Sasagaki (shavings): In 1 hand hold vegetable and cut at it with a knife as if you were sharpening a pencil. A common cut used for carrots, burdock and similar-shaped root vegetables.

Mijin-giri (mincing): Pieces of fish, meat and vegetables are chopped to the finest consistency. They lose their individuality and blend into a single mass. When mincing garlic, fresh gingerroot and green onions, smash them first with the side of the knife to break down fibers and release flavor oils. Garlic skins can be easily lifted off and discarded after smashing.

Hana-gata (flower shapes): Cut vegetables into attractive flower shapes with flower-shaped metal cutters (yasaino nuki-gata). See Assorted Vegetable Flowers, page 30.

Sue hiro (fan shape): Vegetables are cut into fan shapes. See Japanese Eggplant Fans, page 32.

Japanese Knives & Cuts

1	Domino-cut akami tuna		6	Kyoto-style vegetable-cutting knife
2	Kyoto-style fish-slicing knife		7	Onion Flower, page 31
3	Thin-slice-cut sea bass		8	Long shreds of daikon radish and carrot (katsura-muki)
4	String-cut squid		9	Fish-, meat- and chicken-cutting knife
5	Lotus Flower, page 31		10	Beef cubes

Planning a Japanese Menu

The basic Japanese meal is comprised of three parts: soup; side dishes (okazu); and steamed rice with pickles and hot tea. There is no featured main dish, but rice is considered the most important food served during the meal. The side dishes are intended to compliment the delicious pure taste of the cooked rice. The number of side dishes to be served varies according to the formality of the meal.

The saying *ichiju sansai* refers to *soup and three* and is a good guide to follow when planning a special Japanese meal. Select a total of three side dishes from the following categories: Sliced Raw Fish (Sashimi); Charcoal-Grilled & Pan-Grilled Foods (Yakimono); Steamed Foods (Mushimono); Simmered Foods (Nimono); and Deep-Fried Foods (Agemono). Each dish selected should be prepared by a different cooking technique; do not select two dishes from a single category. As an alternative, select a single one-pot dish to replace the side dishes. You can also add a salad from the Dressed-Foods & Vinegared-Salads section (Aemono & Sunomono). Round out the meal with a rice and pickle dish. Fresh fruit, ice cream or custard can be served at the end of the meal, if desired. Noodle dishes are usually served as a separate light meal, unaccompanied by rice.

During the formal Japanese meal, foods are served in a succession of small courses on individual lacquer trays. A less-formal serving style would be more appropriate for the Western kitchen. In this same mood of informality, you can also build your menu referring to the same guidelines you would use in planning a Western-style meal. For example, one of the delicious miso soups or consommés can be offered as the first course and the side dishes,

rice, pickles and tea can be combined into a single course. If you want something for a more-formal occasion, serve warm saké and appetizers from the Zensai chapter before the soup course. A raw-fish course can be added after the soup course, in addition to three or more side dishes for the middle course.

Strive to use fresh seasonal foods with a variety of flavors, colors and textures. Although a single type of food should not usually be repeated within the meal, seafood is so important in Japan, it might be presented two or more times.

With just a little imagination, Japanese dishes can be incorporated within your regular family-style meal. The flavorful meat, chicken and seafood recipes in the chapter on Charcoal-Grilled & Pan-Grilled Foods are superb for family barbecues especially with a Japanese-style salad on the side. What could be better than a dish of refreshing Strawberry-Tofu Sherbet or creamy Kiwifruit-Tofu Ice Cream, page 168, to finish the meal? The recipe amounts in the book have generally been increased to accommodate Western appetites.

A large amount of excellent mellow-tasting domestic beer is drunk in Japan, so it would make a suitable accompaniment to your meal. For a final touch, you can serve each guest with a small amount of plum wine either on its own or over crushed ice. Despite its medicinal properties, particularly for soothing stomach disorders, plum wine is pleasing served as an aperitif or an after-dinner drink.

One of the most important points of etiquette to remember when serving food Japanese-style is to begin the meal with an offering of thanks by saying, *"itadakimasu."* At the end of the meal it is polite to say, *"goshisosama deshita,"* indicating that you have appreciated such a wonderful feast.

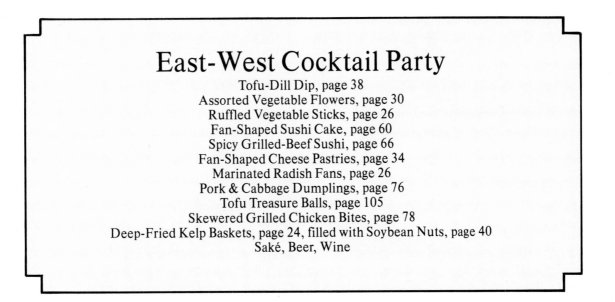

East-West Cocktail Party
Tofu-Dill Dip, page 38
Assorted Vegetable Flowers, page 30
Ruffled Vegetable Sticks, page 26
Fan-Shaped Sushi Cake, page 60
Spicy Grilled-Beef Sushi, page 66
Fan-Shaped Cheese Pastries, page 34
Marinated Radish Fans, page 26
Pork & Cabbage Dumplings, page 76
Tofu Treasure Balls, page 105
Skewered Grilled Chicken Bites, page 78
Deep-Fried Kelp Baskets, page 24, filled with Soybean Nuts, page 40
Saké, Beer, Wine

Tea

Ryokucha, or green tea, is the indispensable beverage of Japan. Green tea is produced by steaming newly harvested tea leaves before drying. This process inhibits the action of an enzyme which causes fermentation and darkening. Naturally fermented black tea is enjoyed in China, India and the Western world. Tea leaves are harvested from May through September. The quality varies depending on the area of production, how early the leaves are picked, the size of the leaves and even the position of the leaves on the bushes. Tea leaves contain a type of amino acid which is a flavor enhancer. It adds a distinct sweetness to the tea. Perhaps this explains the popularity of the dish called *ocha-zuke* which in its simplest form is hot green tea poured over cooked rice.

Green tea is processed into leaf form and powdered form. Top-quality *leaf* tea, called *gyokuro* (jewel dew), comes from the first summer picking of protected young leaves from the tops of the bushes. These leaves will be dried into long thin tightly curled rolls. Gyokuro is expensive and is sipped for appreciation and not to quench thirst. *Matcha* or *hikicha* is *powdered* green tea made from the same leaves as gyokuro. This expensive powdered tea is used mainly for the traditional tea ceremony.

Sencha is a good medium-quality tea picked after the first trim. This excellent tea is served in homes and often in sushi bars. *Bancha* is a popular lower-quality tea made from older leaves picked later in the season. It is served without charge in restaurants as a thirst-quenching beverage. *Kukicha* is the next grade after bancha and is made from the oldest leaves along with the stems and twigs of the bush. This is often rated as the healthiest grade of tea because of the low caffeine content. Bancha and kukicha are often roasted to give them a rich nutty flavor. Roasted bancha is refreshing in the summer when chilled and garnished with lemon or orange slices.

Genmai-cha is sometimes called popcorn tea because it is a combination of bancha and partially popped brown rice. This tea is sometimes served in inexpensive restaurants. Other teas include cold barley tea (mugi-cha) and a festive tea made by pouring hot water over salted preserved cherry blossoms. Medicinal teas, including those made from lotus root, mugwort, dried mushrooms and burdock root, are also popular.

Tea Ceremony

For the Japanese, the act of drinking tea is more than a simple means of taking refreshment. Throughout the past 400 years it has evolved into a highly stylized and refined art known as *cha-no-yu,* or the *tea ceremony.*

Brick-shape loaves of tea were introduced into Japan from China in the eighth century. Powdered green tea (matcha) was brought to Japan by Zen monks returning from China in the 12th century. Originally, tea was consumed for its medicinal properties and used as a mild stimulant to stay awake during all-night meditation. Tea drinking eventually spread to the nobility who freely dispensed it during tea-tasting contests and extravagant social gatherings. Under the influence of the dominant samurai class, the formal etiquette for serving tea evolved. In the 16th century, the tea master, *Sen-no-Riku,* simplified the tea ceremony and developed it into the form we still know today.

There are many types of tea gatherings, held in accordance with the changing seasons, the guests, the time of day and the occasion. Tea ceremonies are held to celebrate occasions, such as sunrise or sunset, New Year's festivities, Girls' Day, a full moon or even the first blossoms of spring. The ceremony is often held in a special tea room or outdoors in a tranquil setting and is frequently preceded by a special light meal (kaiseki). Moist tea sweets (namagashi), such as the jellied sweets in the Desserts & Confectionery section, page 157, are served after the meal. Then the host or hostess prepares frothy thick green tea (koicha) according to the prescribed ritual. The tea is passed in a single bowl and offered to each guest for sipping. Thin tea (usucha), in individual bowls, and dry sweets (higashi) are served next. Each guest receives a cup of thin tea. After the tea has been served, guests spend time examining and appreciating the tea articles, an essential part of the ceremony.

The ceremony is conducted according to a set of rules which might seem complex; each motion has special meaning. The formal manners, the spiritual hush of the occasion and the ritualized ceremony reflect the Zen philosophy that enlightment can be reached only through meditation. The tea ceremony is regarded as a means of physical, mental and spiritual discipline.

The spirit of the tea ceremony is based upon the Zen principle of *oneness with nature.* Followers strive to recognize real beauty in the plain and simple. A moss-covered stone in the tea garden, a perfect flower on display in the tea room, the tranquility of the ceremony and even the astringent taste of the green tea become objects of appreciation. Cha-no-yu is a living tradition in Japan and a symbol of the culture. *Chado (the way of tea)* has effected the everyday lives of the people, as well as the arts, architecture, ceramics, literature and calligraphy of Japan.

Brewing Tea

When brewing a pot of Japanese tea, several factors should be considered. The correct amount of tea leaves must be steeped for an exact amount of time in good-quality water heated to a certain temperature. To brew tea, fill your teapot with hot water to warm it before use. Pour out the warming water; refill the pot with water heated to the correct temperature depending on the type of tea being used, directions follow. Add the leaves and steep them for the recommended amount of time. The tea leaves will begin to sink to the bottom of the teapot when the tea is properly steeped. Never boil the tea leaves in the water. The Japanese prefer their tea without sugar, lemon or milk.

Powdered ceremony tea (matcha) is prepared by the cupful. Blend about 2 teaspoons powdered tea with 1/2 cup hot water. Correct water temperature will vary with the season.

Top-quality leaf tea (gyokuro) is steeped in water heated to between 120F (50C) and 130F (55C) 1 to 2 minutes. One to 2 tablespoons tea are enough for 1 cup water. Correct water temperature is not as high as that required for lower grades of tea. If the water is too hot, it will destroy the aroma and make the taste too strong. Gyokuro is sipped in small amounts.

Good medium-quality leaf tea (sencha) is steeped in water heated to between 175F and 180F (80C) 1 to 2 minutes. One tablespoon tea is enough for about 2-1/2 to 3 cups water. Sencha is sipped in small amounts.

Coarse tea (bancha) is steeped in water heated to between 210F and 215F (100C) 2 to 3 minutes. Two to 3 tablespoons tea are enough for 3 to 4 cups water. The tea leaves can be used a second time.

Barley tea (mugi-cha) is simmered in water 3 to 4 minutes, then strained and chilled before serving. One-half cup roasted barley is enough for 1-1/2 to 2 quarts simmering water.

Chopstick Etiquette

The Japanese custom of eating with chopsticks (hashi) was adopted from China almost 2,000 years ago. It is believed that the first chopsticks were connected and resembled tweezers rather than two separate sticks. Early records indicate that spoons were once used with chopsticks, but eventually the spoons completely disappeared. This was due, in part, to the fact that few except the nobility could afford them since they were made of precious metals. Bamboo, a natural resource, was widely available for making chopsticks.

The rules of chopstick and table etiquette were developed by court aristocracy and Buddhist clergy between the 12th and 15th centuries. Later, during the Edo period (1603-1868), these customs became popular throughout the land.

The simplistic use of a single pair of chopsticks during a Japanese meal is in sharp contrast to the numerous knives, forks and spoons necessary for a Western meal. Each family member has his own personal set of chopsticks and a container for storing them. To facilitate the use of chopsticks, foods are usually precut into bite-sized pieces, or in pieces small enough to be eaten politely in two or three bites. Hard-to-eat foods can be maneuvered by sliding the chopsticks under small portions and lifting the foods to the mouth. It is proper to lift the soup bowl or rice bowl and carry food to the mouth.

Japanese chopsticks can vary in shape but are shorter and lighter than the Chinese kind and easier to use. Chopsticks for everyday use are made of woods such as bamboo, pine, cypress and white birch. Many restaurants use soft wooden chopsticks (warabashi) which are attached at the top and enclosed in a paper wrapping. They are broken apart by the diner, then after the meal, slipped back into the paper wrapping for disposal. More-formal chopsticks are often slightly longer and made of cedar, ivory or lacquered wood inlaid with abalone or mother-of-pearl. Smaller chopsticks are made especially for children and longer chopsticks of metal or bamboo are available for cooking purposes.

Some of the earliest traditional rules governing chopstick etiquette are still in use today:

● At the beginning of the meal, chopsticks should be picked up with one hand then handed to the other hand for eating.

● Slightly wet chopsticks before use by dipping them into soup or hot tea.

● Reverse chopsticks to the clean ends before helping yourself from the communal serving dish. A common pair of serving chopsticks can be provided.

● Do not lean your chopsticks against a food dish. Special chopstick rests (hashi-oki) are available. Place the eating end of chopsticks directly on the rest, pointing to the left.

● Do not scrape your chopsticks together to remove pieces of food.

● Do not point with your chopsticks during a meal.

● Chopsticks have played an important role in religious ceremonies. At Buddhist funerals, special chopsticks are used to pass the cremated bones of the deceased between family members. Because of this custom, food must never be passed from person to person with chopsticks.

● Do not allow your chopsticks to stand upright in dishes of food. A taboo also related to funerary customs.

Garnishes (Mukimono)

A major concern for the Japanese cook is that foods satisfy the soul as well as the body. A high level of technical expertise and creativity enables him to create tantalizing aromas to whet the appetite and an endless variety of textures and natural flavors to please the taste buds. Equally important is his ability to garnish foods skillfully and create a visual appeal which constantly serves to remind us of our close relationship with nature. A taste of an edible Deep-Fried Kelp Basket brimming with lacy seafood tempura will intrigue the palate. But the spirit will be reminded that nature's bountiful expanse of ocean surrounding the Japanese archipelago provides a comfortable haven for marine and plant life.

During the Edo period (1603-1868), Japanese cuisine flourished and became a highly developed art. To decorate and enhance their foods, knife-wielding cooks developed the craft of sculpting vegetables into fanciful shapes (mukimono). The ancient art of food arrangement (moritsuke) dictated that foods be piled up high in individual portions and be colorfully decorated. Evidence of this style still exists in the presentation of some ceremonial foods. Look at the stacked rice cakes (kagami mochi) in the Japanese New Year Menu, pages 106 and 107.

Observe the basic rule of this popular art form to create your own unique style of food presentation and garnishing. Take your cue from nature. Choose the freshest seasonal foods available which will provide a complimentary splash of color and contrasting textures and flavors. Create an element of surprise and decorate your serving platters or tabletop with a crisp Carrot Spider Mum or Lotus Flower. Simple garnishes, such as Scalloped Lemon Slices or a Pine-Needle Garnish, can help make foods more attractive and excite the appetite. Beyond the vast realm of vegetable sculpting, food garnishings can be simplified, yet remain equally effective. Add flavor as well as texture by sprinkling black Dry-Roasted Sesame Seeds, page 150, over rice or colorful vegetables, or Green-Onion Threads over noodle dishes or grilled fish. Fresh, edible, seasonal flowers and leaves are often used to garnish foods as a tribute to nature.

Delicate Egg Chrysanthemums evoke the feeling of autumn and Assorted Vegetable Flowers remind us of new flowers popping up in spring. Edible garnishes do not have to be the final embellishments for food. Portion sizes, background settings, serving dishes and food arrangement all play an important role in building a total visual effect. Make the effort to link each of these aspects of food garnishing to the corresponding season. Strive to delight all the senses of smell, taste, sight and touch thereby creating a gentle mood of well-being.

Useful Garnishing Equipment

Cookie cutters
Canapé cutters
Metal Japanese flower-shaped cutters
Radish-rosette cutter
Combination citrus zester and citrus scorer
Straight paring knife
Curved paring knife
Eight- to ten-inch chef's knife
Japanese vegetable-cutting knife
Crinkle-edged vegetable-cutting knife
Vegetable peeler

Melon baller
Benriner cutter
Saladacco cutting box
Kitchen scissors
Assorted molds and cups for shaping rice
Wooden picks
Oriental bamboo skewers
Spray bottle for misting carved vegetables
Paper towels
Paste food colors
Zip-type plastic bags

Scalloped Lemon Slices

Using a paring knife or lemon zester, remove small vertical strips of peel down the length of a lemon. Cut lemon into thin slices. Use as garnish.

Lemon Baskets

Lemon Kago

Lemon Baskets can be filled with salads, sauces, Fresh Chilled Raw Fish, page 54, or ice cream.

1 large lemon per serving

Cut off a thin slice from stem-end of lemon to make a flat surface for basket to sit on. Plunge a small sharp knife horizontally into middle of lemon or a little above. Cut around lemon, leaving a 1/3-inch strip going over top of lemon to form handle. Carefully cut out pulp from under handle and rest of basket. Refrigerate until serving time.

Variations

Lemon Cups: Photo on page 121.
Cut off upper 1/3 of lemon. Using a small spoon, scoop out pulp from lemon bottom and lid. Fill cups with desired filling. Lean lids at an angle against filled cups.
Lemon Boats: Lay lemon on its side. Cut off upper 1/3 of lemon. Using a small spoon, scoop out pulp from lemon. Fill boats with desired filling.

Baskets can also be made from limes and oranges. Use grapefruit for larger baskets.

Deep-Fried Kelp Baskets

Konbu No Hana Kago

Fill these tasty edible baskets with Lacy Batter-Fried Foods, page 116.

1 (6-inch) square good-quality dried kelp (dashi konbu) per basket
1 (10-inch) dried-gourd strips (kampyo) per basket, soaked in salted water

6 to 8 cups vegetable oil or peanut oil for deep-frying

To soften dried kelp, dip in a large bowl of warm water. Gently flex 2 to 3 minutes or until soft. Dry softened kelp with a clean kitchen towel. To shape a small basket, place kelp on a cutting surface. Place a 5-1/2- to 6-inch saucer on top. Using a small sharp knife, trim around saucer. Press circular piece of kelp into a 4-1/2-inch foil tart pan. Crease kelp around bottom edge of tart pan to help set shape. Press sides into a fluted design, if desired. Using small sharp knife, make a few small slits on bottom of kelp. This will prevent it from blistering and splattering oil when fried. Make a small horizontal slit 1/2 inch from top edge of each side of basket, 2 slits in total. Insert 1 end of a soaked gourd strip into 1 slit; tie it into a knot. Insert other end of gourd strip into opposite slit; tie as before. Handle will be limp until basket is deep-fried. Fill basket with loosely crushed foil to hold up handle and to help shape it. Thoroughly dry basket in tart pan several hours or overnight. In a wok or shallow pan, heat oil to 360F (180C) or until a 1-inch cube of bread turns golden brown in 60 seconds. Remove foil from tart pan. Remove basket from pan. Using long tongs, carefully hold basket upside-down in hot oil a few seconds to set shape of handle. Turn basket and fry side knots. Set basket upright in hot oil. With a large spoon, pour oil inside basket. Tilt basket on all sides for even-browning. Basket will have a rich brown lacquered-wood look after frying. Do not let basket become too brown or it will be bitter. Drain basket on paper towels. Baskets make excellent bowls for Soybean Nuts, page 40, or rice crackers. Larger pieces of dried kelp can be formed into serving bowls. Experiment by making a variety of shapes. Makes 1 basket.

Variations

Deep-Fried Kelp Boats: Form soaked kelp into boat shapes as directed in Steamed Seafood in Kelp Boats, page 88. Make slits in bottom of boats; dry overnight. Deep-fry as above.
Deep-Fried Kelp Trays: Cut a piece of soaked kelp into a 5- to 6- inch square. Deep-fry kelp in a wide shallow skillet until crisp. Drain on paper towels.

Green-Onion Threads

Place green stem portion of a green onion on a cutting board. Cut stem open lengthwise. With the point of a small paring knife, shred stem lengthwise into threads. Place threads in a bowl of iced water to curl. Thickness of threads can be varied.

Variation

Make a cluster of attached green-onion threads. Shred only 3/4 the way down length of an uncut stem, leaving 1/4 of stem uncut. Chill shredded stem in iced water. Use as a garnish.

How to Make Deep-Fried Kelp Baskets

1/Make small horizontal slits on top edge of each side of basket. Insert 1 end of soaked gourd strip into a slit; tie in a knot. Tie other end of strip into opposite slit.

2/Fill baskets with loosely crushed foil to hold up handle and help shape it. Dry several hours or overnight. Deep-fry basket; drain. Fill as desired.

Pinwheel Shrimp

This pretty pair of shrimp will spin merrily in your bowl of hot soup.

2 medium shrimp, per pinwheel　　　　　　**Water**
1 tablespoon cornstarch

Peel shrimp, leaving tails intact. Make a shallow cut lengthwise down back of each shrimp. Rinse out dark vein. On a cutting board, lay 1 shrimp on its side with tail curling up. Place second shrimp on its side with tail curling down. Fit shrimp together with bellies meeting. In a small bowl, make a thick paste with cornstarch and a few drops of water. Put a dab of paste between shrimp. Pin shrimp together with 2 wooden picks. In a medium saucepan, bring water to boil. Add shrimp. Reduce heat to low; poach shrimp pinwheels 2 to 3 minutes. Drain; cool slightly. Remove wooden picks. Makes 1 pinwheel.

Cherry-Tomato Flowers　　　Photo on page 81.

Cut cherry tomatoes into quarter sections without cutting all the way through to stem end. Remove seeds. Petals can be trimmed with scissors. Chill tomato flowers in iced water. Condiments or decorative pieces of vegetable can be inserted in centers, if desired.

Marinated Radish Fans   Photo on page 106.

Aka Kabu Sunomono

Ordinary radishes are transformed into tiny fans which make attractive garnishes or a colorful salad.

Marinade, see below
1 bunch large, well-shaped,
  oval radishes

Marinade:

1/2 cup rice vinegar	**1/2 teaspoon salt**
1/3 cup sugar	**1/2 teaspoon sesame oil**

Prepare Marinade; set aside. Cut off radish tops; trim off root ends. Wash radishes in cool water; pat dry. On a cutting board, place a radish on its side between 2 chopsticks. Top and bottom of radish should be at right angles to chopsticks. Make a series of slices across radish down to chopsticks. Chopsticks will prevent knife from cutting all the way through radish. Repeat with remaining radishes. Add partially sliced radishes to marinade. Refrigerate in marinade at least 30 minutes but no longer than 1 hour. After this time, radishes bleed and turn pink. Remove radishes from marinade; shake off excess liquid. With your fingers, gently spread each radish open into a fan-shape. Serve in small dishes as a salad or use for garnishing foods. Makes 3 to 4 servings.

Marinade:

In a small bowl, combine all ingredients. Stir well to dissolve sugar. Makes 2/3 cup.

Variation

Before slicing radishes, score through skin with a fine-pronged fork or small knife, from end to end. When sliced, radish fans will be notched in a decorative pattern.

For crisp radish-fan decorations, chill cut radishes in iced water 2 to 3 hours; do not marinate.

Ruffled Vegetable Sticks

An easy edible garnish.

Large carrots, scraped	**Jícama, peeled**
Medium to large turnips, peeled	**Zucchini, scrubbed**
Daikon radish, peeled	

Slice selected vegetables into ruffle-shaped sticks using a crinkle-edged vegetable-cutting knife, opposite.

Garnishing equipment, clockwise starting at top left: Benriner cutter; Saladacco cutting box; Metal rice molds and dessert cutters; Small metal vegetable cutters; Rice molds; Combination citrus zester/citrus scorer; Paring knife; Radish-rosette cutter; Crinkle-edged vegetable-cutting knife; Fine grater (oroshi gane).

Egg Chrysanthemums   Photo on page 69.

Tamago Kiku

Decorate your sushi platters or fresh sashimi platters with these attractive egg flowers.

1 extra-large egg per flower
Pinch of salt
1 or 2 drops yellow food coloring
Vegetable oil

Pink, sweetened, dried-fish flakes
   (denbu) or Pickled Pink-Ginger Slices,
   page 153

In a small bowl, beat egg, salt and food coloring. Heat a 10- or 11-inch skillet over medium-high heat. Wipe skillet with a paper towel dipped in oil. Pour beaten egg into oiled skillet. Swirl skillet so egg covers bottom of skillet in a sheet. Reduce heat to low. Cook 1 minute or until egg is set. Remove skillet from heat. Carefully turn egg sheet over; cook 30 seconds. Turn cooked egg out of skillet. Cool 5 minutes. Fold 2 opposite sides of egg sheet so they meet in center. Fold egg sheet in 1/2 again, starting from a folded side. Using a small knife, make short slits, 1/2 inch apart, down double side of folded sheet. Make slits no deeper than 1/4 to 1/2 of width of folded piece. Beginning at 1 end, roll up egg sheet. Set flower on uncut edge. Gently spread open flower petals. Place a small amount of dried-fish flakes in center of each flower; or, cut ginger into thin strips, then add to flower centers. Makes 1 flower.

Variation
Smaller flowers can be made by cutting folded scored egg strip in 1/2 into 2 shorter strips. Roll up each 1/2 into a small flower. Secure each flower with a wooden-pick half.

Vegetable Ikebana Centerpiece

Create this centerpiece for your next Japanese dinner party.

4 or 5 large turnip or daikon-radish flowers
   with carrot centers, page 30
3 or 4 small turnip or daikon-radish
   flowers with carrot centers, page 30

1 (1-1/2- to 2-lb.) well-shaped
   acorn squash
8 to 10 green-onion stems
Separated leek leaves, blanched

Prepare vegetable flowers. Chill in iced water until needed. Wash and dry acorn squash. Cut off top 1/3 from stem end to form container and lid. Scrape seeds and pulp from inside squash and lid. If necessary, cut a small piece from base of squash so it will sit flat. Break several 10-inch bamboo skewers into shorter lengths. Push pieces of green-onion stems over various lengths of skewers to form flower stems. Drain vegetable flowers; pat dry with paper towels. Insert large flowers on longer stems and small flowers on shorter stems. Push skewered flowers into squash vase, arranging them in an attractive manner. It may be helpful to place 1/2 a potato inside squash to hold skewers in place. Place leek stems into the base of the arrangement, securing them with wooden picks, if necessary. Tuck in the ends, creating loops of various sizes to correspond with the arrangement.

How to Make Egg Chrysanthemums & Vegetable Ikebana Centerpiece

Using a small knife, make short slits, 1/2 inch apart, down double side of folded egg sheet. Roll up sheet. Gently spread open flower petals. Place some dried-fish flakes in center of each flower.

Stick skewered flowers into acorn-squash vase, arranging them in an attractive manner. Place leek stems in base of arrangement, securing with wooden picks. Tuck in ends, creating loops.

Scored Shiitake Mushrooms   Photo on cover.

If you are using dried shiitake mushrooms, rehydrate them in warm water 30 minutes or until needed. Cut off and discard tough stems. Using a small paring knife, make a shallow cut across middle of a mushroom cap on top side, slightly at an angle. Make a second cut, at an opposite angle, parallel to the first one. Pull out thin V-shaped piece of mushroom between cuts. Make a similar pair of cuts crossing first cuts in the center at right angles. Remove thin piece of mushroom between cuts. Mushroom cap will be fluted in a cross pattern.

Variation

Star-Fluted Shiitake Mushrooms: Using a small paring knife, make a shallow cut from center top of a mushroom cap to edge, slightly at an angle. Make a second cut, at an opposite angle, parallel to first one. Pull out thin V-shaped piece of mushroom between cuts. Continue making 4 or 5 similar pairs of cuts evenly around mushroom cap. Remove pieces between cuts. Mushroom cap will be fluted in a star-shaped pattern.

Pine-Needle Garnish

Cut a 1-1/4'' x 1/2'' piece of lemon peel. On a cutting surface, place lemon peel with a short side toward you. Using a small sharp knife, make a cut 1/8 inch from right side. Cut should start from bottom and go 2/3 way to top edge of lemon piece. Turn peel and repeat cut on opposite side. Pull up 2 side strips and cross over center section.

Variation
This garnish can also be made with strips of steamed fish loaf, carrot or other vegetables.

Carrot Spider Mum

Cut 10 or 12 (4-inch-long) paper-thin strips from a large carrot, using a Benriner cutter. Using a small knife, make 5 lengthwise cuts, about 2 inches long, in center of each strip. Cut outside strips apart on each slice, trimming ends into a point. Fold ends of carrot strips together. Push a thick carrot slice onto 1 end of a short bamboo skewer. Push a folded carrot strip onto bamboo skewer. Fold remaining strips; push onto same skewer. When all strips are on skewer, push another thick carrot slice onto skewer to hold petals in place. Gently pull alternate carrot strips to left and right on skewer to build a flower shape. Drop flowers into a small bowl of iced water to chill. Before using, trim skewer so it does not show on garnish.

Assorted Vegetable Flowers

Cut 1/2-inch-thick shapes if vegetable flowers are to be cooked with other foods.

Large and small carrots
Turnips
Daikon radish

Jícama
Food coloring, if desired

Cut selected vegetables into 1/4-inch-thick slices. Cut slices into large and small flowers using assorted sizes of cookie cutters; Japanese, metal, flower-shaped cutters; or canapé cutters. Place flower pieces in a bowl of iced water or store in iced water in an airtight plastic bag in the refrigerator until needed. If desired, white flower shapes can be tinted various colors for garnishing. Different sizes, shapes and colors of flowers can be fastened together with wooden picks to form layered flowers. Flowers can be used singly or together in a grouping for garnishing. Do not tint or use wooden picks in vegetable flowers to be cooked or served with dips.

How to Make a Pine-Needle Garnish & Carrot Spider Mum

Make a cut 1/8 inch from right side of lemon piece. Cut should start from bottom and go 2/3 way to top edge. Turn peel and repeat cut on opposite side. Pull up 2 side strips and cross over center section.

Push a thick carrot slice onto 1 end of a short bamboo skewer. Push a folded carrot strip onto skewer. Push remaining strips onto skewer. Push another thick carrot slice onto skewer. Arrange strips to get a flower shape. Chill in iced water.

Onion Flower   Photo on page 18.

Remove outer skin from an onion. Using a paring knife or a **V**-shaped wedge cutting tool, insert knife into center of onion. Make **V**-shaped cuts around middle of onion, cutting about halfway through. Hold onion under hot running water and separate layers. Flowers can be tinted in bowls of water with food coloring added. Various centers can be inserted. For a layered flower, stack layers attractively beginning with largest and ending with smallest.

Variation

Lotus Flower: Photo on page 18.
Peel a large onion; cut a flat area on base. Secure onion for cutting by inserting 2 long metal skewers through bulb close to flat base. Run skewers, parallel to base, in opposite directions. With a sharp knife, slice onion in 1/2, down to skewers, then in quarters, then in eighths. If onion is large, it may be possible to cut it further into sixteenths. Blanch onion 1 to 2 minutes in boiling water. Remove skewers; submerge onion in iced water. When cooled, gently pull petals apart. Store Lotus Flower in iced water until needed; drain well. Garnish with lily-pad leaves or trimmed vegetable leaves.

Scalloped Lotus-Root Flowers   Photo on cover.

Hana Renkon

These make an attractive vegetable garnish for box lunches or for Kansai-Style Mixed Sushi, page 70.

1 (4- to 5-inch) fresh lotus root
Thin curly strips of dried hot
  red pepper, if desired

Peel lotus root. Rinse; cut into thin slices. Drop slices into a medium bowl; add cool water to cover. Add 2 tablespoons rice vinegar to help prevent discoloration. Blanch lotus slices 1 to 2 minutes in boiling water. Drain; place in a bowl of iced water. To shape lotus flowers, use a small paring knife to trim edges of each slice into a scalloped design. Drop flowers back into iced water as you finish trimming them. Refrigerate until needed. Garnish center of lotus flowers with strips of red pepper, if desired. Makes 6 servings.

Variations

Pickled Lotus-Root Flowers: Photo on page 106
In a medium bowl, combine 1/2 cup rice vinegar, 1/2 cup sugar and 1/2 teaspoon salt. Stir well to dissolve sugar. Add blanched scalloped lotus flowers. Cover and marinate in refrigerator 1 hour or longer. Serve as a pickle or use as a garnish.

Lotus root can be cut into a scalloped shape as you cut off outer peel. Slice scalloped root into thin slices. Soak in vinegar water. This method will require more dexterity with a knife.

Lotus flowers can be used white or they can be tinted different colors. Drop slices into small bowls of cool water with 3 or 4 drops food coloring. Or, soak lotus flowers in liquid drained from pickled plums (umeboshi). Pink and white lotus flowers are a popular color combination in Japanese box lunches.

Canned lotus slices can be blanched, then pickled. Lotus slices can also be purchased water-packed in plastic packages. Look in the refrigerator sections of Oriental markets.

Japanese-Eggplant Fans   Photo on cover.

Select well-shaped Japanese eggplants. With a small sharp knife, slice eggplant lengthwise, stopping 1 inch from stem end. Make additional 2 or 3 evenly spaced parallel cuts. Fans can be steamed or deep-fried according to specific recipes.

Variations
If Japanese eggplants are not available, cut fan shapes using 3- to 4-inch-long rectangular pieces cut from regular eggplants. Refer to cutting instructions for Carrot Fans, below.

Carrot Fans: Photo on page 49.
Cut rectangular pieces from a large carrot, 1-1/2 inches long, 1 inch wide and 1/2 inch thick. Blanch pieces 1 minute; drain and rinse with cold water. Using a small paring knife, starting 1/2 inch from edge of 1 long side, make 4 or 5 cuts at right angles to and through opposite long side of each carrot piece. Strips should remain attached. Let stand in iced water to spread open, at least 20 minutes. Or, carrot pieces can be cut flared with top edge 1-1/2 inches long and bottom edge 1 inch long.

Appetizers (Zensai)

Appetizers, or *zensai,* are tantalizing small portions of artistically arranged foods served to stimulate the appetite for the upcoming courses of a meal. They are traditionally served at the beginning of a formal Japanese meal after the first cup of saké and before the clear-soup course. Zensai make excellent snacks and can be served to increase the pleasure of drinking saké. They vary according to the season because, as with all Japanese food, only the freshest and finest ingredients are used.

Preparation of zensai can be as easy as slicing steamed fish loaf, then fashioning the slices into butterfly shapes. Other foods, such as fresh tuna or peeled lotus root, are sliced and served raw. Or, appetizers can be more complex and time consuming, as the occasion demands.

Because of their versatility, many Japanese dishes can be served as appetizers or other parts of a meal. For example, Simmered Burdock & Bacon Rolls can be served as an appetizer or as a simmered food (nimono). Grilled Sesame Shrimp, page 77, fits just as well in a selection of appetizers as in a group of grilled foods (yakimono). For an attractive presentation, try filling Lemon Baskets, page 23, with appetizer items, salads, pickles or small portions of fruit. Thin gyoza skins can be deep-fried into Pastry Baskets and filled with zensai or

coated with sugar and filled with ice cream for dessert. These skins can also be deep-fried into round chips and used as dippers for Tofu-Dill Dip, a Western-style appetizer featuring creamy fresh tofu. Small portions of fresh chilled raw fish (sashimi) or crunchy pickled vegetables make excellent appetizers. Look through the chapters and you will find that many recipes in other categories can be served as zensai. Appetizers make a delcious addition to the Japanese box lunch (bento) because all the food is good served at room temperature.

Japanese-style salads can be served as zensai and are sometimes referred to as *tsukidashi.* In the bars and pubs (nomi-ya and taishu sakaba), bite-sized portions of food, such as Sautéed Tree Oyster Mushrooms or Butter-Grilled Meat, Shellfish & Vegetables, page 74, are served as hors d'oeuvres (otsumami). *O-toshi* are complimentary snacks served before orders for heavier food are placed in drinking establishments. These might include Soybean Nuts, Spicy Glazed Sardines or rice crackers with canapé toppings. More substantial hors d'oeuvres, including Fresh Chilled Raw Fish, page 54, Salt-Grilled Trout, page 79, and many one-pot dishes, are served in the intimate and cozy setting of the *izakaya* or upgraded saké shops.

Fan-Shaped Cheese Pastries

Chizu No Uchiwa Gyoza

These crisp cheese-filled pastries will be a hit at your next cocktail party.

Green-Onion-Miso Dipping Sauce, see below
1 (8-oz.) box pasteurized process cheese
  spread, well-chilled
1 tablespoon cornstarch
1 tablespoon water

1 (10-oz.) pkg. round gyoza skins
  (about 54 skins)
About 6 cups peanut oil or
  vegetable oil for deep-frying

Green-Onion-Miso Dipping Sauce:
2/3 cup sweet white or yellow miso
2 tablespoons Dry-Roasted Sesame Seeds,
  page 150
2 tablespoons sugar

2 teaspoons lemon juice
3 tablespoons mirin
2 green onions, minced

Prepare Green-Onion-Miso Dipping Sauce; set aside. Cut cheese crosswise into 3 equal-sized blocks. Cut each block into 6 slices. Cut each slice into 3 strips. You will have 54 cheese strips. In a small dish, blend cornstarch with water until dissolved. Place a cheese strip on lower 1/2 of a gyoza skin. Fold up bottom portion of skin to enclose cheese. Coat sides of skin with cornstarch mixture. Pick up bottom corner of folded skin; pull up so bottom of skin is flush against end of cheese. Repeat with other corner. Press folded areas firmly so they do not pop open during frying. Place fans on a plate as you form them. Cover with plastic wrap to prevent drying. In a wok or deep pot, heat oil to 360F (180C) or until a 1-inch cube of bread turns golden brown in 60 seconds. Fry fans, a few at a time, in hot oil about 1 minute or until crisp and golden. Drain briefly on paper towels; place on a wire rack to retain crispness while frying remaining fans. Serve hot with Green-Onion-Miso Dipping Sauce. Makes 8 to 10 appetizer servings.

Green-Onion-Miso Dipping Sauce:
In a small bowl, combine all ingredients. Makes about 1 cup.

Variation
Cheese-filled gyoza skins can be shaped into cylinders. Place a cheese strip on lower 1/2 of skin. Fold sides over to enclose cheese. Fold up bottom portion of skin; roll up into a tight cylinder. Seal edges with a tiny amount of cornstarch mixture. Wrap a narrow strip of nori around middle of each cylinder. Dampen ends of nori strips to seal. Deep-fry as directed above.

Pickled Quail Eggs   Photo on page 69.

Uzura Tamago Zuke

Tint quail eggs pink by adding some of the liquid from a jar of red pickled ginger or a can of beets.

12 hard-cooked quail eggs, peeled
1/2 cup rice vinegar

2 tablespoons sugar
1/2 teaspoon salt

Place quail eggs in a small jar. In a small bowl, combine vinegar, sugar and salt. Stir well to dissolve sugar. Pour over quail eggs. Cover and refrigerate 2 to 3 days. For each serving, thread 2 or 3 pickled eggs on a short skewer. Makes 4 to 6 appetizer servings.

How to Make Fan-Shaped Cheese Pastries

1/Place a cheese strip on lower 1/2 of a gyoza skin. Fold up bottom portion of skin. Coat sides of skin with cornstarch mixture. Pick up bottom corner of folded skin; pull up so bottom of skin is flush against end of cheese. Repeat with other corner. Press folded areas firmly.

2/Fry fans, a few at a time, in hot oil about 1 minute or until crisp and golden. Drain briefly on paper towels; place on a wire rack while frying remaining fans. Serve hot with Green-Onion-Miso Dipping Sauce.

Pastry Baskets

Photo on page 37.

Gyoza No Kago

Fill these little pastry baskets with appetizer snacks or sprinkle with sugar and fill with ice cream.

About 6 cups peanut oil or vegetable oil for deep-frying

6 round gyoza skins

In a wok or deep pot, heat oil to 325F (165C) or until a 1-inch cube of bread turns golden brown in 90 seconds. Press each skin into a small tart pan or fluted brioche pan. Place 1 pan in a long-handled wire strainer. Lower pan slowly into hot oil, holding skin in place with a wooden spoon. If oil is too hot, skin will immediately lose its shape and float out of pan. Lift tart pan slightly out of oil and continually spoon hot oil over sides and into bottom of pastry basket. Fry until crisp and golden brown. With wooden spoon, hold basket in pan. Pour out any oil inside. Cool pan and pastry basket 1 to 2 minutes. Lift cooled pastry basket out of pan. Drain briefly on paper towels; cool on a wire rack. Deep-fry remaining skins as above. Cool completely before use. Makes 6 baskets.

Variation

Coat baskets with sugar while warm; cool completely. Fill with ice cream and garnish with small pieces of fresh fruit and tiny fresh flowers.

Spicy Glazed Sardines

Tazukuri

Once you begin nibbling on these tiny sweet fish, you won't want to stop.

**About 4 cups peanut oil or
  vegetable oil for deep-frying**
1 (3-oz.) pkg. dried tiny sardines
1/4 cup soy sauce
2 tablespoons water

2 tablespoons mirin
1/4 cup sugar
**1 tablespoon Dry-Roasted Sesame Seeds,
  page 150**
Seven-Spice Mixture, page 147, to taste

In a wok or deep saucepan, heat oil to 360F (180C) or until a 1-inch cube of bread turns golden brown in 60 seconds. Place sardines in a large wire skimmer. Lower sardines into hot oil. Fry 30 seconds. Drain sardines on paper towels. In a small saucepan, bring soy sauce, water, mirin and sugar to a boil. Reduce heat to medium. Cook 5 minutes or until thick and syrupy; cool 3 to 4 minutes. Add sardines to glaze; mix well. Stir in Dry-Roasted Sesame Seeds and Seven-Spice Mixture. Serve at room temperature. Makes 4 to 6 appetizer servings.

Variations

Sardines can be dry-roasted in a hot skillet 3 to 4 minutes instead of being deep-fried.

Instead of offering as an appetizer, serve small amounts of Spicy Glazed Sardines over hot Steamed Rice, page 139.

Marinated Radish Mums

Kiku Aka Kabu Sunomono

You can use chopsticks to help the cutting as in Marinated Radish Fans, page 26.

Marinade, page 26   **1 bunch large, well-shaped, oval radishes**

Prepare Marinade; set aside. Cut off radish tops. Trim off root ends. Wash radishes in cool water; pat dry. Using a small sharp knife, make close parallel cuts across radish from top to within 1/4 inch of stem. Turn radish 90 degrees; make a series of similar parallel cuts at right angles to first ones. Slice remaining radishes in the same way. Add radishes to marinade. Marinate in the refrigerator 2 to 3 hours. Radishes will open slightly into a flower shape. Red skin of radishes will bleed and tint radishes pink. To serve radishes, tap off excess liquid. Serve in small dishes as a salad or use as a garnish. Makes 3 to 4 servings.

Variations

Turnip Flowers (Kika Kabu): Small turnip flowers can be made following the directions given above. Turnips can be flavored and tinted pink by marinating them in liquid from pickled plums (umeboshi) or Pickled Pink-Ginger Slices, page 153. Add a small spoonful of salmon-roe caviar (ikura) to each flower center.

For crisp radish-mum decorations, chill cut radishes in iced water 2 to 3 hours; do not marinate.

Spicy Glazed Sardines, above; Marinated-Radish Mum, above; Kumquat-stuffed steamed fish loaf, page 41; Pastry Basket, page 35, filled with Mixed Sweet Vegetable Pickles, page 156.

Sea-Shell Appetizers

Kaigara Zushi

These delightful sea creatures can also be stuffed with your favorite creamy seafood salad.

6 extra-large eggs
2 tablespoons mirin
1/2 teaspoon salt

Vegetable oil
1 generous cup Kansai-Style Mixed Sushi,
  page 70, without Toppings

In a medium bowl, beat eggs until blended. Stir in mirin and salt. Strain egg mixture through a fine strainer into a medium bowl. Heat an 8-inch non-stick skillet over medium heat. Wipe surface with a paper towel dipped in vegetable oil. Pour about 1/4 cup egg mixture into hot oiled skillet. Swirl skillet to make a well-shaped egg circle. Reduce heat; cook 1 to 2 minutes or until egg is almost set. Do not brown bottom side. Carefully flip egg circle over; cook 10 seconds longer. Turn egg circle out of skillet; cool. Continue making egg circles with remaining egg mixture. Fold cooled egg circles into quarters. Heat a wooden-handled metal skewer in an open flame. Use hot skewer to brand 3 decorative lines on top of each folded egg circle. Or, you can make decorative marks with a small amount of food coloring. Stuff top folds with a generous tablespoon of Kansai-Style Mixed Sushi. If necessary, press stuffed shells to improve shapes. Serve shells on a serving platter or on individual small plates. Makes 12 to 13 appetizer servings.

Tofu-Dill Dip   Photo on page 75.

Versatile tofu can be combined with other flavors to make a delicious low-calorie dip.

1 large garlic clove
1 (14- to 16-oz.) pkg. silken or
  regular Japanese-style tofu,
  rinsed, patted dry
1/2 pint sour cream (1 cup)
1 tablespoon yellow miso
2 tablespoons fresh minced dill weed or
  dried dill weed

1 tablespoon fresh lemon juice
Seasoning salt to taste
4 green onions, thinly sliced
3 to 4 red-cabbage leaves
Vegetable Dippers, see below

Vegetable Dippers:
Edible pea pods, blanched 30 seconds,
  chilled in iced water
Scalloped Lotus-Root Flowers, page 32
1 (15-oz.) can baby corn, drained, rinsed

Assorted Vegetable Flowers, page 30
Ruffled Vegetable Sticks, page 26
Hand-trimmed radish rosettes made with
  cutter, page 27

Mince garlic in a blender or food processor fitted with a steel blade. Add tofu, sour cream and miso; process until smooth. Add dill weed, lemon juice and seasoning salt. Pour into a medium bowl; stir in green onions. Cover and refrigerate 2 hours or longer for flavors to develop. Prepare Vegetable Dippers of your choice. Form red-cabbage leaves into a bowl shape in the middle of a serving platter. If desired, place an appropriate-sized glass bowl in the center of cabbage cup. Fill cabbage leaves or bowl with dip. Arrange Vegetables Dippers around dip. Makes about 2 cups.

How to Make Sea-Shell Appetizers

1/Fold cooled egg circles into quarters. Heat a wooden-handled metal skewer in an open flame. Use hot skewer to brand 3 decorative lines on top of each folded egg circle.

2/Stuff top folds of egg with a generous tablespoon of Kansai-Style Mixed Sushi. If necessary, press stuffed shells to improve shapes. Serve on a platter or on individual plates.

Bamboo-Shaped Stuffed Fish Rolls   Photo on page 106.

Takenoko Chikuwa

Stuffed fish rolls can be dipped into Tempura Batter, page 116, and deep-fried.

4 small hollow fish rolls (chikuwa)
1 teaspoon Prepared Japanese Horseradish,
   page 154, if desired
1 or 2 fresh string beans, blanched,
   cut in thin slivers

1/2 small carrot, cut in
   1/8-inch-wide strips
1 (1/2-inch-wide) strip red bell pepper,
   cut in thin slivers
Soy sauce

Cut fish rolls in 1/2 crosswise. Using a small knife, spread insides with Prepared Japanese Horseradish, if desired. Trim vegetable strips to length of fish-roll pieces. Hold a strip of each vegetable together in a bunch; push into hollow center of a piece of fish roll. Continue stuffing remaining fish rolls. Slice each piece of fish roll into 2 pieces, using a diagonal cut. Stand stuffed fish-roll pieces on their flat ends. Serve immediately with soy sauce. Or, cover and refrigerate several hours. Makes 16 appetizer servings.

Variations

Stuffed fish rolls can be added to soups and stews.

Karen's Hard-Cooked Eggs Sukiyaki

Gyu Niku No Tamago

My friend, Japanese-cooking expert Karen Green, shared this simple recipe with me.

8 hard-cooked eggs, peeled, chilled
1/2 lb. sukiyaki meat (beef rib-eye steak,
　　sliced paper thin), chilled
1/2 cup saké

2/3 cup soy sauce
2 tablespoons sugar
4 (1/8-inch-thick) slices peeled fresh
　　gingerroot, smashed

Wrap each hard-cooked egg with sukiyaki meat, completely enclosing egg. If eggs and meat are cold, meat will stick easily. In a skillet, combine saké, soy sauce, sugar and gingerroot over low heat. Cook, stirring constantly, until sugar has dissolved. Place meat-covered eggs in saké mixture. Cook gently about 10 minutes, spooning sauce over eggs. Remove eggs from sauce. Place on a rack over waxed paper to cool; excess liquid will drain off. Slice cooled eggs in halves or thirds, so each slice has some egg yolk. Serve room temperature as a first course. Or, refrigerate several hours and use as party appetizers or picnic snacks. Makes 8 to 24 appetizer servings.

Soybean Nuts

Age Daizu

The mild flavor of soybeans lends itself to a variety of seasonings.

1 lb. dried soybeans
About 6 cups peanut oil or
　　vegetable oil for deep-frying

Salt or seasoning salt to taste

In a large bowl, wash soybeans in a large amount of cool water; drain. Cover with about 10 cups water. Soak overnight; drain. In a large saucepan, place beans and about 4 cups water over medium-high heat. When beans come to a boil, reduce heat to low; simmer 15 minutes. Beans will still be slightly crunchy. Drain beans. Spread out beans to dry on 2 or 3 clean kitchen towels. Roll beans over towels to help absorb moisture. Spread out dried beans in a large shallow baking pan. Place in a 250F (120C) oven 1 hour. Stir once or twice. Turn off oven. Leave beans in oven several hours or overnight to dry before deep-frying. In a wok, heat oil to 350F (175C) or until a 1-inch cube of bread turns golden brown in 65 seconds. Place beans, 1 heaping cup at a time, in a large wire skimmer. Lower beans into hot oil. Fry 5 to 7 minutes or until beans are a rich medium-brown color and crunchy. Drain on paper towels. Sprinkle with salt or seasoning salt. Continue frying and seasoning remaining beans. Cool completely. Store in an airtight container. Makes about 7 cups.

Variations

Sweet Spicy Soybean Nuts: To each cup hot fried soybeans, add 2 tablespoons sugar and 1/2 teaspoon ground cinnamon; mix well.

Hot Spicy Soybean Nuts: To each cup hot fried soybeans, add Seven-Spice Mixture, page 147, and salt to taste; mix well.

Soy-Sauce Soybean Nuts: Soak and simmer soybeans as above; place in a large bowl. Add 1 cup soy sauce. Soak beans 2 hours. Drain beans; pat dry. Dry in oven and deep-fry as directed above. Add salt to taste.

Miso Soybean Nuts: Place 1 cup fried soybeans in a medium skillet. Stir in 2 teaspoons red miso. Stir over medium heat until beans are coated with miso.

How to Make Fish-Loaf Butterflies

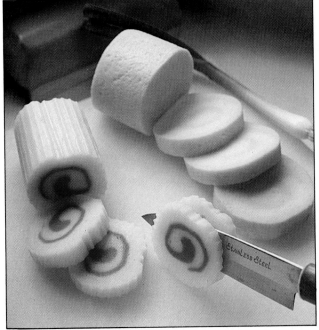

1/Slice fish loaf into 1/2-inch-thick pieces. Slice each piece through the middle to within 1/8 inch of base without cutting all the way through.

2/Place each piece on a cutting surface with attached side to your right. Make a short diagonal cut on attached side in lower 1/2. Slant cut downward at a 45-degree angle. Spread flaps or wings and tuck cut section inside flap. Decorate each butterfly.

Fish-Loaf Butterflies

Cho Cho Kamoboko

This attractive appetizer will fly to your mouth!

1 (6-oz.) pkg. steamed pinwheel or plain fish loaf (narutomaki or kamaboko)
Green-onion stems

Soy sauce to taste
Prepared Japanese Horseradish, page 154, to taste

Slice fish loaf into 1/2-inch-thick pieces. Slice each piece through the middle to within 1/8 inch of base without cutting all the way through. You will have 2 attached flaps of fish loaf. Place each piece on a cutting surface with attached side to your right. Make a short diagonal cut on attached side in lower 1/2. Slant cut downward at a 45-degree angle. Spread flaps or wings and tuck cut section inside flap. Decorate each butterfly with green-onion pieces. Serve with soy sauce mixed with Prepared Japanese Horseradish. Makes 10 to 12 butterflies.

Variation Photo on page 37.

Split slices of fish loaf can also be stuffed with sliced kumquats, whole-bean miso (moromi miso), steamed fermented soybeans (natto), radish slices or other fillings. Serve with soy sauce and Prepared Japanese Horseradish.

Ham & Fish Pinwheels   Photo on page 106.

Create exciting taste combinations by adding strips of Toasted Nori, page 59, or shiso leaves.

Mustard-Miso Sauce, page 156
5 or 6 small hollow fish rolls (chikuwa)
2 (1/8-inch-thick) slices Monterey Jack or
  Swiss cheese

2 (1/8-inch-thick) slices cooked ham
1 tablespoon Prepared Japanese Horseradish,
  page 154

Prepare Mustard-Miso Sauce; set aside. Using a small sharp knife, make a cut from top to bottom on 1 side of each fish roll. When spread open, each roll will be a rectangle. Cut cheese and ham slices into narrow strips to fit rectangular pieces of fish roll. Layer a strip of cheese and a strip of ham on white inside portion of each fish-roll rectangle. Spread a small amount of Prepared Japanese Horseradish over ham layer. Beginning at short end, roll up layers into a cylinder. Secure with 3 evenly spaced wooden picks. Repeat with remaining ingredients. Cut each cylinder into 3 pinwheel slices between wooden picks. Each slice will be held together with a wooden pick. Arrange pinwheel slices on a serving platter. Serve with Mustard-Miso Sauce for dipping. Makes 15 to 18 appetizer servings.

Simmered Burdock & Bacon Rolls

Gobo No Bacon Maki

Yukari Oya, a young Tokyo policewoman, recommends this snack as an accompaniment to saké.

Sauce, see below
4 (5-inch) pieces burdock root (gobo),
  scraped, soaked in water

4 bacon slices

Sauce:
1 cup water
1 teaspoon dashi-no-moto powder
2 tablespoons mirin

2 tablespoons soy sauce
1 tablespoon saké
2 tablespoons sugar

Prepare Sauce; bring to a boil over high heat, then immediately reduce heat to low. Add burdock pieces. Cover and simmer 25 to 30 minutes or until tender. Burdock will retain a firm texture but can still be pierced easily with a knife. Cool in sauce. Drain burdock; reserve sauce. Wrap a bacon slice around each piece of burdock in a spiral fashion. Secure ends of bacon with wooden-pick halves. In a small skillet, fry wrapped burdock over medium-low heat. Turn burdock several times so bacon cooks evenly. Wooden picks can be removed when bacon is half-cooked. Watch carefully to prevent bacon fat from burning. If fat burns, remove burdock; drain and wipe skillet. Return wrapped burdock to skillet and continue frying until bacon is crisp. Pour off any remaining fat. Pour reserved sauce over burdock; coat well. Cut each piece into 5 (1-inch) pieces. Put 4 or 5 pieces on each small serving plate. Spoon remaining sauce over each serving. Makes 4 or 5 appetizer servings.

Sauce:
In a small saucepan, combine all ingredients. Makes about 1-1/3 cups.

Soups (Shirumono)

Soups are among the most simple and satisfying foods of Japan. The classification of soups is called *shirumono*. The two main categories of soup are: *suimono* or *sumashi-jiru*—a clear broth or consommé—and *miso-shiru*—a clear broth which has been thickened with fermented bean paste (miso). Suimono or sumashi-jiru is served after the appetizer course of an elegant Japanese meal. It is an excellent accompaniment to sushi, and doubles as a replacement for a thirst-quenching beverage in the meal. Suimono and miso-shiru are served year round. Through the use of a great variety of fresh ingredients, they have become a reflection of the changing seasons.

Suimono consists of four parts. The first part is the soup base, sea-vegetable and fish stock, known as *dashi*. The subtle yet complex flavor of the dashi will guarantee the success of the soup. The second part is usually a bite-sized piece of protein, such as chicken, fish or tofu. The third part is a secondary solid ingredient which might include a piece of vegetable selected especially to compliment the main ingredient. The fourth part is the garnish. This is the final touch and could feature a special seasoning or a fresh herb selected in honor of the season. Consommé with Ginger Scallops embodies the ideals of a

good clear soup. Clear soup and miso soup are sipped directly from the bowl. The additional ingredients are eaten with a pair of chopsticks.

For centuries, one of Japan's favorite breakfast foods has been a steaming-hot bowl of savory miso soup. Supplemented with protein-rich tofu and a leafy green sea vegetable, it becomes a powerhouse of good nutrition.

Miso soup is based upon two important ingredients, dashi—the soup stock—and miso—fermented-bean paste. The wide variety of miso pastes can be blended at will to create a large range of flavors for miso soup. For example, red and yellow miso can be blended for a pleasing taste combination. Or, the soup can be made with a single type of miso, such as sweet white miso, a favorite in Kyoto. The soup is completed by the addition of solid ingredients and a garnish. For the more-substantial evening meal, the amount of protein in miso soup can be easily increased.

Miso soup is so beloved in Japan that it has been the favorite subject of poets and scholars throughout Japanese history. For centuries it has been the staple food of the disciples of Zen. It is said that a young woman in Japan is ready to become a wife when she is able to make delicious miso soup. I have found that when houseguests are visiting from Japan, a cup of steaming-hot miso soup satisfies the nostalgic craving for a taste of home. The additional ingredients in clear soup and miso soup serve primarily as garnishes. Thicker soups or stews, such as Sparerib Soup with Vegetables, feature the solid ingredients as the principal elements.

The foundation of a good soup in Japan or any other country is the stock. Dashi is one of the great stocks of the world. But unlike meat or chicken stock, its preparation requires only a few minutes of effort. This advantage enables the Japanese to have fresh stock available for the preparation of every meal. For centuries, the use of animal fat was unknown in Japan. Fats serve to add richness, flavor and substance to stock. The ingenious development of dashi was based upon the need to add these qualities to foods without the use of fats. Dried bonito (katsuo-bushi) and dried kelp (konbu) were selected because of their high amino-acid content. This gives a distinctive flavor which enhances food considerably. Dried shiitake mushrooms can also be added to the basic stock to give even more flavor. Sometimes fish stock is made with dried sardines in place of dried bonito. The cuisine of Zen Buddhists, known as *shojin ryori,* bases its stocks upon the use of vegetables, especially kelp. Kelp is a natural source of the amino acids used in the manufacture of monosodium glutamate (ajinomoto). The long life span of the Okinawan people is attributed to the healthful qualities of kelp which is consumed in large quantities.

Sometimes Japanese soups are made with chicken stock, especially when the primary soup ingredient is chicken. It is possible to substitute chicken for sea-vegetable and fish stock in all soups; however, the flavor and character will be greatly altered.

Savory Miso Soup

Miso Shiru

This is the "flavor of Japan" and a great breakfast favorite.

**3-1/2 cups Sea-Vegetable & Fish Stock
    or Instant Sea-Vegetable &
    Fish Stock, opposite
3 tablespoons red miso
About 1 tablespoon yellow miso
1/4 lb. silken or regular Japanese-style
    tofu, rinsed, patted dry,
    or Peanut Tofu, page 112**

**1/2 cup fresh or rehydrated dried
    lobe leaf (wakame)
2 small green onions, minced**

Heat stock over medium-low heat. Place miso in a small bowl; dilute with a small amount of hot stock. Stir diluted miso into stock in saucepan. Leave over medium-low heat. Do not boil or flavors and nutrients in miso could be destroyed. Cut tofu into 1/2-inch cubes. Add tofu, lobe leaf and green onions to soup. Simmer 1 to 2 minutes or until hot. Ladle soup into 4 or 5 lacquer soup bowls. Top with lids. Makes 4 or 5 servings.

Variations

Fish-Cake Miso Soup (Tsuke-age Miso Shiru): Omit tofu and lobe leaf. Substitute 1 cubed piece Fish-Cake Tempura, page 122, and 1/4 pound torn fresh spinach leaves. Add a dash of ground sansho pepper.

Treasure-Ball Miso Soup (Hirousu Miso Shiru): Omit tofu and lobe leaf. Add 1/2 recipe Tofu Treasure Balls, page 105, and cooked, cubed, peeled, 2-inch piece daikon radish. Add a dash of Seven-Spice Mixture, page 147.

Country-Style Miso Soup: Omit tofu and lobe leaf. Soften 2 dried mushrooms in warm water; cut off and discard stems. Thinly slice mushrooms. Sauté 1 chopped medium onion and 1 cup cabbage pieces in vegetable oil until tender. Stir mushrooms, onion and cabbage into miso soup; simmer 1 to 2 minutes or until hot.

Sea-Vegetable & Fish Stock

Ichiban Dashi

This first-quality mild-tasting stock is the basis for many of Japan's delicious soups and sauces.

**1 (5" x 4-1/2") piece good-quality
  dried kelp (dashi konbu)
4 cups bottled spring water
  or tap water**

1/2 cup dried-bonito shavings

Lightly wipe dried kelp with a damp cloth. Make 2 or 3 slits in it with a small knife. In a medium saucepan, place kelp and water over medium-low heat. Heat slowly 8 to 10 minutes or until water reaches simmering point. Do not allow water and kelp to boil at any time or stock will become bitter. Remove kelp; let water come to a full boil. Add bonito shavings and immediately remove pan from heat. Let shavings settle to bottom of pan. After 2 to 3 minutes, strain stock through 3 layers of dampened cheesecloth or a fine strainer. Use stock immediately or refrigerate up to 2 days. Kelp and bonito shavings can be used again for making Second-Quality Sea-Vegetable & Fish Stock, below. Recipe can be doubled. Makes about 3-1/2 cups.

Second-Quality Sea-Vegetable & Fish Stock

Niban Dashi

This stock is suitable for cooking many vegetables and making noodle broth and hearty stews.

**Strained bonito shavings and
  kelp (dashi konbu) from
  Sea-Vegetable & Fish Stock, above**

**3-1/4 cups water
Additional 1/4 cup dried-bonito
  shavings**

In a medium saucepan, heat strained bonito shavings, kelp and water over medium heat. When water is hot, remove pan from heat; steep 30 minutes. After steeping, slowly bring to a boil over medium-high heat. When water boils, add additional bonito shavings. Remove pan from heat. Let shavings settle to bottom of pan. After 4 to 5 minutes, strain stock through 3 layers of dampened cheesecloth or a fine strainer. Use stock immediately or refrigerate up to 2 days. Remaining piece of kelp can be added to braised dishes or stews for enrichment. Makes about 3 cups.

Instant Sea-Vegetable & Fish Stock

Dashi-no-moto

An excellent quick base for soups. Sprinkle dashi-no-moto powder over foods as a seasoning.

6 cups water

1 envelope dashi-no-moto powder

In a 2-quart saucepan, simmer water over medium heat. Stir in dashi powder; simmer 2 minutes. Makes 6 cups.

Consommé with Ginger Scallops

Hotategai No Sumashi Jiru

A simply elegant beginning for a special meal.

1 to 2 oz. tosakanori or
   dried wakame (sea vegetables)
4 or 5 Pine-Needle Garnishes, page 30
Ginger Scallops, below
1 teaspoon light (thin) soy sauce

1 tablespoon saké
Salt to taste
3-1/2 cups Sea-Vegetable & Fish Stock,
   page 45, or Clarified Chicken Stock
   with Ginger, page 48

Place sea vegetable in a small bowl. Add warm water to cover. Soak 30 minutes. Prepare Pine-Needle Garnishes and Ginger Scallops. Add soy sauce, saké and salt to stock. Place 1 Ginger Scallop in each lacquer soup bowl. Remaining Ginger Scallops can be served with soy sauce, if desired. Arrange rehydrated sea vegetable around base of each scallop. Carefully fill bowls with hot soup. Add a Pine-Needle Garnish to each bowl. Top with lids. Makes 4 or 5 servings.

Variations

Pinwheel-Shrimp Consommé: Photo on cover.
Omit Ginger Scallops and sea vegetable. Place 1 Pinwheel-Shrimp, page 25, in each bowl. Add 1 sprig of kinome or watercress to each bowl. Fill bowls with soup.
Kyoto-Style Flower Consommé (Kyo Hana Consommé): Omit Ginger Scallops. Add 2 soaked pieces flower-shaped wheat gluten (fu) to each bowl. Divide rehydrated sea vegetable among soup bowls. Fill bowls with soup.
Cucumber-Mushroom Consommé: Omit Ginger Scallops and sea vegetable. Peel 1 small Japanese cucumber. Cut off ends. Using a long knife or iced-tea spoon, hollow out cucumber. Cut into 8 or 10 rings. Insert a cluster of enokitake mushrooms in pairs of cucumber rings. Place 1 pair of cucumber rings with enokitake mushrooms in each bowl of soup.

Ginger Scallops

Kaiba-shira No Shoga Mushi

Good in soup or as part of a salad.

Vegetable oil
1/2 lb. scallops
1 tablespoon saké
2 tablespoons mirin

1 teaspoon fresh gingerroot juice, page 8
1 small egg white
1/2 teaspoon salt
1 teaspoon potato starch or cornstarch

Spray insides of 8 small scallop shells with non-stick vegetable spray. Puree scallops in a blender or food processor fitted with a steel blade. Add saké, mirin, gingerroot juice, egg white, salt and potato starch or cornstarch; process until smooth. In a wok or deep pot, bring about 4 cups water to a boil. Use some of scallop mixture to spread a thin smooth coating inside each oiled shell. This will give a pretty shell pattern. Spoon remaining scallop mixture into shells; smooth tops. Place filled shells on a steamer tray. Cover and place over boiling water. Reduce heat to medium-low. Steam over gently simmering water 5 minutes or until a small knife inserted into scallop mixture comes out clean. Cool scallops completely. Remove from shells by running a small knife around edge of shell and gently prying out mixture. Serve in soups or as an appetizer. Makes 8 appetizer servings.

How to Make Teapot Soup

1/When stock mixture simmers, add chicken, okra and mushroom slices; simmer 4 to 5 minutes. Add bamboo shoots, shrimp, gingko nuts and wheat gluten, if desired; simmer 1 to 2 minutes. Add green onion and trefoil or watercress.

2/Pour clear broth into teacup-sized bowls. Add some of each solid ingredient to each bowl. Pass lemon wedges for seasoning.

Teapot Soup

Dobin Mushi

In Japan, a unique little teapot with its serving-cup lid is enough for one serving.

**3-1/2 cups Sea-Vegetable & Fish Stock,
   Instant Sea-Vegetable & Fish
   Stock, page 45, or Chicken Stock
   with Ginger, page 50**
1 tablespoon light (thin) soy sauce
1 tablespoon mirin
Salt to taste
1/2 chicken breast, skinned, boned, diced
2 or 3 small okra pods, sliced
**2 large matsutake mushrooms or
   2 large round mushrooms, sliced**

2 oz. bamboo shoots, sliced
4 small shrimp, peeled
4 gingko nuts (ginnan), if desired
**4 pieces ball-shaped or flower-shaped
   wheat gluten (fu), if desired,
   soaked in water**
1 green onion, thinly sliced
4 trefoil sprigs (mitsuba) or watercress
4 lemon wedges

Place stock in a medium saucepan; add soy sauce, mirin and salt. Heat soup over medium-low heat. When it simmers, add chicken, okra and mushroom slices; simmer 4 to 5 minutes. Add bamboo shoots, shrimp, gingko nuts and soaked wheat gluten, if desired; simmer 1 to 2 minutes longer. Add green onion and trefoil or watercress. Pour soup into a 1-1/2-quart, wide-mouth, ceramic teapot. Place lid on top of pot. At the table, pour clear broth into teacup-sized bowls. Add some of each solid ingredient to each bowl. Pass lemon wedges. Makes 4 servings.

Variation

It may be necessary to make an adjustment in the amount of soup, depending on size of teapot available. Measure amount of liquid your teapot will hold before you begin.

New Year's Soup with Grilled Rice Cakes

Ozoni

All the preparation can be done hours ahead; assemble ingredients and add hot soup at the last minute.

3-1/2 cups Sea-Vegetable & Fish Stock,
** Instant Sea-Vegetable & Fish**
** Stock, page 45, or Chicken Stock**
** with Ginger, page 50**
1 tablespoon light (thin) soy sauce
1 tablespoon saké
Salt to taste
5 small fresh or dried shiitake
** mushrooms**
1/2 chicken breast, skinned, boned, diced
1 tablespoon mirin

1 teaspoon light (thin) soy sauce
1 cup sliced Napa cabbage
5 (1/4-inch-thick) slices steamed pinwheel
** fish loaf (narutomaki), if desired**
5 pieces Sweet Glutinous-Rice Cake, page 144
5 Carrot Fans, page 32, or
** 5 carrot flowers, page 30**
10 edible pea pods, blanched
2 small green onions, thinly sliced
5 Pine-Needle Garnishes, page 30

Place stock in a medium saucepan; add 1 tablespoon soy sauce, saké and salt. If using dried mushrooms, place in a medium bowl; add warm water to cover. Soak 30 minutes or until needed. Squeeze mushrooms dry. Cut off and discard tough stems. Using a small sharp knife, score tops of fresh or rehydrated mushrooms in a star pattern, page 29. In a small bowl, marinate chicken in mirin and 1 teaspoon soy sauce about 5 minutes. Heat seasoned stock over medium heat. Add scored mushrooms, marinated chicken, cabbage and fish-loaf slices. Reduce heat; simmer 5 minutes. Grill a Sweet Glutinous-Rice Cake following directions on page 144. Place a piece of grilled rice cake in each of 5 lacquer soup bowls. Ladle hot soup into bowls, dividing solid ingredients among servings. Place a Carrot Fan or carrot flower and 2 pea pods in each bowl. Garnish each serving with green onion and a Pine-Needle Garnish. Makes 5 servings.

Variation

Kogoshimi-Style New Year's Soup with Miso (Kogoshima Miso Zoni): In a small bowl, mix 3 to 4 tablespoons yellow miso with a small amount of hot stock. Stir diluted miso into stock in saucepan. Continue as directed above.

Clarified Chicken Stock with Ginger

Sumashi Jiru

Use as an alternative for Sea-Vegetable & Fish Stock, page 45, in Japanese consommé.

5 qts. Chicken Stock with Ginger,
** page 50, with variation noted below**

2 egg whites, lightly beaten
Shells of 2 eggs, crushed

To use Chicken Stock with Ginger for consommé, it must be be clarified, or cleansed of all impurities. To make a crystal-clear stock, first blanch whole chicken and chicken parts. Cover with cool water in a large pot. Bring water to a full boil. Pour off cloudy water; rinse chicken under cool running water. Continue with recipe. After stock has been strained, chilled and completely defatted, place it in a large clean pot. Bring to a boil. Stir in egg whites and egg shells. Reduce heat; barely simmer 4 to 5 minutes. By boiling stock, impurities are pushed to top of pot and trapped in coagulated egg layer. Strain stock through several layers of dampened cheesecloth. Cool stock, uncovered, 1 hour. Refrigerate up to 3 days. Stock should be brought to a boil before use. Stock can also be frozen in smaller amounts 1 month. Makes 5 quarts.

Sparerib Soup with Vegetables

Gomoku Soki Soba

Meaty spareribs, flavorful vegetables and noodles are simmered together in this hearty Okinawan soup.

3 qts. Chicken Stock with Ginger,
  below
2 (1/8-inch-thick) slices peeled fresh
  gingerroot, smashed
2 green onions, smashed
1 large garlic clove, smashed
1 lb. pork spareribs
2 oz. fresh mushrooms, sliced
1 small carrot, cut sen-giri, page 18
1/2 lb. Napa cabbage, sliced

1/4 bunch spinach, well-rinsed
1/4 cup soy sauce
Salt to taste
1/4 teaspoon ground sansho pepper or
  ground black pepper
3/4 lb. fresh ramen noodles
1 teaspoon sesame oil
4 green onions, thinly sliced
6 quail eggs, if desired, hard-cooked,
  peeled

In a large stockpot, simmer stock, gingerroot, 2 smashed green onions and garlic over medium heat 10 minutes. Separate spareribs by cutting through meat between bones. In a medium saucepan, blanch ribs in boiling water 1 minute; drain. Add ribs to stock mixture. Reduce heat; simmer 1-1/2 hours or until meat is tender. Remove spareribs from stock mixture. Cut meat off bones; discard bones. Return meat to stockpot. Spoon off excess fat floating on top. Add mushrooms and carrot; simmer 10 minutes. Add cabbage, spinach, soy sauce, salt and pepper; simmer 5 minutes. In a large pot, bring about 3 quarts water to a boil. Add fresh noodles; cook 1 minute. Drain well. Add sesame oil; toss until coated. Divide noodles among 6 deep soup bowls. Ladle soup with meat and vegetables on top of noodles. Sprinkle with sliced green onions. Add a quail egg to each serving, if desired. Makes 6 servings.

Chicken Stock with Ginger

Tori No Sumashi Jiru

This alternative to Sea-Vegetable & Fish Stock, page 45, is an excellent base for many Japanese soups.

1 (3-1/2- to 4-lb.) chicken
2 to 3 lbs. chicken parts
  (backs, necks, wings)
5 green onions or 2 leeks,
  cut in 1/2, well-rinsed

4 (1/4-inch-thick) slices peeled fresh
  gingerroot, smashed
About 5 qts. bottled spring water or
  tap water

Rinse chicken and chicken parts under cool running water. Remove any fat pads. Place all ingredients in a stockpot over medium-high heat. When stock bubbles, immediately reduce heat to low. Simmer, uncovered, 30 minutes, skimming off foam which forms on top. Do not boil or stir stock. After 30 minutes, remove breast and thigh meat from whole chicken, if desired; reserve for another use. Continue simmering stock 1-1/2 to 2 hours longer. If water level becomes low, add a little more water. Strain into a large pan; discard solids. For greater clarity, stock can be strained again through a strainer lined with several layers of dampened cheesecloth. Cool stock, uncovered, 1 hour. Refrigerate up to 3 days. Skim off surface fat before using stock. Stock should be brought to a boil before use. Defatted stock can also be frozen in smaller amounts 1 to 2 months. To concentrate stock flavor, boil it to reduce by 1/3 to 1/2. Salt stock as you use it in cooking, adding salt amounts suggested in recipes. Recipe can be halved. Makes about 5 quarts.

How to Make Creamy Corn Potage with Crabmeat

1/Push pureed corn back into stock through a fine strainer. Discard corn pulp left in strainer.

2/Stir crabmeat into thickened soup. Remove from heat. Drizzle in beaten egg white, stirring with chopsticks. Add green onions. Ladle hot soup into bowls.

Creamy Corn Potage with Crabmeat

Tomorokoshi No Kani Jiru

On the island of Okinawa, this delicate creamy soup is a great favorite in restaurants.

3-1/2 cups Chicken Stock with Ginger,
   opposite
1 cup fresh whole-kernel corn from
   2 large ears, or 1 (9-oz.) pkg.
   frozen whole-kernel or cream-style corn
1 tablespoon saké
1/2 teaspoon sugar
1 teaspoon salt

Dash of ground black pepper
1 tablespoon minced baked ham
2-1/2 tablespoons cornstarch
1/4 cup cold chicken stock or water
2 to 3 oz. flaked crabmeat,
   well picked over
1 large egg white, slightly beaten
2 small green onions, thinly sliced

In a medium saucepan, heat stock and corn over medium heat 5 minutes. Strain hot stock mixture into a medium bowl. Puree corn in a blender or food processor fitted with a steel blade. Add a small amount of stock. Push pureed corn back into stock through a fine strainer. Discard any corn pulp left in strainer. Heat stock mixture over medium heat. Stir in saké, sugar, salt, pepper and ham. In a small bowl, blend cornstarch and 1/4 cup chicken stock or water. Increase heat. When soup boils, add cornstarch mixture, stirring constantly 1 minute as soup thickens. Reduce heat to low. Stir in crabmeat. Remove from heat. Drizzle in beaten egg white, stirring with chopsticks in a circular motion. Add green onions. Ladle hot soup into bowls. Makes 6 to 8 servings.

Sliced Raw Fish & Vinegared-Rice Dishes (Sashimi & Sushi)

Freshness makes its most subtle statement in the form of fresh chilled raw fish (sashimi). My first inquisitive taste of Japan's most beloved food was in Tokyo several years ago. With a flash of steel, the sushi chef (shokunin) deftly performed his magic act with great precision cutting exceptionally fresh fish into a variety of attractive slices. Several pieces were arranged carefully upon a bed of garnishes, or *tsuma*. Garnishes play an important role by adding color, texture and flavor. They are often selected to represent the season. A tiny dish of soy sauce and a cone of hot Prepared Japanese Horseradish (wasabi) were served on the side with my sashimi. My first bite of fish was a pleasant surprise! The taste was clean and mild, the texture tender and the smell resembled a fresh ocean breeze. There was no hint of the fishiness so often tasted in "fresh fish" bought at home. I would caution that your first taste of Japanese horseradish be approached as if entering a steaming hot Japanese tub. Don't leap in; inch your way in a little bit at a time!

Sashimi represents the freshest and highest quality of seasonal fish available in Japan. Freshness is so desirable that the concept is often carried to an extreme. The preparation of *ikizukuri,* for example, requires that a portion of the flesh of a fish be carved while still alive. The fish is garnished and served so quickly that the gills are still heaving as the fish is presented for serving. Another dish, dancing shrimp (odori), requires that live prawns are quickly cleaned and served for immediate consumption; the fresh flavor is enhanced only by the prawn's spirited wiggle!

Housewives in Japan have developed a skill for recognizing the freshest fish at its flavorful best. You can duplicate sashimi in your own kitchen if you observe the golden rule: Select only the freshest seasonal fish and live shellfish with tightly closed shells. Good sashimi can be made using the seasonal best of whatever fish is available in your area. It is best to use only saltwater fish for sashimi; freshwater fish could harbor parasites.

Seek the advice of a trusted fishmonger who will guide you in making your fish selections. If you request it, he will scale, gut and fillet your fish in preparation for slicing. Try to avoid frozen fish. Give careful thought to slicing your fish for serving. The shape and firmness of each fish will help determine the proper cut. The firmer the flesh, the thinner it can be sliced. The thickness of each cut can effect the fish's final flavor. The method for preparing sashimi is sometimes varied by grilling the fish for a few seconds over an open fire, by blanching in boiling water or by a quick chilling in iced water.

The merits of sashimi depend upon the freshness, flavor and texture of the fish alone, but *sushi* depends upon a careful blending of fresh fish with sweet vinegared rice. Sushi originated in Southeast Asia as a method for preserving fish. Fresh fish were layered with large amounts of salt. Later they were pressed between layers of steamed rice. The formation of organic acids caused the rice to ferment and flavor the fish. Harmful bacteria were destroyed during the fermentation process. At first, the rice was discarded, but eventually it was eaten, too. Layered carp and rice (funa-zushi) is a descendant of the earlier type of pressed sushi. It is still made today at Lake Biwa, near Kyoto. Pressed-box sushi (oshi-zushi) became increasingly popular in the Kyoto area where it is a specialty today. Fan-Shaped Sushi Cake and the Happy-Birthday Cake Japanese-Style are my modernized versions of the traditional pressed layered sushi.

Impatient to devise a quicker method for making sushi, the Japanese added vinegar to the rice to create the sour taste. Vinegared fish and even beef were pressed on top. These were a form of pickled foods (namasu). Spicy green horseradish (wasabi) was added to the sushi as an antibacterial agent as well as for its good flavor.

Fresh sliced tuna is an excellent choice for topping sushi rice. *Otoro* tuna is the grade containing most fat. The pale marbled flesh is located near the belly section of the fish. Otoro is highly prized and expensive. *Chutoro* tuna is a less fatty grade located in the midsection. Bright red *akami* tuna is the leanest part of the fish located near the backbone. It is an excellent choice for dieters.

If you want to enjoy sushi made without raw fish, try Spicy Grilled-Beef Sushi, Stuffed Golden Tofu Pouches or Kansai-Style Mixed Sushi. The latter is the most popular type made in Japanese homes.

A skillful sushi chef can prepare sushi with amazing speed. He instinctively gathers the correct amount of vinegared rice to prepare hand-pressed sushi and molds it with one hand into a perfectly shaped bite-sized oval. Apprentice chefs spend years perfecting these skills, often practicing with huge tubs of soybean pulp (okara) instead of wasting precious rice. Each movement has been calculated and the timing must be exact. Every grain of rice must be coaxed into the same direction.

The expertise of the sushi chef is the result of years of apprenticeship and hard work. The skill cannot be duplicated but the taste of delicious sushi can be recreated in your own kitchen. The secret bears repeating—prepare the finest ingredients with care and reverence. The essence of such careful food preparation is in itself a religion, a belief in the total supremacy of nature.

Sashimi Roses Photo on cover.

Bara Sashimi

Size of roses can be varied according to width and thickness of the fish strips.

Lemon-Soy Dipping Sauce, page 54
1 fresh, firm, white fish fillet,
    skinned, about 1-inch thick
3 to 4 oz. thinly sliced smoked salmon
    or lox, cut in 2" x 1" strips

Shredded daikon radish
Fresh shiso leaves
Prepared-Japanese-Horseradish Leaves or
    Cones, page 154

Prepare Lemon-Soy Dipping Sauce; set aside. Cut fish into rectangular pieces about 2 inches wide. Slice each piece diagonally across the grain into 1/8-inch-thick slices. Lay 6 slices in a long row with short ends overlapping. Leave about 1/4 of top of each piece showing. Starting at the bottom, carefully roll up pieces into a single roll. Set roll upright. Bend back tops of slices to resemble rose petals. Shape smoked-salmon strips into roses using this method. Or, roll a single slice loosely into a cone shape and stand it upright. Wrap remaining slices around cone shape, overlapping them to resemble a rose. Carefully bend back tops of slices to resemble rose petals. On each serving plate, place 1 white and 1 pink Sashimi Rose. Garnish with shredded daikon, shiso leaves and a Prepared-Japanese-Horseradish Leaf or Cone. Pour a small dish of Lemon-Soy Dipping Sauce for each serving. Dip fish petals into sauce before eating. Makes 3 to 4 servings.

Fresh Chilled Raw Fish

Sashimi

Present an array of your favorite sashimi cuts chilled and decorated in a bed of crushed ice.

Paper-Thin Cut (Usu-Zukuri):
Firm-fleshed white fish fillets, such as halibut and sea bass, can be cut into 1/16-inch paper-thin diagonal slices across the grain. These slices are often placed overlapping on a platter in a circular flower-shape. A decorative edible garnish is usually placed in the center.

Thin-Slice Cut (Sogi-Zukuri):
Similar to paper-thin cut but slices are slightly thicker, about 1/8 inch.

Domino Cut (Hira-Zukuri):
This common rectangular cut is excellent for many fish such as tuna, flounder, red snapper and yellowtail. Make clean 3/8-inch straight cuts across the grain through rectangular pieces of fish. Firmer-fleshed fish can be cut into thinner slices. Pieces can be cut slightly at an angle, if desired. Use the blade of the knife to push slices to the side as they are cut, creating a stacked domino effect. Five or 6 pieces are usually enough for each serving.

A similar cut, called *hiki-zukuri,* is used for fragile fish which require careful handling. Each cut piece of fish is lifted to the plate instead of being pushed to the side of the board with the knife.

String Cut (Ito-Zukuri):
An excellent method for cutting squid or other thin pieces of fish fillets. Slice fish into thin strips; place a small pile on each serving plate. Hollowed-cucumber cups or tiny leaf-lined baskets are handy serving containers for string-cut fish.

Cube Cut (Kaku-Zukuri):
Tuna and other thick fillets of fresh fish can be cut into a cube cut. Cut slices about 3/4 inch wide, then cut slices into 3/4-inch cubes.

Lemon-Soy Dipping Sauce

Ponzu

Serve this tangy sauce with Chicken Hot Pot, page 99, or with your favorite sushi or sashimi.

1/2 cup soy sauce
1/4 cup fresh lemon juice
2 tablespoons mirin
3 tablespoons water

2 tablespoons rice vinegar
1 tablespoon dried-bonito shavings,
    if desired

In a small bowl, combine all ingredients. Cover and steep 2 to 3 hours. Strain before use. Sauce can be steeped longer for a more pronounced bonito flavor. Makes about 1 cup.

Variation

Use the following combination of ingredients for a milder sauce: 1/2 cup soy sauce; 2 tablespoons mirin; 2 tablespoons water; 1/4 cup rice vinegar; and 2 tablespoons saké. Makes about 1 cup.

Domino-Cut Akami Tuna, above, garnished with a Prepared-Japanese-Horseradish Leaf, page 154, caviar and shredded daikon radish, carrot and cucumber.

Treasure-Ship Sashimi   Photo on page 106.

Takara Bune

Celebrate New Year with this festive dish or cook the fish whole as in Salt-Grilled Trout, page 79.

**1 (1-1/2- to 2-lb.) very fresh, whole,
    undressed, red snapper or sea bream
Finely shredded daikon radish and carrot
Scalloped Lemon Slices, page 23, halved
Prepared-Japanese-Horseradish Cone,
    page 154**

**Fresh shiso leaves, if desired
Other garnishes such as Onion Flowers,
    page 31, and edible fresh flowers
Soy sauce**

Rinse fish under cool running water. Place damp fish on a damp surface. Grasp fish by the tail and run a fish scaler or sharp knife toward head of fish. Continue scraping all around fish until it has been completely scaled. Rinse fish well. Wipe cutting board clean. Replace scaled fish on cutting board with head to the left and belly facing you. Slide knife under pectoral fin near head; cut off head. A larger fish may require another cut on the opposite side. Reserve head. Using a sharp knife, slit open belly of fish; remove viscera. Rinse out cavity under cool running water. Be sure air bladder and any clots of blood have been removed. When cavity is thoroughly rinsed, pat fish dry. Fillet it using the *three-piece cut (sanmai-oroshi)* as follows. Using a sharp boning knife, make a shallow slit just above the backbone, going from head to tail. Make firm steady cuts along slit, separating meat from backbone and ribs. Hold cut edge of fillet and raise it as separation progresses. When fillet is completely separated, turn fish over to the other side. Cutting from neck area, repeat process. Cut skeleton crosswise just above tail. Reserve tail with head. To skin fillets, place them on cutting surface, skin-side down. Using a serrated fish knife, make a small cut separating tip of tail flesh from skin. Grasp skin with your left hand. In your right hand, knife should be laying almost parallel to skin and cutting board. Begin cutting flesh away from skin, sawing knife gently from right to left. Pull skin tightly as flesh is being scraped away. Check fillets for any small bones and remove with tweezers or a sharp knife. Trim fillets to even them into rectangular shapes. Wide fillets can be cut in 1/2 lengthwise. Make clean 3/8-inch cuts across grain of fillets. Some portions of fillets can be cut into cubes, if desired. Place a pile of shredded daikon and carrot on a serving plate. Arrange cut fish attractively with Scalloped Lemon Slices. Put reserved fish head and tail back into place on platter to resemble uncut fish. Add a Prepared-Japanese-Horseradish Cone, shiso leaves and other garnishes, as desired. Onion Flowers and edible fresh flowers are appropriate garnishes. Serve immediately with small dishes of soy sauce. Makes 4 to 6 servings.

Variation

Fish fillets can be sliced and arranged on the platter omitting the head and tail.

Note: Fish can be filleted and refrigerated several hours in advance. Do not skin and slice fillets until just before serving time.

The fishmonger will be happy to clean and fillet your fish. Be sure the fish you select is extremely fresh.

Stuffed Golden Tofu Pouches   Photo on page 106.

(Inari Zushi)

Carry these in a basket to your next tailgate picnic.

1/2 recipe Sweet Vinegared Rice, page 58
1 tablespoon Dry-Roasted Sesame Seeds,
    page 150
2 (1-1/2-oz.) pkgs. fried tofu pouches
    (12 abura-age)

Simmering Sauce, see below
Shredded red pickled ginger (beni shoga)
Radish sprouts (kaiwari daikon) or
    kinome leaves, if desired

Simmering Sauce:
1-1/2 cups water
1 teaspoon dashi-no-moto powder
1/4 cup sugar

2 tablespoons light (thin) soy sauce
1 tablespoon mirin
1 tablespoon saké

Prepare Sweet Vinegared Rice. Sprinkle rice with Dry-Roasted Sesame Seeds; carefully mix together. In a small bowl, combine 1/2 cup water and 2 tablespoons rice vinegar for moistening your hands. Wet your hands; shake dry. With damp hands and a damp measuring tablespoon, divide rice into 24 portions. Each portion should measure about 1 generous tablespoon. With damp hands, gently form each portion into an oval shape, about 2 inches long. Place rice ovals on a platter. To prevent drying, cover with plastic wrap until needed. Bring about 4 cups water to a boil in a large skillet. Blanch tofu pouches 1 to 2 minutes to remove excess oils. Cover pouches with a drop-lid or press them under water several times with a wooden spoon. Turn pouches once or twice. Drain; press out excess liquid. Cool. Prepare Simmering Sauce; bring to a boil over medium-high heat. Stir once to dissolve sugar. Reduce heat to medium-low; add cooled tofu pouches. Simmer 12 to 15 minutes, turning occasionally. Sauce should be almost evaporated. Cool pouches in remaining sauce. Drain off excess sauce. Pouches should remain moist. Cut each pouch apart to make 2 rectangles. Fill each piece with a rice oval. Top rice with a few shreds of pickled ginger. Add a few radish sprouts or a kinome leaf, if desired. Serve immediately or cover loosely with plastic wrap and serve within 3 to 4 hours; do not refrigerate. Makes 24 pieces.

Sauce:
In a medium saucepan, combine all ingredients. Makes about 1-3/4 cups.

Variations

To make 12 large stuffed tofu pouches, blanch and simmer whole pouches as above. Use kitchen scissors to cut them open on 1 side. Divide rice into 12 oval portions. Fill pouches and garnish as directed above. Or, overlap cut edges enclosing rice. Place closed pouches on serving platter, cut-sides down. Recipe can be doubled.

Stuffed Tofu-Pouch Rolls: If you can obtain 6 to 8 double-length fried tofu pouches, blanch them, then simmer in Simmering Sauce. Cut pouches open on 1 long side and 2 short sides, making a large sheet. Place each sheet on a bamboo sushi mat covered with plastic wrap. Spread Kansai-Style Mixed Sushi, page 70, over 3/4 of sheet. Use mat to help roll up filled sheet into a cylinder. Tie each roll with 3 Glazed Dried-Gourd Strips, page 93. Cut roll between tied strips into 3 pieces. Each serving will be tied with a tasty gourd ribbon.

Sweet Vinegared Rice

Sushi Meshi

This delicately seasoned rice is the basic ingredient of all sushi.

2 cups short-grain rice
2-1/3 cups bottled spring water or
    tap water

1 (3-inch) piece dried kelp (konbu),
    wiped
Dressing (Awaze-Zu), see below

Dressing (Awaze-Zu):
1/4 cup rice vinegar
2 tablespoons sugar
1 tablespoon mirin

1 tablespoon saké
1-1/2 teaspoons salt

Wash rice as for Steamed Rice, page 139. Place drained rice in a 3-quart saucepan with 2-1/3 cups water. Sushi rice should have a firmer bite than regular steamed rice. Add dried kelp and soak 30 minutes. Cook rice as directed on page 139; remove kelp just before water boils. Prepare Dressing. Rinse a cedar rice-mixing tub (hangiri) or other odorless shallow wooden bowl with water. You can also use a large glass or pottery bowl. Using a dampened wooden rice paddle or spatula, scoop cooked rice into rinsed tub or bowl. Hold rice paddle over rice; sprinkle a little dressing onto rice paddle, letting it drip onto rice. Do not add entire amount at 1 time because it may not be needed. Toss rice with a gentle cutting and tossing motion. Do not crush grains. As dressing is added, constantly fan rice to cool it and remove moisture. Fanning rice will impart an attractive sheen to it as it cools. It is helpful to have a partner to help with fanning while you are tossing rice. A small electric fan also works. Continue sprinkling in dressing, a little at a time. Use only as much dressing as rice will absorb without becoming damp. Cover rice with a damp cloth. Do not refrigerate. Use rice the same day it is cooked. Makes about 6 cups.

Dressing:
In a small saucepan, combine all ingredients over low heat. Stir until sugar is dissolved. Cool to room temperature before using. Makes about 1/2 cup.

Lemon Dressing

Lemon Sosu

Sushi chefs often use this mayonnaise-type dressing for binding sushi fillings.

1 large egg, room temperature
1 tablespoon rice vinegar
1/4 teaspoon salt or to taste

1/2 teaspoon freshly grated lemon peel
1 cup almond oil or other
    top-quality vegetable oil

In a blender or food processor fitted with a steel blade, process egg 15 seconds. Add rice vinegar, salt and lemon peel; process 5 seconds. With machine running, drizzle in over 1/2 of oil. Remaining oil can be added in a slow steady stream. Continue processing until all oil is added. Dressing will become thick. Scrape it into an airtight container or handy squeeze-tube bottle for easy use. Refrigerate up to 10 days. Makes 1-1/8 cups.

How to Make Sweet Vinegared Rice

1/Hold rice paddle over rice; sprinkle a little dressing onto rice paddle, letting it drip onto rice. Do not add entire amount at 1 time. Toss rice with a gentle cutting and tossing motion.

2/As dressing is added, constantly fan rice to cool it and remove moisture. Continue sprinkling in dressing, a little at a time. Use only as much dressing as rice will absorb without becoming damp.

Toasted Nori

Yaki-Nori

For the best flavor, toast the sea-vegetable sheets just before use.

Nori
Pressed pink bonito sheets (teimaki katsuo),
  plain or plum flavored

Sheets of nori or pink bonito must be toasted before use to enhance their natural flavors and to tenderize their texture. To toast a sheet, pass shiny side 2 or 3 times over the flame of a gas stove, or quickly over an electric burner set on high heat. Nori sheets will lighten in color, gaining a greenish iridescence. Do not overtoast sheets or they will crack when rolled.

Variation
Some sheets of nori come pre-toasted or seasoned with soy sauce. Toast these sheets as directed above to refresh the flavor and recrisp the texture.

Fan-Shaped Sushi Cake

Sensu Zushi

A spectacular conversation piece for your next cocktail buffet!

Vinegared Cucumber Slices, see below
1-1/2 recipes Sweet Vinegared Rice, page 58,
    using 3 cups short-grain rice
3-1/4 cups water
1 to 2 tablespoons Prepared Japanese
    Horseradish, page 154

1 to 2 tablespoons Dry-Roasted Sesame
    Seeds, page 150
6 to 8 oz. smoked salmon, thinly sliced
Suggested Garnishes, see below

Vinegared Cucumber Slices:
2 tablespoons fresh lemon juice
2 tablespoons rice vinegar
1/4 cup sugar

1/4 teaspoon salt
1 European-style or large regular cucumber,
    rinsed, dried, sliced paper-thin

Suggested Garnishes:
Toasted Nori, page 59, for decorations
Black or red caviar
Salmon-roe caviar (ikura)
Leek or green-onion stems,
    cut to resemble bamboo leaves and
    pine needles

Sieved hard-cooked egg yolk

Line a round, 12-inch baking pan with foil. Lightly oil foil. Prepare Vinegared Cucumber Slices. Prepare Sweet Vinegared Rice using 3-1/4 cups water for soaking and cooking rice. In a small bowl, combine 1/2 cup water and 2 tablespoons rice vinegar for moistening your hands. Wet your hands; shake dry. Gently but firmly, pat 1/2 of rice evenly over bottom of prepared pan. Spread Prepared Japanese Horseradish over rice. Sprinkle with Dry-Roasted Sesame Seeds. Place a layer of drained cucumber slices over horseradish and sesame seeds. Place slices 1 inch from edge of rice from center portion down. Sides will be trimmed off later to form fan. Place a thin layer of smoked-salmon slices on top of cucumber. Pat remaining rice over salmon layer in small handfuls. Pat rice smoothly and evenly over top. Place a piece of plastic wrap directly on top of rice. Place a slightly smaller round baking pan on top of rice. Add about a 1-pound weight. Press 5 minutes. During pressing time, begin preparing a selection of Suggested Garnishes to decorate top of rice fan. Remove weight, pan and plastic wrap from top of rice. To unmold rice, place a large serving tray over top. Position pan slightly above center of tray. Grasp pan and tray firmly; invert quickly. Rice mold will fall out onto tray. Using a large, wet, sharp knife, cut off each side of rice circle to form fan shape. Position knife at an angle from center of sides down to 1 inch from bottom center. Clean and wet knife between cuts. Bottom 1/2 of rice cake will form a **V** shape. Carefully pack layered rice trimmings into a round, 3-1/2-inch cookie cutter. Unmold circle and place trimmed portion snugly against **V**-shaped end of rice fan. Circle will form handle of fan. With damp hands, press sides of fan neatly into place, if necessary. Decorate fan using prepared garnishes. After decorating, fan should be served as soon as possible. Leftovers can be refrigerated; let stand, covered, at room temperature 30 minutes before serving. Makes 12 to 14 servings.

Vinegared Cucumber Slices:
In a medium bowl, combine lemon juice, rice vinegar, sugar and salt. Stir well to dissolve sugar. Add cucumber slices. Cover and marinate in the refrigerator 3 to 4 hours. Drain well before use. Makes about 1 cup.

How to Make Fan-Shaped Sushi Cake

1/Using a large, wet, sharp knife, cut off each side of rice circle to form fan shape. Position knife at an angle from center of sides down to 1 inch from bottom center. Clean and wet knife between cuts.

2/Carefully pack layered rice trimmings into a cookie cutter; unmold. Press snugly against V-shaped end of rice fan. Decorate fan using prepared garnishes.

Sushi-Roll Fillings

Use some of these suggested fillings to create your own special sushi-roll combination.

Fresh tuna, yellowtail, red snapper or flounder
  fillets, cut in strips
Canned tuna or salmon
Chopped poached shrimp
Crabmeat
Caviar
Steamed fish loaf (kamaboko), cut in strips
Sweetened pink or green dried-fish flakes (denbu)
Avocado strips
Enokitake mushrooms, blanched

Cooked asparagus tips
Cooked whole string beans
Cooked carrot strips
Cucumber strips
Strips of bamboo shoots
Spinach Logs, page 125
Pickled burdock root
Rehydrated freeze-dried tofu
Steamed fermented soybeans (natto)
Cooked green-tea noodles

To round out a meal of sushi, serve steaming bowls of clear soup or miso soup, and a surprise side dish (tsudidashi). Side dish could come from the Dressed Foods & Vinegared Salads, or Appetizer sections.

Kokeshi-Doll Sushi

Kokeshi Zushi

An edible replica of the charming wooden doll so dear to little girls throughout Japan.

Sweet Vinegared Rice, page 58
4 (8" x 7-1/2") sheets Toasted Nori or
   toasted pink bonito sheets
   (toasted teimaki katsuo), page 59
Threads of arame sea vegetable, if desired

Shredded red pickled ginger (beni shoga),
   if desired
Candy flowers, if desired
Small paper umbrellas, if desired

Prepare Sweet Vinegared Rice. In a small bowl, combine 1/2 cup water and 2 tablespoons rice vinegar for moistening your hands. Wet your hands; shake dry. Divide rice into 5 equal portions. Pinch off 1/4 of each portion to form heads. Roll large portions of rice into oblongs, about 4" x 2". Shape them a little wider at the bottom; these will be dolls' bodies. Roll small portions of rice into round balls. Flatten them slightly at top and bottom; these will be dolls' heads. Cut sheets of Toasted Nori or bonito in 1/2. Use 1/2 sheet to form a kimono for each rice doll. Trim length of nori or bonito sheets to wrap neatly around rice bodies, flaring slightly at the bottom. Using kitchen scissors, snip a small **V** shape at each neck. Cut 5 (4" x 3") nori or bonito pieces for hair. Using small scissors, trim out a 1-1/2- to 2-inch square at the bottom of each piece for face. Fit nori or bonito pieces over small rice balls; faces should be uncovered. Smooth nori or bonito over heads. Trim sides of hair so it slants toward mouth. Trim tiny pieces for eyes. If desired, use small threads of arame sea vegetable for eye lashes. Use tiny pieces of red pickled ginger for mouth, if desired. A tiny candy flower can be placed in each doll's hair. Use your imagination to think of different ways in which you and your children can decorate the dolls. Moisten base of rice-ball head with water and press it gently onto doll's neck; tilt head at an angle, if desired. A paper umbrella can be used to decorate each doll. Makes 5 dolls.

Variations

Other designer touches can be added to the kimonos. Make them from Egg Pancakes, page 80, if your child doesn't care for nori or bonito. A pickled plum (umboshi) or a sour cherry makes an excellent top knot.

Treat your little girl and her friends to a Kokeshi-doll-making birthday party. Supply all the ingredients and let the children create dolls and design the edible accessories.

Note: Dolls are an especially charming addition to a picnic lunch (bento), or to an *okosama-ranchi,* which is a very special children's lunch in Japan. Dolls can be propped up inside the little box lunches with the tiny umbrellas secured over their heads.

In Japan, sushi is never refrigerated because the rice becomes too firm. But leftovers should be refrigerated to prevent spoilage. Bring to room temperature before serving.

How to Make Kokeshi-Doll Sushi

1/Trim length of nori sheets to wrap neatly around rice bodies, flaring slightly at the bottom. Snip a small V shape at each neck. Cut nori pieces for hair. Trim out a square for face.

2/Fit nori piece over small rice ball; face should be uncovered. Smooth nori over head. Trim sides of hair so it slants toward mouth. Trim tiny pieces for eyes. Add eye lashes and other decorations, if desired. Moisten base of head and press gently onto doll's neck.

Skewered Shrimp

Yude Ebi

Skewering them before poaching gives attractive straight-backed shrimp for making sushi.

1 lb. large shrimp, not peeled, (16 to 18)

Run a short bamboo skewer through the length of each shrimp on belly side between shell and flesh; be careful not to pierce flesh. In a large saucepan, bring about 1 quart water to a boil over high heat. Add shrimp; reduce heat to low. Simmer shrimp 2 to 3 minutes or until pink and firm. Drain; cool. Remove skewers from cooled shrimp. Peel shrimp, leaving tails intact. To butterfly shrimp, cut them lengthwise down belly sides, about 3/4 of the way through. Do not cut into tail sections. Carefully remove any large veins. Use shrimp for sushi. Makes 1 pound shrimp.

Variation

Salt-Grilled Shrimp (Ebi Shio Yaki): In a shallow baking pan, place shrimp and 3 tablespoons saké; mix well. Drain shrimp. Using 8-inch skewers, skewer shrimp as directed above. Sprinkle shrimp generously with salt until well-coated. Leave shrimp at room temperature 30 minutes. Grill shrimp until pink. To serve shrimp, remove skewers and shells. Serve with soy sauce and lemon wedges.

Hand-Rolled Sushi Cones

Te-maki Zushi

Arrange the ingredients on platters and invite your guests to roll their favorite sushi combinations.

1/2 recipe Sweet Vinegared Rice, page 58
1 (1-lb.) salmon fillet with skin
6 to 12 large Skewered Shrimp, page 63,
 poached
12 (8" x 7-1/2") sheets Toasted Nori,
 page 59, cut in 24
 (5-1/2" x 3-1/4") pieces
12 (7" x 4") pieces toasted pink bonito
 sheets (toasted teimaki katsuo),
 page 59, if desired, plain or
 plum flavored
Lemon-Soy Dipping Sauce, page 54
3 tablespoons Prepared Japanese
 Horseradish, page 154
36 fresh shiso leaves or
 torn bibb-lettuce leaves
1 small avocado, peeled,
 cut lengthwise in thin strips,
 sprinkled with lemon juice

1 Japanese cucumber, rinsed, dried,
 sliced diagonally 1/4 inch thick,
 cut in 1/4-inch-wide strips
1 small red or yellow bell pepper,
 cut in thin strips
Egg Pancake, page 80, shredded
1 medium carrot, cut in thin strips
Shredded daikon radish
Salmon-roe caviar (ikura)
1 bunch enokitake mushrooms,
 blanched 10 seconds, separated
1 bunch small green onions, thinly sliced
Pickled Pink-Ginger Slices, page 153
1 pkg. radish sprouts (kaiwari daikon),
 if desired, separated
3 tablespoons Dry-Roasted Sesame Seeds,
 page 150
1/2 cup dried-bonito thread shavings

Prepare Sweet Vinegared Rice. In a small bowl, combine 1/2 cup water and 2 tablespoons rice vinegar for moistening your hands. Wet your hands; shake dry. With a damp measuring tablespoon, shape rice into 36 neat portions, using 1 level tablespoon rice per portion. Place on a tray; cover loosely with plastic wrap until serving time. Although best done close to serving time, rice portions can be prepared 1 to 2 hours ahead. Place salmon, skin-side up, in a broiler pan; broil 4 to 5 minutes. Skin will become crisp. When fish is opaque when probed in thickest portion and just begins to flake, remove from broiler. Finely chop salmon or flake with your fingers. Remove any bones. Place fish in a serving bowl. Prepare remaining ingredients; arrange on serving trays in separate piles. Toasted Nori and toasted bonito sheets can go into small baskets. Scrap pieces of nori can be crumbled or shredded for a rice topping. Put Lemon-Soy Dipping Sauce in a small soy-sauce pot for pouring. To fill a cone, place a shiso leaf or piece of lettuce at an angle on 1 side of a sheet of nori or bonito. Bottom of leaf should be pointed toward bottom center of sheet. Top with a portion of rice. Spread rice with about 1/4 teaspoon Prepared Japanese Horseradish. Add a small amount of salmon or a shrimp and a small amount of each of desired remaining ingredients. To fold sheet into a cone, pull bottom lefthand corner up over ingredients. Then wrap long side around bundle and pull tightly into a cone shape. Sprinkle a few drops of sauce inside cone. Eat cone immediately. Invite guests to fill their own cones after you have demonstrated making 1. Makes 36 pieces.

Variation

If pink bonito sheets are not available, use an additional 6 sheets Toasted Nori, cut into 12 (5-1/2" x 3-1/4") pieces.

Spicy Grilled-Beef Sushi

Bulgogi Zushi

Immensely popular in Japan, this superb Korean version of sushi requires unseasoned cooked rice.

Steamed Rice, page 139
5 (8" x 7-1/2") sheets Toasted Nori,
   page 59, with variation noted below
Sesame oil
4 medium, fresh shiitake mushrooms
2 teaspoons soy sauce
1 (8-inch) strip pickled daikon radish
1/3 cup rice vinegar
Spicy Beef Strips, see below

1 (1/2-lb.) bunch fresh spinach with stems,
   well-rinsed, roots trimmed
1 teaspoon sesame oil
4 to 5 tablespoons Dry-Roasted Sesame
   Seeds, page 150
Condiments, page 99
Shredded red pickled ginger (beni shoga),
   if desired

Spicy Beef Strips:
About 3/4 lb. beef tenderloin
3 tablespoons soy sauce
1/2 teaspoon sugar
1 green onion, minced

1 large garlic clove, minced
Dash of ground black pepper
1 teaspoon sesame oil
2 tablespoons vegetable oil

Prepare Steamed Rice; cool. Cover with a damp cloth; set aside. Before toasting nori, rub sheets sparingly with a tiny amount of sesame oil. Cut off tough stems from mushrooms. Slice mushroom into strips. Place in a small bowl; sprinkle with soy sauce. Cut pickled daikon into strips, 8 inches long and 1/2 inch square at each end. In a shallow glass bowl, place pickled-daikon strips and vinegar; marinate 30 minutes. Prepare Spicy Beef Strips. Blanch spinach 30 seconds. Rinse in cool water. Gently squeeze water from spinach. Lay spinach on paper towels in a long bunch; pat dry. Drizzle with 1 teaspoon sesame oil. Cover with plastic wrap until needed. Drain pickled-daikon strips. Arrange Toasted Nori, Spicy Beef Strips, pickled daikon, mushroom strips, spinach and Dry-Roasted Sesame Seeds on a tray. Prepare Condiments; set aside. On the rolling edge of a bamboo sushi mat, place a sheet of nori, shiny-side down, with longest side running horizontally. In a small bowl, combine 1/2 cup water and 1/2 teaspoon salt for moistening your hands. In a damp measuring cup, measure 1 generous cup rice. Unmold rice in middle of nori sheet. Wet your hands; shake dry. Pat rice over 3/4 of nori sheet, leaving top 1/4 uncovered. Lay 2 strips beef, 2 strips pickled daikon, several mushroom strips and several spinach leaves in a long strip down center of rice. Sprinkle 2 to 3 teaspoons sesame seeds over ingredients and rice. To form roll, lift edge of mat with your thumbs. Holding filling ingredients in place, roll mat and nori away from you to enclose filling. Roll to far edge of rice only, leaving uncovered portion of nori extended. Be careful not to catch end of mat in sushi roll. Tuck in any escaping grains of rice. Press mat firmly a few seconds to set shape. Moisten extending edge of nori with water and complete roll. Wrap mat completely around rice roll and press gently a few seconds. Remove bamboo mat. Tap ends on counter, if necessary, to even them up. Continue making rolls with remaining ingredients. Cut rolls and serve immediately or store uncut in a loosely covered rectangular pan 1 to 2 hours; do not refrigerate. To cut rolls, wet a large sharp knife. Place rolls on a cutting board, seam-side down. Cut each in 1/2 with a swift clean cut. Clean and moisten knife between cuts. Cut each 1/2 into 3 or 4 pieces. Place pieces on a serving tray, cut-sides up. Serve with Condiments and pickled ginger, if desired. Makes 30 to 40 pieces.

Spicy Beef Strips:
Cut meat into 1/2-inch-thick slices. Stack slices; cut into 1/2-inch-wide strips. In a bowl, mix beef strips and remaining ingredients except vegetable oil. Marinate 10 minutes; drain well. Heat vegetable oil in a skillet over high heat. Add drained meat strips; stir-fry 1 to 2 minutes or until meat is almost done but still slightly pink inside. Remove from skillet; cool completely.

How to Make Spicy Grilled-Beef Sushi

1/Lay 2 strips beef, 2 strips pickled daikon, several mushroom strips and a long strip of spinach down center of rice. Sprinkle 2 to 3 teaspoons sesame seeds over ingredients and rice.

2/Lift edge of mat with your thumbs. Holding filling ingredients in place, roll mat and nori away from you to enclose filling. Roll to far edge of rice only, leaving uncovered portion of nori extended.

3/Press mat firmly a few seconds to set shape. Moisten extending edge of nori and complete roll. Wrap mat completely around rice roll and press gently a few seconds. Remove bamboo mat.

4/Using a large, wet, sharp knife, slice each roll into 6 to 8 pieces. Serve with Condiments and red pickled ginger, if desired.

Happy-Birthday Cake Japanese Style

Tan-joo-bi 0-me-de-too

For the sushi-lover, this could be the best birthday cake ever.

Vinegared Cucumber Slices, page 60
Sweet Vinegared Rice, page 58
Salmon Filling, see below
Egg Pancake, page 80, using 1 large egg
3 or 4 Egg Chrysanthemums, page 28

Leaf lettuce, if desired
Stems and leaves made from trimmed,
**   blanched green vegetables**
Hand-trimmed radish rosettes made with
**   cutter, page 27, if desired**

Salmon Filling:
1/2 lb. fresh salmon fillet, skinned
1 cup water
2 tablespoons saké
1 (1/4-inch-thick) slice peeled
**   fresh gingerroot, smashed**

1/4 cup Lemon Dressing, page 58
2 green onions, minced
1/4 teaspoon salt or to taste
1 to 2 tablespoons capers

Line a round, 8-inch deep-sided baking pan or springform pan with foil. Lightly oil foil; set aside. Prepare Vinegared Cucumber Slices, Sweet Vinegared Rice, Salmon Filling and Egg Pancake. In a small bowl, combine 1/2 cup water and 2 tablespoons rice vinegar for moistening your hands. In a damp measuring cup, measure 3 cups rice. Unmold rice in bottom of prepared pan. Wet your hands; shake dry. Pat rice evenly over bottom of pan. Trim Egg Pancake; fit into pan on top of rice. Add a layer of Salmon Filling. Drain cucumber slices. Place a layer of drained cucumber slices over salmon layer. Dot top of cucumbers with remaining rice. With damp hands, spread rice evenly over layered ingredients. Firmly but gently press rice cake. Place a piece of plastic wrap directly on rice. Place a slightly smaller pan on top of rice; add a 1- or 2-pound weight. Press 2 to 3 minutes. Remove pan and plastic wrap. Prepare Egg Chrysanthemums, in various sizes, and vegetable leaves. To unmold cake, place a serving plate on top of cake in pan. Grasp pan and plate securely; invert quickly. Cake will fall out onto plate. Peel off foil. Arrange a spray of Egg Chrysanthemums on top of cake. Garnish with green stems and leaves. Arrange leaf lettuce and radish rosettes around cake, if desired. To serve, slice cake into wedges using a large, wet, sharp knife. Makes 8 to 10 pieces.

Salmon Filling:
Trim off any dark parts from salmon. In a small saucepan, bring water, saké and gingerroot to a boil over high heat. Reduce heat to low. Add salmon; poach 5 to 8 minutes or until done. Do not overcook. Remove fish from poaching liquid; cool completely. With your fingers, flake fish into small pieces. Remove any bones. Add remaining ingredients to fish; mix well. Use filling immediately or refrigerate until needed. Makes about 1-1/2 cups.

Variations

Valentine's-Day Sushi Cake: Substitute an 8- or 9-inch heart-shaped pan for round pan. Prepare cake as directed above. Trim Egg Pancake into a heart shape. Decorate as desired.
Merry-Christmas Sushi Cake: Sprinkle finely chopped fresh parsley over bottom of an oiled Christmas-tree-shaped pan. Prepare cake as directed above. When unmolded, top of sushi tree will be green. Decorate top with edible Christmas ornaments using ingredients such as Pickled Pink-Ginger Slices, page 153, red pickled ginger, vegetable slices and caviar.

Happy-Birthday Cake Japanese-Style, above; Pickled Quail Eggs, page 34; Vinegared Cucumber Slices, page 60.

Kansai-Style Mixed Sushi   Photo on pages 106 and 107.

Chirashi Zushi

In the Kyoto area, this type of sushi is seldom made with raw seafood.

1/2 recipe Sweet Vinegared Rice,
    page 58
1/2 recipe Sweet Simmered Mushrooms,
    page 93
Cooking Sauce, see below
2 oz. fresh string beans,
    cut diagonally in thin strips
1/2 medium carrot, cut sen-giri, page 18

1/4 cup thawed, frozen, baby, green peas
2 green onions, thinly sliced
1/4 lb. seafood (tiny shrimp,
    flaked poached salmon, crabmeat or
    strips steamed fish loaf)
1 tablespoon Dry-Roasted Sesame Seeds,
    page 150
Toppings, see below

Toppings:
1 ripe avocado, peeled, cubed
1 teaspoon fresh lemon juice
Egg Pancake, page 80, shredded
1 (7-1/2" x 2") piece Toasted Nori or
    toasted pink bonito sheet
    (toasted teimaki katsuo), page 59,
    cut in thin strips

Pickled Lotus-Root Flowers, page 32,
    if desired
Sashimi Rose, page 53, if desired
Green-Onion Threads, page 24, if desired
Scalloped Lemon Slices, page 23, halved
Pickled Pink-Ginger Slices, page 153

Cooking Sauce:
1 cup water
1/2 teaspoon dashi-no-moto powder
1 teaspoon light (thin) soy sauce

1 tablespoon mirin
1 tablespoon saké
2 tablespoons sugar

Prepare Sweet Vinegared Rice and Sweet Simmered Mushrooms. Slice mushrooms into strips; set aside. Prepare Cooking Sauce; bring to a boil over high heat. Reduce heat to medium; add string beans. Simmer 1 to 2 minutes or until tender. Using a slotted spoon, remove beans. Bring sauce back to a boil; add carrot. Simmer 1 to 2 minutes or until tender. Remove carrot from sauce; cool completely. Assemble remaining ingredients and Toppings. Sprinkle avocado cubes with lemon juice. In a medium bowl, toss rice, mushroom strips, string beans, carrot, peas, green onions, seafood and Dry-Roasted Sesame Seeds. Mound mixture on a large serving tray. Scatter avocado cubes, shredded Egg Pancake and strips of Toasted Nori or bonito over top of rice. Place Scalloped Lotus-Root Pickles over mound. Add Sashimi Rose to top of mound, if desired. Arrange Green-Onion Threads around rose for greenery. Place halved Scalloped Lemon Slices and flower-shaped piles of Pickled Pink-Ginger Slices around base of rice mixture. Serve immediately. Makes 4 to 6 servings.

Cooking Sauce:
In a small saucepan, combine all ingredients. Makes about 2-1/4 cups.

Variation

Stuffed-Avocado Sushi: Peel and remove seeds from 5 or 6 large ripe avocados. Omit avocado listed in recipe above. Enlarge avocado shells by spooning out a small amount of avocado flesh. Chop flesh; mix with sushi rice. Pack about 1/2 cup rice mixture into each avocado shell. Omit egg strips, nori, lotus root and Sashimi Rose. Garnish each serving with a pile of Pickled Pink-Ginger Slices, Green-Onion Threads and a halved Scalloped Lemon Slice. Makes 10 to 12 servings.

Charcoal-Grilled & Pan-Grilled Foods (Yakimono)

The oldest recipe known to man is meat roasted over an open flame. The Japanese have refined this basic idea and expanded it to create a category of cooking methods known as *yakimono* or *food seared with intense heat*. Charcoal-grilling (barbecuing), pan-grilling, oven-broiling and baking are included in this category. The last two are not often used in home cooking because of the scarcity of ovens in Japanese homes.

Before grilling, sometimes foods are inserted with two or more bamboo or metal skewers of the appropriate length. Skewering techniques vary according to the size and shape of the food. Skewers help balance the foods as they are turned on the grill. Skewers inside cooked foods can also be used to help determine the degree of doneness. If the skewer can be twisted easily with little resistance, the food is properly cooked. To test fish, insert a bamboo skewer into the thickest portion of the flesh. Cooked fish yields easily; uncooked fish offers greater resistance. Be careful not to overcook fish; it continues cooking after it is removed from the grill. Experience will be your best guide to cooking fish to perfection.

Soak bamboo skewers in cool water 30 minutes before using. The ends of the skewers can be wrapped in foil before grilling. Reusable flat metal skewers hold foods more securely than round ones.

Foods prepared in the *yakimono* style are lightly seasoned and then rarely marinated more than 30 minutes, if at all. Foods can be grilled plain or they can be basted with a sweetened soy-sauce mixture, vegetable oil or sometimes butter. A splash of saké will prevent foods from burning over too hot a fire and add a hint of flavor. Whichever method of yakimono you use, the end product should always be the same—a tender juicy inside and a crusty exterior enhanced by the natural flavors.

Small whole fish are often laced with skewers before grilling and sometimes curved into a swimming motion. One of the most succulent methods of preparing skewered fish is Salt-Grilled Trout. The fish are seasoned with a generous amount of coarse salt, then after a period of 30 minutes, grilled over a hot charcoal fire. The skin becomes crisp and the flesh is basted by the dripping fat coming from just underneath the skin.

In traditional Japanese cooking, the side of the fish to be presented at the table is the first side to be placed on the hot grill. Fillets with skin are grilled skin-side down, then served skin-side up for an attractive presentation. For oven-broiling, fillets with skin are cooked skin-side up (close to the heat source), then turned if necessary, to complete the broiling. Serve broiled fish skin-side up.

Foods prepared for *dengaku* are skewered, grilled and coated with a sweet miso mixture. After a final broiling, they are served on the skewers. The two-pronged flat bamboo skewers used for dengaku are reminiscent of entertainers from many centuries earlier who performed on a single stilt at festival time.

Teriyaki or grilled glazed foods have found favor in the Western kitchen. Meat, fish, seafood and tofu can be charcoal-grilled or pan-grilled. The glazing mixture is never added until about halfway through the grilling or in the final minutes of cooking to prevent burning.

Pan-grilling (teppan yaki) is a recently developed cooking technique in which top-grade meats, seafood and vegetables are skillfully cut and cooked on grill-topped tables. In restaurants, this equipment gets the chef out of the kitchen and allows him to demonstrate his cutting skills before an admiring audience. *Bata yaki* is a variation of teppan yaki in which the foods are grilled in butter. Use a Japanese flat iron pan (teppan) or a heavy cast-iron skillet, over a portable tabletop gas burner. You can also use an electric griddle at the table or a stovetop griddle in the kitchen. The rectangular *tamago yaki nabe* is an essential pan for making pan-grilled Sweet-Omelet Roll. Like any good omelet pan, it has to be carefully seasoned to give perfect results.

Charcoal-grilling can be accomplished on a regular-sized barbecue grill, hibachi or portable tabletop gas grill. Be sure to start the charcoal fire 30 to 40 minutes in advance so the coals will be hot enough at cooking time. Preheat the tabletop gas grill two to three minutes. A Japanese stovetop fish-grilling pan (sakanayaki) has been designed to hold fish securely between two wire grids for an occasional turn over the base pan. Several models are fitted with a ceramic heating element. As an alternative to charcoal-grilling, foods can be broiled successfully in the oven by placing them on a rack fitted into a broiling pan. For more-even cooking, preheat the pan and broiler before the food is added. The foods should be placed four to five inches from the heat source.

Broiled Eggplant with Peanut-Miso Sauce

Nasu Dengaku

Simmered daikon radish or sweet-potato slices are delicious prepared this way.

1 (1-1/2-lb.) eggplant, peeled	Peanut-Miso Sauce, see below
2 tablespoons vegetable oil	2 green onions, minced

Peanut-Miso Sauce:

2 tablespoons cocktail peanuts	2 tablespoons saké
1/2 cup sweet white miso	2 teaspoons light (thin) soy sauce
2 tablespoons brown sugar	

Soak 12 to 14 (2-prong) pine-needle skewers or 24 to 28 thin (6- to 8-inch) bamboo skewers in water 30 minutes. Cut eggplant crosswise into round 1-inch-thick slices. Cut each slice into 2 semicircles. Push 1 pine-needle skewer or 2 bamboo skewers into the end of each piece. Brush both sides of skewered eggplant slices with oil. In a wok or deep pot, bring about 4 cups water to a boil over high heat. Place eggplant on a steamer tray. Cover; place over boiling water. Steam 10 minutes or until tender. Remove from heat. Remove steamer tray. Cool eggplant 5 minutes. Preheat broiler and broiling pan. Prepare Peanut-Miso Sauce. Spread sauce over 1 side of each eggplant slice. Refrigerate leftover sauce. Oil hot broiling pan. Place coated eggplant on oiled pan, sauce-side up. Broil 4 to 5 inches from heat source 1 to 2 minutes or until sauce begins to be lightly speckled. Do not allow sauce to burn. Scatter green onions over eggplant. Eat hot eggplant from skewers or remove them, if desired. Makes 5 to 6 servings.

Peanut-Miso Sauce:
In a grinding bowl or food processor fitted with a steel blade, grind peanuts to a paste. Add remaining ingredients; blend well. Use sauce immediately or cover and refrigerate until needed. Makes about 2/3 cup.

Grilled Miso Chicken

Tori No Miso Yaki

Serve this delicious barbecue favorite with Tree Oyster-Mushroom Rice, page 139.

Miso Marinade, see below
8 chicken thighs with skin, boned

1-1/2 tablespoons Dry-Roasted Sesame
 Seeds, page 150

Miso Marinade:
1/4 cup soy sauce
1/4 cup saké
2 tablespoons mirin
3 tablespoons sugar
1/4 cup red miso

4 green onions, smashed, slivered
1 teaspoon minced fresh gingerroot
1 garlic clove, minced
Seven-Spice Mixture, page 147, to taste

Prepare Miso Marinade; pour into a shallow baking dish. Add chicken to marinade; turn until coated. Marinate 30 minutes, turning several times. Preheat a hibachi, portable tabletop grill or charcoal grill. Remove chicken from marinade. Shake excess marinade back into pan. Place chicken, skin-side down, on hot grill. Grill 3 to 4 minutes; turn chicken to the other side. Grill 3 to 4 minutes or until chicken is done and no longer pink inside. Baste with remaining marinade, if desired. Sprinkle chicken with Dry-Roasted Sesame Seeds. Makes 4 to 8 servings.

Miso Marinade:
In a small bowl, combine all ingredients. Makes about 1 cup.

Lemon-Miso Broiled Fish

Sakana No Lemon-Miso Yaki

A delicate lemon flavor permeates the fish during marination.

1 lb. fish fillets (red snapper, sea bass,
 halibut, rock cod)
1 tablespoon sea salt
Lemon-Miso Marinade, see below

2 green onions, thinly sliced
Lemon wedges
5 to 6 cups hot Steamed Rice, page 139

Lemon-Miso Marinade:
1-1/3 cups sweet white miso
Freshly grated peel of 2 small lemons

2 tablespoons mirin
1/3 cup sugar

Lay fish fillets in a shallow baking pan. Sprinkle salt evenly on both sides of fish. Cover and refrigerate 30 minutes. Prepare Lemon-Miso Marinade. Spread enough marinade over top of fish to cover. Turn fish and spread with marinade to cover. Fish should be completely covered with marinade. Cover tightly and refrigerate 24 to 48 hours. At cooking time, scrape marinade off fish. Lightly wipe with paper towels. Do not rinse. Preheat broiler and broiling pan. Oil hot broiling pan. Place fish on oiled pan. Broil fish 4 to 5 inches from heat source 5 to 10 minutes or until it barely flakes, depending on thickness of fish. Turn fish once halfway through cooking time. Watch fish carefully so it does not overcook and become dry. Fish can also be grilled over a preheated hibachi or portable tabletop grill. Cut each fillet into 2 or 3 serving pieces. Garnish with green onions and lemon wedges. Serve in pieces with hot Steamed Rice or flaked as a topping over rice. Makes 4 to 6 servings.

Butter-Grilled Meat, Shellfish & Vegetables

Bata Yaki

Okinawan restaurants use generous amounts of butter and garlic for this teppan-yaki style of cooking.

Dipping Sauce, see below
Peanut-Miso Sauce, page 72
1 medium Bermuda onion, halved,
   cut in 1/4-inch slices
1-1/2 to 2 lbs. beef tenderloin or
   sirloin, cut in 1-inch cubes
2 large potatoes, peeled, cubed,
   parboiled, cooled
1 lb. large shrimp, peeled, deveined
2 small bell peppers, cut in thin strips
1/2 lb. round mushrooms, sliced

3 ears fresh corn, parboiled,
   cut in 3-inch pieces
1/2 lb. fresh bean sprouts, rinsed, drained
8 to 10 whole small green peppers
   (ao-togarashi), if desired
About 1/4 cup vegetable oil
About 1/2 cup butter, room temperature
3 garlic cloves, finely minced
Salt and ground black pepper to taste
5 to 6 cups hot Steamed Rice, page 139

Dipping Sauce:
1/2 cup soy sauce
1 teaspoon dashi-no-moto powder

1 cup water
Red-Maple Radish, page 155, to taste

Prepare Dipping Sauce and Peanut-Miso Sauce; pour each sauce into individual bowls for each guest. Arrange vegetables, meat and shrimp on serving platters. At the table, heat a portable tabletop griddle or electric skillet to high heat. Add 1 tablespoon oil and 1 tablespoon butter. Add 1/3 of garlic and onion. Add 1/3 of meat; cook on all sides to desired doneness. Add portions of remaining foods in the order listed. Keep food in separate piles. Brush pieces of corn with butter before grilling. Continue adding oil and butter as needed. Turn foods as they cook and season with salt and pepper. Invite diners to help themselves to some of each food as it is cooked. Replenish griddle or skillet as foods are eaten. Instruct diners to dip bites of meat and shrimp into their bowls of sauce. Serve with hot Steamed Rice. Makes 4 to 6 servings.

Dipping Sauce:
In a small bowl, combine soy sauce, dashi-no-moto powder and water; stir in Red-Maple Radish.

Sautéed Tree Oyster Mushrooms

Shimeji Itame

Prepare fresh shiitake mushrooms or the highly prized matsutake mushrooms this way.

1 lb. tree oyster mushrooms
2 tablespoons vegetable oil
1-1/2 teaspoons minced fresh gingerroot
1 garlic clove, minced

Pinch of salt
2 tablespoons unsalted butter
1 tablespoon Japanese chives (nira) or
   regular chives

Quickly rinse clumps of tree oyster mushrooms under cool running water. Drain well; pat dry on paper towels. Slice clumps of mushrooms into smaller pieces. In a large skillet, heat oil over high heat. After 30 seconds, add mushrooms, gingerroot and garlic; toss and stir mushrooms constantly 1 to 2 minutes. Add salt. Reduce heat; add butter. Stir mushrooms until coated with melted butter. Stir in chives. Serve mushrooms on a heated serving plate. Makes 4 servings.

Dee's Marinated Fruit Kabobs, page 82; Butter-Grilled Meat, Shellfish & Vegetables, above; and Tofu-Dill Dip, page 38.

Pork & Cabbage Dumplings

Gyoza

For a fun evening, invite a group of friends over for a do-it-yourself dumpling-making party!

Dipping Sauce, see below
Pork & Cabbage Filling, see below
1 (10-oz.) pkg. round gyoza skins
 (about 54 skins)

1 tablespoon cornstarch
1 tablespoon water
1/4 cup vegetable oil
About 1/2 cup chicken stock or water

Dipping Sauce:
1/2 cup soy sauce
1 tablespoon water
2 teaspoons sugar
2 tablespoons rice vinegar
1 green onion, minced
1 garlic clove, minced

1/2 teaspoon sesame oil or to taste
1 generous teaspoon Dry-Roasted Sesame
 Seeds, page 150, if desired
Dried hot red-pepper flakes or
 hot red-pepper sauce,
 if desired, to taste

Pork & Cabbage Filling:
1 cup minced green cabbage
1 teaspoon salt
1 lb. ground pork
3 tablespoons saké
3 tablespoons soy sauce
1 garlic clove, minced

1 teaspoon minced fresh gingerroot
2 green onions, minced
1 teaspoon potato starch or cornstarch
1/4 teaspoon sesame oil
2 to 3 dashes ground black pepper
1/2 teaspoon sugar

Prepare Dipping Sauce; set aside. Prepare Pork & Cabbage Filling. Place 1 teaspoon filling in center of each gyoza skin. Fold skins in 1/2, forming semicircles. In a small bowl, blend cornstarch and water. If desired, before sealing dumplings, pleat top curved edges. Seal edges with cornstarch mixture. Place dumplings on a tray; press bottoms to flatten slightly. As dumplings are filled, cover loosely with plastic wrap to prevent drying. In a large non-stick skillet, heat 2 tablespoons oil over medium-high heat. Place about 1/2 of dumplings in hot oil. Fry 2 to 3 minutes or until golden brown. Add 1/4 cup chicken stock or water to dumplings. Cover skillet with a tight-fitting lid or foil. Steam dumplings 2 to 3 minutes. Remove cover; cook until any remaining liquid has evaporated. Fry dumplings a few seconds longer to crisp bottoms. Wipe skillet clean. Repeat with remaining dumplings. Serve with Dipping Sauce. Makes 8 servings.

Dipping Sauce:
In a small bowl, combine all ingredients. Let stand 30 minutes at room temperature for flavors to develop. Makes 3/4 cup.

Pork & Cabbage Filling:
Place cabbage in a small bowl. Sprinkle with salt. Let stand 1 hour. Rinse cabbage in a fine strainer; drain well. In a bowl, combine cabbage and remaining filling ingredients. Mixture should be moist and soft, not dry and tightly packed. Use immediately. Makes about 2-1/2 cups.

Variation

Simmered Pork & Cabbage Dumplings: Drop dumplings, a few at a time, into a large pot of boiling chicken stock or water until all dumplings are added. Immediately reduce heat to low; gently simmer 2 to 3 minutes. If necessary, add 1 cup cold water to reduce water temperature. Serve dumplings in individual serving bowls with Dipping Sauce or add to soups or stews.

How to Make Pork & Cabbage Dumplings

1/Place 1 teaspoon Pork & Cabbage Filling in center of each gyoza skin. Fold skins in 1/2, forming semicircles. If necessary, seal edges with cornstarch mixture. If desired, before sealing dumplings, pleat top curved edges.

2/Fry dumplings 2 to 3 minutes or until golden brown. Add chicken stock or water. Cover and steam 2 to 3 minutes. Cook, uncovered, until liquid has evaporated. Fry dumplings a few seconds to crisp bottoms.

Grilled Sesame Shrimp

Goma Ebi Yaki

Serve these tasty shrimp as appetizers or as part of a multi-course meal.

**Fan-Shaped Shrimp, page 122, prepared,
   not marinated**
Marinade, see below

1/2 cup butter, melted
**1 tablespoon Dry-Roasted Sesame Seeds,
   page 150**
3 small green onions, finely minced

Marinade:
1/4 cup soy sauce
2 tablespoons saké
2 tablespoons mirin

2 teaspoons sugar
2 teaspoons fresh lemon juice

Soak 32 to 36 (10-inch) bamboo skewers in water 30 minutes. Insert 2 skewers up through tail of each shrimp. Run 1 skewer through right side of fan cut. Run the other skewer through left side of fan cut shrimp. Prepare Marinade. Marinate skewered shrimp at least 15 minutes, turning at least once. Or, shrimp can be cut and marinated in the refrigerator 3 to 4 hours in advance. Brush shrimp on both sides with melted butter. Sprinkle with Dry-Roasted Sesame Seeds. Arrange shrimp on a serving platter. Add any leftover butter to remaining marinade. Invite guests to grill shrimp over a portable tabletop grill. Cook 1 to 2 minutes on each side or until firm. Brush with marinade mixture. Sprinkle cooked shrimp with green onions. Makes 8 or 9 appetizer servings.

Marinade:
In an 11'' x 7'' baking dish, combine all ingredients. Makes about 1/2 cup.

Skewered Grilled Chicken Bites

Yakitori

Chicken thighs are flavorful and tender in this nationally popular Japanese snack.

Yakitori Sauce, see below
6 chicken thighs, skinned, boned
2 bunches green onions, white parts only
Seven-Spice Mixture, page 147, to taste

2 tablespoons Dry-Roasted Sesame Seeds, page 150
Ground sansho pepper, to taste

Yakitori Sauce:
1/2 cup soy sauce
1/4 cup sugar
1/2 cup mirin
1/4 cup saké
1 garlic clove, crushed

1 (1/8-inch-thick) slice peeled fresh gingerroot, smashed
1 tablespoon water
1 generous tablespoon cornstarch

Soak 16 (8- to 10-inch) bamboo skewers in water 30 minutes. Prepare Yakitori Sauce; set aside. Cut each chicken thigh into 8 cubes for a total of 48 cubes. Cut white parts of green onions into a total of 32 pieces. Onto each skewer, thread 3 chicken pieces alternately with 2 green-onion pieces. Preheat a portable tabletop grill or outdoor charcoal grill. Grill several skewers of chicken and green onion 1 to 2 minutes. Turn once or twice. With a basting brush, baste skewers with Yakitori Sauce on both sides. Continue grilling skewers 2 to 3 minutes longer or until chicken is done, turning and basting chicken frequently. Remove skewers from grill. Brush a final time with Yakitori Sauce before serving. Cook remaining skewers in the same manner. Serve 4 skewers per serving. Invite guests to season their portions with a choice of Seven-Spice Mixture, Dry-Roasted Sesame Seeds or sansho pepper. Makes 4 servings.

Yakitori Sauce:
In a small saucepan, combine soy sauce, sugar, mirin, saké and garlic; add gingerroot. Cook over medium-high heat 3 to 4 minutes. In a small bowl, blend water and cornstarch. Stir cornstarch mixture into soy-sauce mixture. Cook until thickened, stirring constantly. Strain sauce. Keep at room temperature up to 24 hours. Refrigerate leftover sauce. Makes about 1 cup.

Variations

Chicken breasts can be substituted for thighs. Do not overcook or they will become dry.

A double recipe of Yakitori Sauce can be put into a tall narrow jar. Conveniently coat skewers by dipping them into sauce.

Other vegetables can be substituted for green onion, such as 1 large cubed bell pepper or 8 small quartered fresh or rehydrated black forest mushrooms.

One-half pound cubed chicken livers can be divided among skewers of chicken, if desired.

To serve as an appetizer, cut each thigh into 12 small pieces. Use 3 bunches green onions to give 48 pieces. You will have a total of 24 skewers.

Substitute small scallops or small to medium shrimp for chicken.

How to Make Salt-Grilled Trout

1/Insert a metal skewer into head of fish behind eye. Bring skewer out near gills on same side. Do not pierce skin on opposite side. Insert skewer again midway into side of fish. Bring it out near tail.

2/Place fish over hot grill on unskewered sides. Cook on each side 4 to 5 minutes, depending on thickness of fish.

Salt-Grilled Trout

Shio Yaki

Salt crisps the skin and helps draw out the layer of fat under it so it melts, keeping the fish moist.

4 fresh, whole, small trout
About 2 tablespoons kosher salt or
   sea salt

Shredded daikon radish
Lemon wedges

Rinse fish and cutting surface. Slit open bellies of fish; remove viscera. Rinse empty cavity under cool running water. Apply about 1 generous teaspoon salt to each side of fish, adding an extra-thick layer on tails and fins. Spread open fins. Let stand at room temperature 30 minutes. Place fish on a flat surface with heads to the right. Insert a metal skewer into head of a fish behind eye. Bring skewer out near gills on same side. Do not pierce skin on opposite side. Insert skewer again midway into side of fish. Bring it out near tail. Tail and fins can be covered with foil to prevent burning, if necessary. Fish will appear to be in a swimming motion with head and tail up. Skewer remaining fish as described. Preheat a hibachi, portable tabletop grill or charcoal grill. Place fish on hot grill on unskewered side. Cook 4 to 5 minutes; turn and cook 4 to 4 minutes or until fish barely flakes, depending on thickness of fish. Serve on a bed of shredded daikon. Garnish with lemon wedges. Makes 4 servings.

Sweet-Omelet Roll

Ama Tamago Maki

A rectangular tamago pan is recommended for this dish; a similar roll can be made in a small skillet.

4 large eggs
1 tablespoon light (thin) soy sauce
1/4 teaspoon salt
1 tablespoon mirin
3 tablespoons Instant Sea-Vegetable &
  Fish Stock, page 45

1 to 2 teaspoons sugar
Vegetable oil
Additional soy sauce, if desired
Finely shredded daikon radish, if desired

In a medium bowl, lightly beat eggs with a pair of chopsticks or a fork. Add 1 tablespoon soy sauce, salt, mirin, stock and sugar; blend only until combined. Heat a well-seasoned, rectangular, 6-1/2" x 5" tamago nabe over medium heat. Use a folded piece of cloth or paper towel to wipe pan evenly with oil. In Japan, a small oil brush is used for this job. After use, brush is stored in a small colorful oil-storage cup. Pour 1/4 of egg mixture into hot pan. Cook egg sheet 1 minute or until it is about 85 percent set. It may be necessary to adjust heat to prevent bottom of sheet from browning. Beginning at back of pan, use a spatula to fold egg sheet into a narrow flat roll. Carefully push roll to back of pan. If pan has been properly seasoned, roll will slide easily. Wipe front portion of pan with more oil. Pour in another 1/4 of egg mixture. Lift edge of roll in back of pan and let egg mixture run under, forming a layer. Cook egg sheet until almost set. Fold up rolled egg sheet inside second egg sheet, rolling toward you. Again, push multi-layered roll to back of pan. Oil pan and continue process, forming 2 more egg-sheet layers around large egg roll. Tilt completed roll out of pan onto a bamboo sushi mat. Mat can be lined with foil or plastic wrap for easy cleaning. Enclose roll securely inside mat. Cool egg roll in mat at least 30 minutes. Remove mat. Cut roll into slices. Serve with soy sauce mixed with finely shredded daikon, if desired. Or, cut roll into 1/2-inch-wide strips for use as an ingredient in rolled sushi. Makes 4 or 5 servings.

Egg Pancake

Often shredded as a garnish in Japanese cooking.

2 large eggs
1/4 teaspoon salt

1/4 teaspoon sesame oil
1/2 teaspoon sugar

Place all ingredients in a small bowl; beat with a fork. Heat a 10- or 11-inch non-stick skillet over medium-high heat. Wipe skillet with a paper towel dipped in vegetable oil. Pour egg mixture into oiled skillet. Swirl skillet so egg mixture covers bottom of skillet in a sheet. Reduce heat to low. Cook egg mixture 1 minute or until set. Remove skillet from heat. Carefully turn pancake over; cook 30 seconds. Turn pancake out of skillet to cool before cutting. Makes 1 (10- or 11-inch) Egg Pancake.

How to Make Sweet-Omelet Roll

1/Carefully push egg roll to back of pan. Pour in another 1/4 of egg mixture. Lift edge of roll in back of pan; let mixture run under, forming a layer. Cook egg sheet until almost set. Fold up rolled egg sheet inside second egg sheet, rolling toward you.

2/Tilt completed roll out of pan onto a bamboo sushi mat. Enclose roll inside mat. Cool roll in mat at least 30 minutes. Remove mat. To serve, cut egg roll into slices.

Marinated Grilled Meat

Sumi Yaki Niku

Leftover grilled meat can be added to stir-fried rice and noodle dishes.

Sesame Marinade, see below
1 lb. beef rib eye or other tender beef,
   sliced 1/8 inch thick

Sesame Marinade:
1/3 cup soy sauce
3 tablespoons sugar
2 green onions, slivered
1 or 2 garlic cloves, minced
1 tablespoon saké

1 teaspoon Dry-Roasted Sesame Seeds,
   page 150
1 teaspoon sesame oil
1/4 teaspoon ground sansho pepper or
   ground black pepper

Prepare Sesame Marinade. Dip slices of meat into marinade. Arrange attractively on a serving platter for cooking. If necessary for convenience, cover and refrigerate 30 minutes. Shake excess marinade off slices. Preheat hibachi, portable tabletop grill or griddle. Grill meat slices to desired doneness, turning once or twice. Meat will cook in about 30 seconds. Makes 3 or 4 servings.

Sesame Marinade:
In a medium bowl, combine all ingredients. Use immediately. Makes about 1/3 cup.

Dee's Marinated Fruit Kabobs   Photo on page 75.

Kushi Yaki

These tangy bites of fruit go well with grilled foods.

Assorted Fresh Fruit, see below
Plum-Wine Marinade, see below

Plum-Sauce Dip, page 170

Assorted Fresh Fruit:
**1 cup melon balls (watermelon,
   cantaloupe, honeydew)**
1 (10-oz.) can lychee fruits, drained
1 cup fresh strawberries, hulled

1 or 2 peaches, peeled, cubed
1 large banana, cubed
1 cup fresh-pineapple cubes

Plum-Wine Marinade:
1/4 cup unsalted butter, melted
1/2 cup Japanese plum wine

1 teaspoon freshly grated orange peel
2 tablespoons fresh tart orange juice

Prepare Assorted Fresh Fruit. Prepare Plum-Wine Marinade. Place skewered fruit in a 13" x 9" baking pan. Add marinade. Marinate 15 minutes, turning fruit once or twice. Prepare Plum-Sauce Dip. Drain fruit. Preheat a hibachi or portable tabletop grill. Set skewers over hot grill 3 to 4 minutes or until hot. Serve fruit with Plum-Sauce Dip. Makes 6 servings.

Assorted Fresh Fruit:
Soak 6- to 8-inch bamboo skewers in water 30 minutes. Select 3 or 4 types of fruit for skewering. With the exception of canned lychees, select fruits which are ripe but not too soft. Lace fruits on skewers, 3 to 4 pieces per skewer.

Plum-Wine Marinade:
In a small bowl, combine all ingredients. Makes about 3/4 cup.

Salmon Teriyaki

Saké Teriyaki

Salmon pieces can also be broiled on a rack in the oven.

**1 lb. fresh salmon fillets,
   cut in 2-inch-square pieces**
3 tablespoons saké

1 tablespoon soy sauce
Yakitori Sauce, page 78

Soak 8 to 10 (6- to 8-inch) bamboo skewers in water 30 minutes. Place salmon pieces in a small shallow pan. Pour saké and soy sauce over fish. Cover and refrigerate 15 minutes. Prepare Yakitori Sauce. Drain fish well. Insert 2 skewers, running parallel, through each piece of fish. Preheat a hibachi or portable tabletop grill. Grill fish 2 minutes, turning once. Brush both sides of skewered fish pieces with Yakitori Sauce. Continue grilling until fish barely flakes, 3 to 6 minutes depending on thickness of fish. Watch fish carefully so it does not overcook and become dry. Use skewers to turn fish for even cooking. Brush again with sauce. Remove skewers to serve. Serve warm or at room temperature. Makes 4 to 5 servings.

Steamed Foods, Simmered Foods & One-Pot Dishes
(Mushimono, Nimono & Nabemono)

Steaming is a popular and healthful cooking method used throughout Japan. Foods are suspended over boiling water in a closed container, surrounded by intense moist heat. The advantages of steaming are many. It is a clean, quick and economical method of cooking which preserves natural flavors, colors and nutrients. Steamed foods are self-basting so moisture is retained. For all these reasons, steaming is an excellent method for reheating leftovers. Saké-marinated chicken, fish and vegetables lend themselves well to steaming. Steamed Lemon-Egg Custard with Seafood, a savory custard-soup, and items like steamed buns and steamed fish are among Japan's favorite steamed foods. In Japan, steamed foods are valued for their warming effect upon the body during cold weather.

Steaming units are available in aluminum, stainless steel and bamboo. Sturdy metal steamers have a deep base with 1 or 2 perforated stacked trays and a tight-fitting lid. Aluminum steamers are recommended because the metal is an excellent heat conductor. Condensation can be a problem with metal steamers; dripping liquid will often ruin your food. If the food isn't covered inside the steamer, wrap a towel around the lid and secure the four corners at the top. The Chinese bamboo steamer is a handsome addition to the kitchen and will last for years with proper care. The tiers fit into a wok or other suitable pan filled with boiling water. Bamboo steamers should be used regularly to keep them moist to prevent cracking and splitting. The wood is extremely porous and will absorb condensation, preventing soggy foods.

If you don't own a steamer, one can easily be improvised. Round, perforated, metal, steaming trays which fit inside a wok are available in Oriental markets and some cookware stores. Or, try crossing 2 wooden slats or bamboo chopsticks in the bottom of a wok to improvise a tray for holding up the dish of food. This type of arrangement limits the space for the water, but is an adequate substitute. A covered stockpot or roasting pan will serve as a substitute steamer. Place an inverted bowl or empty can inside for holding the plate of food out of the water. Be sure the can isn't too tall or it will prevent the lid from fitting securely in place.

A slight adjustment in steaming time may be necessary, depending upon the type of steamer used and how close the food is to the water. All the recipes in this book were tested on the bottom tray of a bamboo steamer.

Simmered Foods

Simmered foods are prepared daily in Japan. Seasonal vegetables, seafood and fresh meats are bathed in a flavorful seasoning liquid and gently simmered until tender and lightly glazed. There are dozens of variations for the seasoning liquid including the use of plain water. Sea-vegetable and fish stock (dashi) is often used as the base liquid; flavoring is added in the form of saké, mirin, fresh gingerroot, miso, sugar and light and dark soy sauce. All of the ingredients might be used, or only one or two. The foods are usually added all at once to the seasoning liquid and cooked until the liquid is greatly reduced. An *otoshi-buta* or drop-lid is placed on top of the foods to ensure even heat circulation. Sometimes the components of a dish are simmered separately in the way which is best for each food. They are blended for a few final minutes of cooking or simply arranged together in individual serving dishes. The resulting dish is an exciting contrast of tastes and textures bound together by a unifying sauce.

Simmered foods are often cooked in two parts, first sautéed or blanched, then simmered in the seasoning liquid. This way, foods cook more evenly and strong flavors are mellowed. Blanching vegetables first makes them absorb seasonings from the broth more readily. Sukiyaki Beef Rolls is an example of a recipe prepared by this double method of sautéing then simmering. This method is called *itame-ni,* and is part of the Japanese name of this recipe.

For a lovely bowl
Let us arrange these
Flowers . . .
Since there is no rice   *Basho*

One-Pot Dishes

Nabemono includes a variety of country casserole-type dishes prepared by simmering a variety of foods in a pot of savory broth. *Sukiyaki* and Chicken Hot Pot are two of the most well-known examples. In Japan, they are great wintertime favorites. The beauty of a nabemono dish is in the arrangement of the raw materials when presented to guests for cooking. The cooking is done at the table which allows the guests to participate. As the foods are added to the pot, guests can help themselves. While there is no denying that nabemono dishes are delicious, part of their charm lies in the fact that guests will cook and eat together from the communal pot. The Japanese view this as an important time for relaxation, and for bonding new and strengthening old friendships. In earlier years, it was believed that the personalities of people would instantly merge together when they touched food from a common pot with their chopsticks. Although frowned upon in polite society, the habit of using individual chopsticks in a common pot persisted, especially among families and close friends. Today it is accepted practice, except at formal meals. If your guests are adventurous, perhaps they will be willing to chance such a convivial experience to enjoy the delicious and dramatic culinary tradition of nabemono.

Sukiyaki is traditionally cooked in a *sukiyaki nabe,* a heavy cast-iron pot with low sides. It is excellent for braising many foods. Treat it like your cast-iron skillet. After use, dry it well, oil lightly, then heat it over low heat for two to three minutes. A *donabe* is an earthenware casserole glazed only on the inside. It is excellent for simmering nabemono dishes, such as Chicken Hot Pot. Soak the pot in water one hour before use. Drain it and dry well. Add the stock. Place the pot over low heat, raising the temperature gradually so the pot will not crack. Never put an empty pot directly on the heat. A *tetsunabe* is a deep cast-iron cooking pot with a curved handle and a wooden lid for keeping foods warm after cooking. It is excellent for serving Savory Rice Stew. All of the pots mentioned above require the use of a portable tabletop burner for cooking and warming. A gas tabletop burner is a common item found in most Japanese homes. They are available in Oriental markets and by mail order, page 175.

Steamed Lemon-Egg Custard with Seafood

Chawan Mushi

If you don't have chawan mushi cups, substitute custard cups, china rice bowls, or Western teacups.

2-1/3 cups Sea-Vegetable & Fish Stock
    or Instant Sea-Vegetable &
    Fish Stock, page 45
1 tablespoon light (thin) soy sauce
1/2 teaspoon salt
1 tablespoon mirin
1 teaspoon sugar
1 teaspoon freshly grated lemon peel
4 large eggs

1 cup water
6 uncooked Fan-Tail Shrimp, page 88
4 chunks crabmeat
4 gingko nuts (ginnan), if desired
1 small clump tree oyster mushrooms,
    blanched, separated
4 trefoil sprigs (mitsuba), each stem
    knotted, or 4 edible pea pods
4 Pine-Needle Garnishes, page 30

In a medium bowl, combine stock, soy sauce, salt, mirin, sugar and grated lemon peel. In a small bowl, slightly beat eggs. Gently stir eggs into stock mixture. Strain mixture through a fine strainer into a medium bowl. In a wok or deep pot, bring about 4 cups water to a boil. In a small saucepan, bring 1 cup water to a boil; reduce heat to low. Add shrimp to small saucepan; simmer 30 seconds. Drain shrimp; set aside. Divide crabmeat and gingko nuts, if desired, among 4 chawan mushi custard cups with lids. Pour strained stock mixture into cups. Cover with lids. If you are not using chawan mushi cups, cover containers of choice with small pieces of foil for steaming. Place cups on a steamer tray. Cover tray; place over boiling water. Reduce heat to medium. Steam custard over gently simmering water 10 minutes. Uncover cups. Add 1 shrimp, 2 or 3 mushrooms, 1 knotted trefoil sprig or 1 pea pod, and a Pine-Needle Garnish to each custard; cover and steam 5 to 8 minutes longer. Custards are done when a small knife inserted in center comes out clean. Serve custards along with a pair of chopsticks and a small spoon for eating. Makes 4 servings.

Variations

Steamed Lemon-Egg Custard with Chicken: Substitute Chicken Stock with Ginger, page 50, for Sea-Vegetable & Fish Stock. Substitute 1 skinned, diced, chicken-breast half for crabmeat. Marinate chicken 5 minutes in additional 1 tablespoon mirin. Divide among custard cups with gingko nuts. Continue recipe as directed above.

Custard can be steamed in 8 to 10 Japanese teacups for appetizer servings. Increase seafood and other ingredients as necessary; divide among teacups.

Other types of mushrooms can be substituted for tree oyster mushrooms.

Substitute sliced poached scallops for chunks of crabmeat.

A few cooked drained white wheat noodles (udon) or flat wheat noodles (kishimen) can be added to each custard cup before filling.

Steamed Pattypan-Squash Flowers

Seiyo Uri No Buta Ebi Zume

Partial cutting of the squash before steaming makes eating them with chopsticks a snap!

8 to 10 well-shaped pattypan squash, rinsed
Shrimp & Pork Filling, see below

Mushroom Sauce, see below

Shrimp & Pork Filling:
4 medium shrimp, peeled,
   deveined, chopped
1/4 lb. ground pork
1 tablespoon saké
1 tablespoon mirin

1/2 teaspoon minced fresh gingerroot
1 tablespoon light (thin) soy sauce
1/4 teaspoon sesame oil
1/4 teaspoon sugar
1/8 teaspoon salt, if desired

Mushroom Sauce:
1 large dried shiitake mushroom
1/3 cup warm water
1-1/2 cups chicken stock
2 tablespoons soy sauce
2 teaspoons brown sugar

1 tablespoon saké
1/4 teaspoon dashi-no-moto powder
1-1/2 tablespoons cornstarch
1/2 teaspoon sesame oil

Using a small sharp knife, cut off rounded blossom ends of squash. Reserve for caps. Scoop out insides, forming hollow shells. Trim a small piece off stem ends so squash will sit flat. Make a shallow 1/4-inch cut across stem end of each squash. Turn squash 90 degrees and make another cut. Do not cut all the way through or squash will fall apart. Prepare Shrimp & Pork Filling. Mound a small amount of filling into each hollowed squash. In a wok or deep pot, bring about 4 cups water to a boil. Place stuffed squash and reserved caps in a shallow heatproof pan. Place pan on a steamer tray; cover tray. Place over boiling water; steam 15 minutes or until tender. While squash is steaming, prepare Mushroom Sauce. If desired, stir drippings from cooking squash into sauce. Place 2 squash on each serving plate. Serve with Mushroom Sauce. If desired, place 1 cap at an angle on top of each stuffed squash. Makes 4 to 5 servings.

Shrimp & Pork Filling:
In a small bowl, combine all ingredients. Makes about 3/4 cup.

Mushroom Sauce:
Place mushroom in a small bowl; add warm water. Soak 30 minutes or until needed. Squeeze mushroom dry, reserving mushroom liquid. Cut off and discard tough stem. Slice mushroom into strips. In a small saucepan, combine chicken stock, soy sauce, brown sugar, saké and dashi powder over medium-high heat. In a small bowl, blend cornstarch and reserved mushroom soaking liquid. Stir into sauce. Cook until thick, stirring constantly. Stir in sesame oil and sliced mushroom. Makes about 2 cups.

How to Make Steamed Pattypan-Squash Flowers

1/Scoop out insides of squash, forming hollow shells. Mound a small amount of filling into each hollowed squash.

2/Steam filled squash 15 minutes or until tender. Place 2 squash on each serving plate. Serve with Mushroom Sauce.

Steaming Foods

To steam foods successfully, select a dish at least 1 inch smaller than the diameter of the steamer so the steam can circulate freely around the dish of food. Do not add the food until the water has come to a rolling boil over high heat. It will be necessary to reduce the heat to steam egg dishes and delicate custards gently. Simmer a kettle of water on the side to replenish the steamer, if necessary, during long periods of steaming. Several marbles in the bottom of the pan would be a noisy reminder to refill the pan!

Dumplings and buns can be placed directly on a steamer tray lined with dampened cheesecloth, lettuce leaves or cabbage leaves, depending on the type of filling to be steamed. Do not remove the lid during the steaming time unless indicated in a recipe. Remember that the food on the bottom steamer tray near the simmering water will cook faster than food in the upper trays. Remove the steamer from the heat before lifting a steamer tray. Lift the lid *away* from you to avoid scalding burns.

Steamed Seafood in Kelp Boats

Sakana No Konbu Bune

Seafood forms its own delicious dipping sauce, enhanced by the natural flavor boosters in the kelp.

1/3 lb. littleneck or cherrystone clams
  (about 4 clams)
4 to 8 mussels
1 (3-oz.) pkg. wide good-quality dried kelp
  (dashi konbu), cut in
  4 (6" x 8") pieces
8 (7-inch) dried-gourd strips (kampyo),
  soaked in salted water
4 to 8 sea scallops, halved,
  or 1/4 lb. baby scallops

8 to 12 medium shrimp, peeled, deveined
2 or 3 fresh or thawed frozen king crab
  legs, if desired, cut in 3-inch pieces
4 teaspoons saké
4 teaspoons light (thin) soy sauce
4 teaspoons unsalted butter
Scalloped Lemon Slices, page 23

Using a stiff brush, scrub clams under cool running water. Discard any which are not closed or do not clamp shut as you begin to scrub them. Scrub mussels under cool running water. If necessary, pull off beard or strands coming from shells. Make sure mussels are tightly closed; discard any which are not closed. Refrigerate mussels until needed. Place clams in a large bowl; add 2 teaspoons salt and cool water to cover. Soak 3 to 4 hours. To soften dried kelp, dip pieces into a large bowl of warm water. Gently flex pieces 1 minute or until they begin to soften. Do not soak too long or kelp will become too soft and lose its flavor in soaking water. Pat softened pieces dry. Gather each end of a piece of kelp; tie with strips of soaked gourd. Form kelp into a boat shape. Form 3 more boats with remaining kelp pieces and gourd strips. Into each boat, put 1 clam, 1 or 2 mussels, 4 half pieces of scallop or several baby scallops, and 2 or 3 shrimp. Using kitchen scissors, snip open shell of each piece of crab leg; leave meat in shell. Add 1 or 2 pieces to each boat. In a wok or deep pot, bring about 4 cups water to a boil. Place seafood boats on a steamer tray. Add 1 teaspoon saké, 1 teaspoon soy sauce and 1 teaspoon butter to each boat. Cover tray. Place over boiling water; steam seafood 5 to 8 minutes or until clams and mussels have opened. Garnish with Scalloped Lemon Slices. Serve boats immediately. Instruct diners to dip seafood into delicious broth which has formed in bottom of boats. Makes 4 servings.

Variation

Types of seafood can be varied according to availability. Small cubed pieces of fish fillets can be substituted for any of the suggested seafood.

Fan-Tail Shrimp

Oogi Ebi

Shrimp tails spread open into fan shapes.

Large or jumbo shrimp, as needed

Peel shrimp, leaving tails intact. Make a shallow cut lengthwise down back of each shrimp. Rinse out dark vein. Pull away strips of loose skin on each side of cut. Make a slit about 1 inch long through middle of deveined shrimp. Bend head backwards through slit, pulling tail up into place. Secure with a wooden pick. Spread tail open into a fan. Poach shrimp in salted simmering water 1 minute. Remove wooden picks. Use shrimp as a garnish or as directed in recipes.

How to Make Steamed Seafood in Kelp Boats

1/Gather each end of a piece of softened kelp; tie with strips of soaked gourd. Form kelp into a boat shape.

2/Arrange seafood in each kelp boat. Place filled boats on a steamer tray. Add saké, soy sauce and butter to each boat. Cover and steam 5 to 8 minutes. Serve immediately.

Sesame Sauce

Goma Sosu

Good as a dipping sauce for Beef Hot Pot, page 98, or a dressing for noodles.

1/2 cup Dry-Roasted Sesame Seeds, page 150
3 tablespoons soy sauce
1/4 cup rice vinegar
1-1/2 tablespoons sugar

1/2 teaspoon salt
1 teaspoon vegetable oil
1 garlic clove, if desired, minced

For best flavor, dry-roast sesame seeds just before use. In a grinding bowl or blender, grind roasted seeds to a paste. Blend in remaining ingredients until sauce is smooth. Pour into small individual bowls. Sauce can be made 1 to 2 days ahead and refrigerated. Makes about 1/2 cup.

Steamed Buns with Miso-Pork Filling

Miso Buta Manju

In Okinawa, children often head for corner markets after school to snack on these warm soft buns.

Miso-Pork Filling, see below
2-1/2 cups cake flour
1 tablespoon baking powder
1/2 cup sugar
1/2 teaspoon salt

1/4 cup butter or vegetable shortening,
  cut in small pieces
1/2 cup evaporated milk
Vegetable oil

Miso-Pork Filling:
1 tablespoon vegetable oil
3 green onions, minced
1 teaspoon minced fresh gingerroot
1 large garlic clove, minced
1/2 lb. ground pork
3 to 4 dashes ground sansho pepper

2 tablespoons red miso
1 tablespoon saké
1 tablespoon sugar
1 tablespoon soy sauce
1 teaspoon mirin

Prepare Miso-Pork Filling; cool completely, then set aside. In a medium bowl, sift flour, baking powder, sugar and salt. Rub butter or shortening into flour mixture until fine crumbs. Pour evaporated milk over flour mixture; stir until blended. Dough will be very soft. Scrape dough onto a lightly floured surface. Coat dough with flour, kneading lightly several seconds. Pat dough into a ball; rub lightly with oil. Cover with a small bowl; let dough rest 20 minutes. Divide dough in 1/2. Gently roll each 1/2 into a sausage-shaped roll. Cut each roll into 6 equal-sized pieces. With your fingers, press each piece into a circle about 3-1/2 to 4 inches in diameter. Pat circles to make sure dough is well-blended and very smooth. Dough with cracks could split during steaming. This will not harm the bun except for appearance. Place 1 heaping teaspoon filling in center of each circle. Shape dough around filling. Pinch edges tightly closed to seal buns. Rub buns lightly with oil. Cut 12 squares of foil or waxed paper slightly larger than buns. Rub squares lightly with oil. Place 1 bun, seam-side down, on each square. In a wok or deep pot, bring about 4 cups water to a boil. Place buns on foil or waxed paper on a steamer tray, about 3/4 inch apart; cover. Place over boiling water. Reduce heat to medium-high; steam 10 to 12 minutes. Remove foil or paper from buns. Serve warm or at room temperature. Store leftover buns in an airtight plastic bag in the refrigerator. Reheat in a microwave oven or resteam. Makes 12 filled buns.

Miso-Pork Filling:
In a medium skillet, heat vegetable oil over medium-high heat. Add green onions, gingerroot and garlic; stir-fry several seconds or until aromatic. Add pork; stir-fry until crumbly and no longer pink. Add sansho pepper. Reduce heat to medium. In a small bowl, stir together miso, saké, sugar, soy sauce and mirin. Add to meat mixture; cook 3 to 4 minutes, stirring often. Scrape mixture onto a plate; cool before using. Makes about 1 cup.

Note: Tops of steamed buns can be decorated by branding them with a small clean stamp or cutter dipped in red food coloring. Stamps can be found in oriental shops or stationery stores. Look for birds, flower designs or Japanese characters. Or, stamp a flower design using a single drinking straw dipped in food coloring.

How to Make Steamed Buns with Miso-Pork Filling

1/Place 1 heaping teaspoon filling in center of each dough circle. Shape dough around filling. Pinch openings tightly closed to seal buns. Place 1 bun, seam-side down, on each foil square in steamer.

2/Cover and steam buns 10 to 12 minutes. Tops of steamed buns can be decorated by branding them with a small stamp or cutter dipped in red food coloring.

Chicken Simmered with Dried Daikon Radish

Tori No Kiriboshi Daikon

My sister, Dee Bradney, learned to cook dried daikon from a neighbor when she lived in Misawa, Japan.

1-1/2 oz. shredded dried daikon radish
   (kiriboshi daikon)
   (2 cups rehydrated)
2 tablespoons vegetable oil
2 green onions, slivered
1 medium carrot, cut sen-giri, page 18
1 chicken-breast half, skinned,
   boned, diced

1-1/2 cups water
1/2 teaspoon dashi-no-moto powder
2 tablespoons mirin
1 tablespoon sugar
1/4 cup soy sauce
1 tablespoon rice vinegar
Hot red-pepper sauce to taste, if desired

Place shredded dried daikon in a medium bowl; add water to cover. Soak 1 hour. Rinse and drain daikon several times. Squeeze out excess water. Cut pieces once or twice to make shorter lengths. In a medium saucepan, heat oil over medium-high heat. Add green onions and carrot; stir-fry 1 minute. Add chicken; stir-fry 30 seconds. Add rehydrated daikon; stir and toss mixture 30 seconds. In a medium bowl, combine 1-1/2 cups water, dashi powder, mirin, sugar and soy sauce. Pour over chicken and vegetables. Cover saucepan with a tight-fitting lid. Simmer over low heat 20 minutes. Remove lid; cook 2 to 5 minutes longer or until all liquid has evaporated. Stir in vinegar. Serve warm or at room temperature in small serving dishes. Serve with hot-pepper sauce, if desired. Makes 3 to 4 servings.

Braised Spicy Burdock Root   Photo on pages 106 and 107.

Kimpira Gobo

Mrs. Mieko Kaiede of Toki City, Japan, prepared this delicious crunchy vegetable dish for me.

2 (15- to 18-inch) pieces burdock root
   (gobo)
Braising Sauce, see below
2 tablespoons vegetable oil

Seven-Spice Mixture, page 147,
   or red (cayenne) pepper, to taste
1 heaping tablespoon Dry-Roasted Sesame
   Seeds, page 150

Braising Sauce:
2-1/2 tablespoons soy sauce
2 tablespoons saké
1 tablespoon mirin

2-1/2 tablespoons sugar
1/2 teaspoon dashi-no-moto powder

Using a vegetable brush, scrub off earthy brown covering from each piece of burdock root. Cut pieces in 1/2; soak in a pan of cool water 10 minutes. Cut each piece into 2-inch lengths, then cut in julienne strips. Return strips to pan of water. In a large skillet, boil burdock strips in 4 cups water over high heat 5 minutes; drain well. Prepare Braising Sauce. In skillet, heat vegetable oil over high heat. Add drained burdock root; stir-fry 2 minutes. Reduce heat to medium-low. Pour in Braising Sauce. Cook and stir until sauce has almost all evaporated. Add Seven-Spice Mixture or red pepper. Place braised burdock root in a serving bowl. Sprinkle with Dry-Roasted Sesame Seeds. Makes 5 to 6 servings.

Braising Sauce:

In a small bowl, combine all ingredients. Makes about 1/2 cup.

Variation

One or 2 large carrots can be substituted for 1 piece of burdock root.

Simmered Carrot Flowers   Photo on cover.

Hana Ninjin No Nimono

These make a colorful addition to a bento *or Japanese box lunch.*

1-3/4 cups water
1 teaspoon dashi-no-moto powder
1/4 cup sugar
2 tablespoons mirin

1 tablespoon light (thin) soy sauce
3 to 4 large carrots, cut in 1/2-inch-thick
   flower shapes, page 30

In a medium saucepan, combine water, dashi powder, sugar, mirin and soy sauce; bring to a boil over high heat. When mixture boils, add carrot flowers. Reduce heat to medium-high; cook carrots 20 minutes or until tender. Makes 6 servings.

Variation

Carrot Bundles: Cut carrots into strips, 2-1/2 to 3 inches long and 1/4 inch square at each end. Tie strips together in bundles with pieces of dried-gourd strips (kampyo) which have been soaked in salted water. Simmer until barely tender in seasoned stock.

Sweet Simmered Mushrooms

Shiitake No Nimono

Serve with Simmered Carrot Flowers, opposite, and blanched edible pea pods.

4 medium to large dried shiitake mushrooms   **Simmering Sauce, see below**

Simmering Sauce:
1 cup water   **2 tablespoons mirin**
1/2 teaspoon dashi-no-moto powder   **2 tablespoons soy sauce**
2 tablespoons sugar   **2 tablespoons saké**

Place mushrooms in a medium bowl; add warm water to cover. Soak 30 minutes. Prepare Simmering Sauce. Squeeze mushrooms dry. Cut off and discard tough stems. Add mushroom caps to sauce. Bring to a boil over medium-high heat. Reduce heat to medium-low. Simmer mushrooms 15 to 20 minutes or until liquid has almost all evaporated and mushrooms are well-seasoned. Mushrooms can be served warm or at room temperature. Divide with remaining sauce between 2 small serving bowls. Recipe can be doubled. Makes 2 servings.

Simmering Sauce:
In a small saucepan, combine all ingredients. Stir well to dissolve sugar. Makes about 1-1/3 cups.

Variations
Simmered Devil's-Tongue-Jelly Braids: Photo on cover.
Cut 1 block devil's-tongue jelly (konnyaku) into braid shapes as directed on page 18. Blanch in boiling water 2 to 3 minutes; drain well. Cook in Simmering Sauce as directed above.
Glazed Dried-Gourd Strips: Soak 1 (3/4-ounce) package dried-gourd strips (kampyo) in 2 cups water with 1 teaspoon salt 20 minutes; rinse well. Cut into desired lengths. Simmer pieces in Simmering Sauce as directed above. Longer strips can be used for tying foods or as an ingredient inside rolled sushi. Minced, seasoned, soaked gourd can be added to rice dishes.

If desired, score mushroom tops according to directions on page 29.

Serving One-Pot Dishes

One-pot dishes (nimono) are delicious placed on top of steamed rice in large bowls. Or, serve one-pot dishes and rice separately. On the side, serve a salad such as Sweet & Sour Mandarin Shrimp, page 130. Warm saké, hot green tea or cold beer can be served. Soft drinks and cold water are always welcomed and should be kept on hand for those who become extra thirsty from the soy sauce. End the meal with a refreshing dish of Strawberry-Tofu Sherbet, page 168.

As a final thoughtful touch, provide steaming hot perfumed towels. Soak small towels in water to which you have added some drops of rose water or a favorite perfume. Squeeze out towels and tightly roll up. Heat until steaming in the microwave or a steamer. Guests can refresh themselves, Japanese-style, by wiping their hands and faces.

Sweet Simmered Squash

Kabocha No Nimono

A favorite Japanese vegetable dish which can also be made with Hubbard, butternut squash or pumpkin.

1 small acorn squash (about 1-1/2 lbs.), unpeeled	3 tablespoons sugar
1-1/2 cups water	1 tablespoon mirin
1 teaspoon dashi-no-moto powder	1 tablespoon saké
1 tablespoon soy sauce	1 green onion, minced

Rinse and dry squash. Using a large sharp knife, cut squash in 1/2; remove seeds. Cut squash into 1-inch pieces. Pour water into a medium saucepan. Stir in dashi powder, soy sauce, sugar, mirin and saké. Bring to a boil over medium-high heat. Stir a few seconds to dissolve sugar. Add squash; reduce heat to low. Place a drop-lid or small saucepan lid on top of squash; simmer 25 to 30 minutes. Liquid will reduce and squash will become slightly glazed. Garnish with green onion. Makes 4 servings.

Sukiyaki

Sukiyaki (Pan-Simmered Beef & Vegetables, page 96) is one of the most savory and robust of Japanese foods. The flavors of succulent meat and fresh vegetables are enhanced when simmered together in a sweetened soy-sauce mixture. A complex yet delicious taste is created, not to be found in other Japanese foods.

No one is exactly sure how sukiyaki (pronounced skee-yaki) originated. One popular theory states that hungry peasants and farmers working in the fields illegally caught small game and other animals to eat. Eating meat had been forbidden in the seventh century by the teachings of Zen Buddhism. Since the snared animals had to be consumed on the spot, they were cut up and grilled on spades or plows over an open fire. *Suki* means *plow* or *spade; yaki* means *to broil.* Today, sukiyaki is prepared using a combination of two cooking techniques: *nabemono* (one-pot cooking) and *nimono* (simmered in seasoned liquids.)

Sukiyaki, as we know it, was created during the Meiji period (1867-1912) as an attempt to encourage people to eat beef for its nutritional value. Today, some of the finest beef in the world are the Kobe and Matsuzaka beef in Japan. Beer-fed and massaged, the pampered beef is so tender that the meat and fat seem homogenized into one. Traditionally not a beef-eating nation, the Japanese have produced the best! Unfortunately, it is so costly that only a privileged few can enjoy it.

To save time, have your butcher slice the beef for *sukiyaki* or other dishes requiring thinly sliced meats. For sukiyaki, request meat be sliced from 1/6 inch to 1/8 inch thick. Oriental markets carry top-quality meats, sliced especially for these dishes. The thickness of meats could vary slightly from market to market. This is due to personal preference and the ethnic background of the market. Paper-thin slices of *shabu-shabu* meat are too thin to be used in sukiyaki. Korean *bulgogi* beef is slightly thicker than sukiyaki beef. It is usually about 1/4 inch to 1/6 inch thick requiring slightly increased cooking time.

Sukiyaki is a highly individualized dish and can be changed to suit your tastes. Feel free to vary the suggested vegetable amounts or substitute other vegetables. All types of mushrooms, edible pea pods, bean sprouts and water chestnuts are good additions. However, be careful not to use too many vegetables with a high water content at one time. The delicious sauce will be diluted considerably.

Sukiyaki Beef Rolls

Sukiyaki Niku Itame-ni

For an appetizer, each Sukiyaki Beef Roll can be cut into 4 or 5 pieces and served with wooden picks.

Marinade, see below
1 lb. beef rib eye, sliced 1/8 inch thick
   across the grain (about 16 slices)
About 1 tablespoon Prepared Japanese
   Horseradish, page 154
2 (8" x 7-1/2") sheets nori,
   cut in 16 (4" x 1-3/4") strips

1 bunch green onions,
   white parts only, cut in 4-inch slivers
1/2 cup potato starch or cornstarch
Cooking Sauce, see below
2 tablespoons vegetable oil
1 egg per person, if desired

Marinade:

1/4 cup soy sauce
2 tablespoons mirin

2 tablespoons sugar

Cooking Sauce:

1/2 cup water
1/2 teaspoon dashi-no-moto powder
2 tablespoons soy sauce

2 tablespoons sugar
2 tablespoons mirin

Prepare Marinade. Add beef slices; marinate 10 minutes. Remove a slice of beef from marinade; shake off excess liquid. Place on a flat surface. Carefully spread about 1/4 teaspoon Prepared Japanese Horseradish over beef. Place 1 nori strip on top of horseradish. Place 2 or 3 slivers green onion at 1 end of beef slice. Beginning at end with green onion, roll up beef slice. Secure roll with wooden picks. Roll in potato starch or cornstarch. Place on a platter. Continue making beef rolls. Reserve remaining marinade. Prepare Cooking Sauce. Combine Cooking Sauce and reserved marinade. In a medium, non-stick skillet, heat oil over high heat. Add beef rolls; sauté on all sides 3 to 4 minutes. Reduce heat to low; pour in sauce mixture. Simmer rolls 8 to 10 minutes or until sauce becomes glazed. Remove wooden picks from beef rolls. If desired, break 1 egg into a small dipping-sauce bowl for each person; slightly beat each egg. Cut beef rolls in 1/2 and serve warm. Instruct guests to dip each bite into beaten egg, if desired. Makes 4 servings.

Marinade:
In a shallow dish, combine all ingredients; stir until sugar is dissolved. Makes about 1/2 cup.

Cooking Sauce:
In a small bowl, combine all ingredients. Makes 3/4 cup.

Pan-Simmered Beef & Vegetables

Sukiyaki

Guests gather around the communal pot to share the tabletop cooking duties.

1-1/2 lbs. beef tenderloin or rib eye,
   partially frozen for easy slicing
Sukiyaki Vegetables, see below
Cooking Sauce, see below

1 egg per person, if desired
5 to 6 cups hot Steamed Rice, page 139
1 to 2 oz. beef suet or
   3 tablespoons vegetable oil

Sukiyaki Vegetables:

1 bunch green onions,
   cut diagonally in 1-1/2-inch pieces
2 medium Bermuda onions,
   halved, thinly sliced
6 medium, fresh shiitake mushrooms,
   scored in a star-fluted pattern,
   page 29
1 large carrot flower, page 30
1 (1-lb.) Napa cabbage, cored, sliced
1 (15-oz.) can peeled straw mushrooms,
   drained

1/2 lb. Grilled Tofu, page 103,
   cut in 1-inch cubes
1 bunch garland chrysanthemum, rinsed,
   large stems removed, or
   1 bunch spinach, well-rinsed
1/2 lb. devil's-tongue-jelly noodles
   (shirataki) or 1 oz. dried bean-
   thread noodles

Cooking Sauce:

2 cups Sea-Vegetable & Fish Stock,
   page 45, or beef stock
1 cup soy sauce

1/3 to 1/2 cup sugar
1/4 cup saké

Using a large sharp knife or an electric knife, slice meat across the grain as thinly as possible. Arrange meat attractively on a serving platter. Prepare Sukiyaki Vegetables. Blanch noodles 1 minute in boiling water; drain well. If using dried bean threads, soak in water 30 minutes. If noodles are bound by rubber bands, do not remove until after soaking. Snip into shorter lengths, then cut away rubber bands. Arrange Sukiyaki Vegetables on a large serving platter. Cover and refrigerate until needed. Meat and most vegetables can be prepared several hours ahead. It is best to cut onions at the last minute. Prepare Cooking Sauce. Cool; refrigerate until serving time. If desired, break 1 egg into a small dipping-sauce bowl for each person; slightly beat each egg. Serve with bowls of hot Steamed Rice. At the table, heat a sukiyaki-nabe over a portable tabletop burner. Or, use an electric wok or electric skillet heated to medium then adjusted to medium-low, if necessary. Sauté suet; discard suet when most of fat is rendered. Or, add oil. Add ingredients in thirds, beginning with green onions and Bermuda onions. As they become aromatic, add 1/3 of sliced meat. Add a portion of shiitake mushrooms, carrot, cabbage and straw mushrooms. Be sure to keep foods in separate piles in pot. Pour in about 1/3 of Cooking Sauce. When foods begin to simmer, add some tofu, garland chrysanthemum or spinach and noodles. These require less cooking time. Simmer foods 4 or 5 minutes, turning as necessary. Guests can begin helping themselves from pot. Instruct guests to dip each bite into beaten egg, if desired. Cook should replenish pot halfway through first batch of Sukiyaki. Continue cooking as instructed above. Makes 6 servings.

Cooking Sauce:

In a medium saucepan, combine all ingredients over medium-low heat. Heat and stir until sugar is dissolved. Makes about 3-1/2 cups.

Beef Hot Pot

Shabu-Shabu

The name is said to come from the soft swishing sound made when the meat slices are dipped in the broth.

12 fresh or dried shiitake mushrooms
1 small head Napa cabbage
1 Spinach Log, page 125
Sesame Sauce, page 89,
   or Peanut-Miso Sauce, page 72
Lemon-Soy Dipping Sauce variation,
   page 54, with variation noted below
2 tablespoons fresh orange juice
Condiments, see below
1 large onion, cut in thin wedges
1 bunch green onions,
   cut diagonally in 2-inch pieces
1 large carrot, thinly sliced diagonally
1 block Grilled Tofu, page 103,
   cut in 1-inch cubes

6 to 8 oz. dried white wheat noodles (udon)
   or flat white wheat noodles
   (kishimen), cooked, rinsed in
   cool water
1-1/2 to 1-3/4 lbs. top-quality
   well-marbled beef rib eye or sirloin,
   cut across the grain in paper-thin slices
6 cups Sea-Vegetable & Fish Stock,
   page 45, any other stock
Hot Steamed Rice, page 139
Seven-Spice Mixture, page 147, to taste
Salt and pepper to taste

Condiments:
Red-Maple Radish, page 155
3 or 4 green onions, minced

2 to 3 tablespoons grated fresh gingerroot

If using dried mushrooms, place in a small bowl; add warm water to cover. Soak 30 minutes or until needed. Squeeze mushrooms dry. Cut off and discard tough stems from fresh or rehydrated mushrooms. Select 2 or 3 leaves from cabbage. Blanch 1 minute in boiling water; trim tough stems from leaves. If desired, slice remaining cabbage and use in recipe. Prepare Spinach Log. Roll Spinach Log as directed in the variation, page 125, using blanched cabbage leaves instead of Toasted Nori and Egg Pancake. Slice roll into 1-inch pieces. Prepare Sesame Sauce or Peanut-Miso Sauce. Prepare variation from Lemon-Soy Dipping Sauce, adding orange juice to sauce. Prepare Condiments; place in separate small bowls. On a large platter, arrange sliced cabbage roll, sliced cabbage, if desired, onions, carrot, mushrooms and cubed Grilled Tofu. Add a pile of cooked drained noodles. Arrange sliced beef attractively on another platter; meat can be folded for easy handling. Give each guest a pair of chopsticks, a small dish for meat and vegetables, a rice bowl, 2 small dipping-sauce bowls and a soup bowl. Pour stock into a hot pot (hokonabe), a soaked earthenware donabe for use with a tabletop burner, or an electric wok or skillet; bring stock to a boil. Place platters of meat and vegetables, Condiments, individual bowls of dipping sauces and bowls of hot Steamed Rice on the table. Begin cooking by adding some sliced cabbage, if used, onions, carrot and mushrooms to hot stock. After several minutes, invite diners to use their chopsticks and swish pieces of beef through stock until cooked to desired doneness; meat will cook in seconds. Add some cabbage rolls and tofu. Diners should help themselves to vegetables in pot as they cook. Stir small amounts of desired Condiments into small individual bowls of Sesame Sauce or Peanut-Miso Sauce, and Lemon-Soy Dipping Sauce for dipping meat and vegetables. Add more meat and vegetables to hot stock as needed. When all meat and vegetables have been cooked, add noodles to broth in pot and heat through. Divide noodles and broth among soup bowls for a soup course. Sprinkle soup with Seven-Spice Mixture, salt and pepper. Any remaining Condiments or sauce can be stirred in for flavoring. Makes 6 servings.

Chicken Hot Pot

Mizutaki

A rich and delicious hot pot I enjoyed at an inn high in the snowy mountains of Kyoto.

Hot-Pot Ingredients, see below
Condiments, see below
6 cups Chicken Stock with Ginger, page 50
1/4 cup red miso
2 tablespoons yellow miso
1/4 cup saké

1 teaspoon dashi-no-moto powder
1 tablespoon sugar
Salt to taste
Pickled daikon radish (takuan), sliced
5 to 6 cups hot Steamed Rice, page 139

Hot-Pot Ingredients:

1 (1-lb.) Napa cabbage, cored, sliced
6 medium, fresh shiitake mushrooms,
    scored in a star-fluted pattern, page 29
2 medium carrots, diagonally sliced
1 medium onion, halved, thinly sliced
2 medium, new potatoes,
    sliced 1/3 inch thick
3 small Japanese eggplants or 1 small
    regular eggplant, cut in strips
1/2 lb. Grilled Tofu, page 103, cubed,
    or 1/2 lb. firm Chinese-style tofu,
    rinsed, patted dry, cubed

1 bunch green onions, diagonally sliced
3 chicken-breast halves, skinned, boned,
    cut in 1-inch cubes
1 small pkg. fresh enokitake mushrooms,
    rinsed, drained
8 oz. ramen noodles or
    white wheat noodles, cooked,
    rinsed in cool water
Ti leaf

Condiments:

1/2 cup grated Red-Maple Radish, page 155
1 lemon, cut in wedges

1 bunch small green onions, thinly sliced
Soy sauce

Prepare Hot-Pot Ingredients. Prepare Condiments; place in small bowls. In a large stockpot, heat stock over medium heat until hot. Place miso in a medium bowl; dilute with a small amount of hot stock. Stir diluted miso back into stock. Stir in saké, dashi powder, sugar and salt. Heat broth over low heat; do not boil. Pour broth into a soaked earthenware donabe. At the table, place donabe on a portable tabletop burner. Adjust heat so broth simmers. Place Hot-Pot Ingredients, Condiments, bowls of pickled daikon and bowls of hot Steamed Rice on the table. Add some cabbage, shiitake mushrooms, carrots, onion and potato to simmering broth. As foods cook, add some eggplant, Grilled Tofu or Chinese-style tofu, green onions, chicken and enokitake mushrooms; these require less cooking time. Invite diners to help themselves from pot. Instruct diners to dip bites of Hot-Pot Ingredients into their individual small bowls of mixed Condiments. When chicken, vegetables and rice have been eaten, add noodles to pot. Simmer until hot, then spoon noodles and broth into rice bowls for a soup course. Makes 6 servings.

Hot-Pot Ingredients:

Prepare ingredients. To arrange them on a large serving platter, pile cabbage on 1 side of platter and noodles in center. Place remaining foods around and on top of noodles. Across front of platter, place a well-rinsed ti leaf. Pile chicken cubes on leaf. Fan enokitake mushrooms; arrange them in front.

Variation

Dried shiitake mushrooms can be substituted for fresh ones. Soak dried shiitake mushrooms in warm water 30 minutes or until needed. Squeeze mushrooms dry. Cut off and discard tough stems. Using a small sharp knife, score tops in a star-fluted pattern, page 29.

Tofu

Tofu is an important inexpensive protein alternative to meat in Japan. Not only is it rich in vitamins, minerals and important amino acids, but it is low in calories—an 8-ounce piece contains less than 150 calories. Tofu is also 95 percent digestible and low in sodium and fat.

To produce this extraordinary food, soaked soybeans are ground with water to produce soy milk, a nutritious liquid in itself. After straining the milk, high-protein soybean pulp remains called *okara*. The soy milk is then combined with a coagulating agent to produce curds and whey, similar to the cheese-making process. The curds are pressed until firm, then covered with cool water until eaten. Instructions for making tofu are on page 102.

It is believed that tofu, like tea, was introduced to Japan by Buddhist clergy traveling from China. At first, tofu was the food of the nobility. Its use was expanded and refined in Buddhist monasteries because animal-protein foods were forbidden. Tofu Treasure Balls and Monk's Tofu Loaf are examples of tofu foods created during this period. When Buddhism spread throughout the land, so did the knowledge and use of tofu. Tofu-making shops sprang up all over the countryside and tofu evolved into the quality product we are familiar with today. Several varieties of tofu were invented, many of which are still in popular use.

Blocks of regular Japanese-style tofu (momen-goshi) and silken-style tofu (kinu-goshi) can be purchased in sealed water-packed tubs. Package weights of each type will vary a few ounces throughout the country. Regular Japanese-style tofu is also referred to as *cotton-style tofu* because it will have an impression of the cotton cloth used to line the molding box during production. This type is firmer than the silken-style tofu.

Softer than Chinese-style tofu, regular Japanese-style tofu should be wrapped and pressed to remove liquid and firm up the texture before cooking. Press the blocks whole or sliced, as directed in the recipes. Pressing times will vary depending on the texture required for each recipe. If time permits, tofu can be firmed up by wrapping it in two layers of clean kitchen towel and refrigerating it overnight for the next day's use. Silken Japanese-style tofu has a softer delicate consistency unsuitable for frying without long careful pressing. Take advantage of its silken texture and use it for making custards, dips, sauces and ice cream. Another widely available brand of soft tofu custard or pudding is sold in the refrigerator section in small sealed Tetra-Pak containers. It is best used like silken Japanese-style tofu. It has a shelf life of six months.

Tofu is available in other forms. Large thick blocks of deep-fried tofu (atsu-age) are prepared daily in Japan. To use them, cut into smaller pieces and add to soups and stews. Thin deep-fried tofu pouches or bags (abura-age) can be stuffed with sushi rice or meat and vegetable mixtures; see Stuffed Golden Tofu Pouches, page 57. Blanch these two forms of deep-fried tofu in boiling water before use to remove the taste of the frying oils. Grilled, regular, Japanese-style tofu is known as *yaki-dofu*. *Yuba* is the highly nutritious residue from soybean milk; it is dried into sheets then used as a protein-packed meat substitute in dishes.

Purchase fresh tofu from Oriental markets or from local supermarkets. Look for well-chilled packages with fresh clear packing water. Packages should be stamped with a pull-date for quality control. Do not purchase tofu out of date. At home, remove the tofu from its container, rinse it, then submerge it in a bowl of cool water. Refrigerate up to seven days, changing the water daily. Older, slightly sour tofu can be refreshed by blanching it for a few minutes in boiling water. Older tofu is best used in dishes which require cooking. Some recipes call for the use of crumbled tofu. For best results, wrap and press the tofu first, then squeeze in cheesecloth to break up the texture and remove any additional water.

Tofu can be frozen but the consistency becomes spongy and porous after thawing. Squeeze out the liquid and shred this protein-packed food for use as a meat substitute in casseroles, sauces and stir-fry dishes. Freeze-drying is a traditional method of preserving tofu. The resulting *koya-dofu* is produced on a large scale today in Japan. In the West, it is referred to as *textured vegetable protein*. Soak commercially freeze-dried tofu in warm water before use.

For a taste of tofu in its purest and finest form, prepare Bubbling Tofu Hot Pot or Chilled Summer Tofu. To savor the taste of freshly made tofu, follow the directions for making your own. The finest tofu in Japan is made with natural spring water and is eaten the day it is made. The Japanese ideal for preparing tofu is little or no cooking so the natural taste can be enjoyed to the fullest.

The Soybean Culture of Japan

Since ancient times soybeans have played an important role in the cuisine of Japan. They have influenced the social, religious and economic aspects of daily life. Rich in proteins, soybeans are often referred to as "the meat of the fields." They contain the eight essential amino acids of the 21 which form the protein building blocks of the body. The body is able to utilize the eight essential amino acids to produce the rest, qualifying soybeans as a complete protein food.

Soybeans in any form must always be cooked to inactivate the trypsin inhibitor which prevents the body from digesting their protein. Whole dried soybeans, available in health-food stores and Oriental markets, are eaten simmered, roasted and deep-fried. Fresh green soybeans are simmered and popped out of the pod for eating. Soybeans are made into roasted flour for confections, and germinated into sprouts.

Three ancient soybean foods form the foundation of the Japanese cuisine. They are fermented-bean paste (miso), soy sauce (shoyu) and tofu.

Tofu

Tofu made with natural spring water will have a pure clean taste.

1 lb. dried soybeans (2-1/2 cups)
Bottled natural spring water or tap water
4 teaspoons hydrated magnesium sulfate
  (Epsom salts), 3 teaspoons unrefined
  magnesium chloride (nigari) or
  2 teapoons calcium sulfate

In a large bowl, rinse soybeans in cool water. Discard any black, broken or discolored beans. In a large bowl or pot, soak beans in about 8 cups water 10 to 12 hours or overnight. Cut open a bean to determine if it is the same color throughout. This indicates the beans are evenly soaked. Drain beans; rinse under cool running water. In a blender or food processor fitted with a steel blade, grind beans in 5 (1-1/2-cup) batches. Add 1 cup boiling water to each batch; process 1 to 2 minutes. **Beans will become a thick slightly granular mixture.** Add each batch to a 6- to 8-quart soup pot. Stir in 3 quarts water. Bring to a boil over medium-high heat. Stir soybean mixture several times. Watch thick foam forming on top to be sure it does not boil over. When mixture boils, reduce heat to low; simmer 5 minutes. Remove from heat; cool slightly. Line a large metal colander with a dampened tofu-pressing sack, unbleached muslin or several layers of cheesecloth. Place lined colander in a large metal bowl. Pour in soybean mixture. Wearing insulated rubber gloves to protect your hands from the heat, gather edges of cloth; squeeze tightly to press out all soy milk. Slightly open pouch. Pour 3 cups water into remaining soy pulp. Squeeze tightly to press out remaining milk into a large bowl. Wash soup pot; return soy milk to clean pot. Scrape soy pulp from pressing cloth; reserve for making Sugar & Spice Okara and other cooking purposes. Rinse out pressing cloth. Bring soy milk to a boil over medium-high heat. Reduce heat slightly; simmer 5 minutes. In a small bowl, combine 1 cup water and magnesium sulfate or magnesium chloride. Remove milk from heat. If a thick skin layer has formed, skim it off. This is called *yuba* and is the basis for many delicious dishes in Japan. **Pour 1/3 of coagulating agent into hot milk.** Using a wooden spoon, gently cut through milk 6 to 8 times. Let milk stand, undisturbed, 2 minutes so curdling action can begin. Add 1/2 of remaining coagulating agent; cut through milk 3 or 4 times. Check curds after second addition. If thick white curds are floating in clear yellow whey, curdling action is finished. If whey is milky and there is not a definite division between curds and whey, add remaining coagulating agent. Let mixture stand, undisturbed, 5 minutes. Too much coagulating agent could cause curds to become heavy and sink to the bottom, resulting in very firm tofu. Some people might prefer their tofu this way. Curds will vary with each batch, depending on several factors, including age and type of soybeans. **Line a wooden tofu-pressing box or another small perforated container with damp pressing cloth.** A small round, square, or rectangular perforated pan can be substituted for wooden pressing box. Tofu shape and thickness will vary with shape of mold. This factor should be taken into consideration if a specific shape is necessary for a recipe. Place lined box in the sink or in a pan if you wish to retain whey. Using a medium strainer, scoop curds out of whey. **Drain off excess whey; tap curds into box.** When box is filled with curds, smooth top. Smooth pressing cloth over top. Place pressing-box lid on top. Use an appropriate-sized saucer or a piece of trimmed plywood to fit your home-made pressing container. **Add 2 to 3 pounds of weight; press 30 minutes.** For firmer tofu, increase weight slightly; press as long as 2 hours for very firm tofu. Pressing weight must be increased gradually so tofu does not break up. Check curd occasionally to determine desired degree of firmness. Firm tofu gives a smaller yield but has a higher concentration of protein. For frying purposes, firm tofu is the best type to use. Carefully turn tofu out of pressing box into a pan of cool water. Store in water in the refrigerator 7 to 10 days, changing water daily. Makes 2-1/2 to 3 pounds regular-firm tofu or about 1-1/2 pounds extra-firm tofu.

How to Make Grilled Tofu

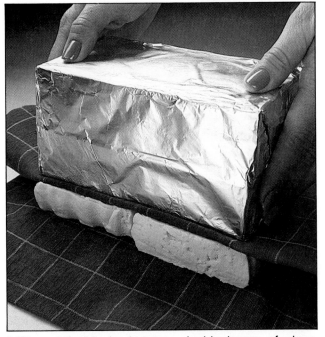

1/Place tofu blocks between double layers of clean kitchen towels. Set weight on top to press out excess liquid and firm tofu for grilling. Press up to 4 hours, changing towels once.

2/Rub oil over tofu. Heat oil in a cast-iron skillet with raised ridges. Add tofu to hot skillet; sear 1 to 2 minutes. Turn tofu once when grill marks are golden brown.

Grilled Tofu

Yaki-Dofu

Prepare hard-to-find grilled tofu in a special, stovetop, cast-iron skillet with ridges.

Regular Japanese-style tofu blocks, rinsed, patted dry   **Vegetable oil**

Cut tofu blocks in 1/2 horizontally or leave whole. Place between double layers of clean kitchen towels or several layers of paper towels. Place 1 to 2 pounds of weight on top to press out excess liquid and firm tofu for grilling. Press at least 1 hour or up to 4 hours. Change towels once while pressing. Using your fingers, rub oil on both sides of each tofu block. Add a small amount of oil to a medium, heavy skillet or well-seasoned cast-iron skillet with raised ridges inside for stovetop grilling. Use a folded piece of cloth or paper towel to wipe skillet evenly with oil. Place over medium-high heat. When hot, place 2 or 3 pieces tofu in skillet. Sear 1 to 2 minutes. If using ridged skillet, lift 1 end of tofu to check grill marks. When marks are medium golden brown, turn tofu over. Do not turn tofu more than once or attractive grill marks from skillet will be uneven. Use tofu immediately or cool, cover and refrigerate for use within 1 to 2 days. Grilled tofu will not fall apart when simmered in one-pot dishes.

Bubbling Tofu Hot Pot   Photo on page 121.

Yudofu

This is one of the purest examples of Kyoto temple cooking and very popular in Japan today.

6 cups water
Dipping Sauce, see below
Condiments, see below
1 (5-inch) square good-quality dried kelp
   (dashi konbu), wiped
2 (14- to 16-oz.) pkgs. silken or
   regular Japanese-style tofu,
   rinsed, patted dry

1 large carrot flower, page 30
3 or 4 trefoil sprigs (mitsuba) or
   watercress, blanched,
   stems knotted together

Dipping Sauce:
1/3 cup soy sauce
1/2 teaspoon dashi-no-moto powder

1/3 cup water
1 tablespoon mirin

Condiments:
2 to 3 tablespoons grated fresh gingerroot
4 small green onions, thinly sliced
2 to 3 tablespoons grated daikon radish

2 tablespoons dried-bonito thread shavings
1 tablespoon Dry-Roasted Sesame Seeds,
   page 150

One hour before cooking, fill a 2- to 2-1/2-quart earthenware donabe with water; soak 1 hour. Or, fill a regular 2- to 2-1/2-quart stovetop casserole. Prepare Dipping Sauce and Condiments; set aside. Using a small knife, make 2 or 3 slits in dried kelp. Add to water in donabe or casserole. Heat 10 minutes over low heat; remove kelp. Cut tofu blocks in 1/2; add to seasoned water. If necessary, adjust heat so water simmers gently. Tofu will be heated through after 3 to 4 minutes. Do not boil or overcook because tofu will toughen. Garnish with carrot flower and trefoil or watercress. Bring donabe or casserole to the table to serve. Place a block of tofu in a serving dish for each diner. Invite diners to season tofu with small amounts of Dipping Sauce mixed with the desired Condiments. Makes 4 servings.

Dipping Sauce:
In a small bowl, combine all ingredients. Pour into a small pottery bowl to be served at the table. Makes 3/4 cup.

Condiments:
Prepare Condiments; place in separate tiny glass or pottery dishes. Guests can help themselves at the table.

Variation
Create a different taste by simmering tofu in Chicken Stock with Ginger, page 50, instead of water. Use stock later for making soup.

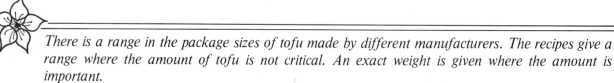

There is a range in the package sizes of tofu made by different manufacturers. The recipes give a range where the amount of tofu is not critical. An exact weight is given where the amount is important.

Tofu Treasure Balls   Photo on page 106.

Hirousu

This Kyoto specialty can be eaten warm with a dipping sauce or added to soups and stews.

Mustard-Miso Sauce, page 156
1 (14- to 16-oz.) pkg. regular
  Japanese-style tofu, rinsed
  patted dry
1 medium, dried shiitake mushroom
2 (1/8-inch-thick) slices peeled
  fresh gingerroot
4 small green onions
1/2 medium carrot
1 (4-inch) piece burdock root (gobo),
  if desired

1 tablespoon vegetable oil
2 tablespoons Dry-Roasted Sesame Seeds,
  page 150
2 teaspoons soy sauce
1/2 teaspoon salt
2 teaspoons mirin
1 tablespoon grated mountain yam
  (yama-imo) or 1 tablespoon cornstarch
About 4 cups peanut oil or
  vegetable oil for deep-frying
Additional soy sauce

Prepare Mustard-Miso Sauce; set aside. Cut tofu horizontally into 3 slices. Place between double layers of clean kitchen towels or several layers of paper towels. Place 2 to 3 pounds of weight on top to press out excess liquid and firm tofu. Press 3 to 4 hours. Change towels once while pressing. Place mushroom in a small bowl; add warm water to cover. Soak 30 minutes or until needed. Squeeze mushroom dry. Cut off and discard tough stem. Mince mushroom, gingerroot and green onions. Shred carrot. If used, scrape, rinse and shred burdock root. Place shredded burdock in a small bowl; add water to cover. Add 1 tablespoon rice vinegar to help prevent discoloration. Drain and pat dry before using. In a small skillet, heat 1 tablespoon oil over medium-high heat. Add mushroom, gingerroot, green onions, carrot and burdock, if using; stir-fry 1 to 2 minutes. Cool. In a grinding bowl or other medium bowl, thoroughly mash tofu. Mix in stir-fried vegetables. Add Dry-Roasted Sesame Seeds, 2 teaspoons soy sauce, salt, mirin and grated mountain yam or cornstarch. If you are not using a grinding bowl, it is helpful to combine mixture thoroughly by blending it with your hands. Mixture can be made into balls immediately or covered and refrigerated up to 2 hours. Use 1 heaping tablespoon mixture per ball. Oil your fingers and pat balls into shape. In a wok or shallow saucepan, heat about 4 cups oil over medium heat to 350F (175C) or until a 1-inch cube of bread turns golden brown in 65 seconds. Fry balls, several at a time, 3 to 5 minutes or until slightly puffed and golden brown. Turn several times for even browning. Drain fried balls on paper towels. Serve warm or at room temperature with small bowls of soy sauce and Mustard-Miso Sauce. Balls can be recrisped with a second frying. Heat oil to 370F (190C) or until a 1-inch cube of bread turns golden brown in 50 seconds. Fry balls 1 to 2 minutes. Drain and serve immediately. Makes about 15 balls.

On the following pages a Japanese New Year Menu, starting from left to right: Jubako box containing: Stuffed Golden Tofu Pouches, page 57; Pickled Lotus-Root Flowers, page 32; Gingko nuts; Marinated Radish Fans, page 26; Tofu Treasure Balls, above; Bamboo-Shaped Stuffed Fish Rolls, page 39; Ham & Fish Pinwheels, page 42; Steamed fish loaf; and Black beans. Continuing left to right: Braised Spicy Burdock Root, page 92; Steamed Red Beans & Rice, page 143; Deep-Fried Ginger Oysters, page 117; Treasure-Ship Sashimi, page 56; Kansai-Style Mixed Sushi, page 70; Strawberries in Snow, page 158; Persimmon & Daikon Salad, page 126; Pineapple-Yam Jelly, page 171; Red-Bean Jelly with Macadamia Nuts, page 169; Plum-Wine Jelly, page 170; and in the background traditional stacked rice cakes (kagami mochi), page 138.

Monk's Tofu Loaf

Gisei-Dofu

Created by the Buddhist monks to conceal forbidden eggs, this savory tofu hides many treasures.

2 (14- to 16-oz.) pkgs. regular
   Japanese-style tofu, rinsed,
   patted dry
2 medium, dried shiitake mushrooms
1 (5-inch) piece burdock root (gobo),
   if desired
3 eggs
2 tablespoons mirin
1 tablespoon light (thin) soy sauce

1 teaspoon salt
1 tablespoon sugar
2 tablespoons vegetable oil
2 teaspoons minced fresh gingerroot
1/4 cup finely diced carrot
2 green onions, minced
1/4 cup thawed, frozen, petit green peas
2 tablespoons vegetable oil
Mushroom Sauce, page 86, if desired

Line an 8-inch-square baking pan with foil; grease foil. Cut tofu blocks in 1/2 horizontally. Place between double layers of clean kitchen towels or several layers of paper towels. Place 2 to 3 pounds of weight on top to press out excess liquid and firm tofu. Press 1 hour. Change towels once while pressing. Place mushrooms in a small bowl; add warm water to cover. Soak 30 minutes or until needed. Squeeze mushrooms dry. Cut off and discard tough stems. Dice mushrooms. Scrape and rinse burdock root, if using. Dice into small pieces. Place diced burdock in a small bowl; add water to cover. Add 1 tablespoon rice vinegar to help prevent discoloration. Drain and pat dry before using. **In a blender or food processor fitted with a steel blade, place pressed tofu, eggs, mirin, soy sauce, salt and sugar; process until smooth.** Scrape mixture into a medium bowl; set aside. In a medium skillet, heat 2 tablespoons oil over medium-high heat. Add diced mushrooms, diced burdock, if using, gingerroot, carrot and green onions. Sauté 1 to 2 minutes; add peas. Sauté 30 seconds longer; cool. **Stir cooled vegetables into tofu mixture.** Pour mixture into prepared pan; cover with foil. In a wok or deep pot, bring about 4 cups water to a boil over high heat. Place pan on a steamer tray. Cover tray; place over boiling water. Reduce heat to medium. **Steam over gently simmering water 20 minutes or until set.** Test tofu mixture by inserting a small knife in center; it should come out clean. Remove tray from water. Cool to room temperature. Turn loaf out of pan. Remove foil. Cut tofu loaf in 1/2, then into 1-inch strips. Add 1 tablespoon oil to a medium, heavy skillet or well-seasoned cast-iron skillet with raised ridges for stovetop grilling. Use a folded piece of cloth or paper towel to wipe skillet evenly with oil. Place over medium-high heat. **When hot, place 1/2 of tofu pieces in skillet.** Sear 1 to 2 minutes. If using ridged skillet, lift 1 end of tofu to check grill marks. When marks are medium golden brown, turn tofu over. Do not turn tofu more than once or attractive grill marks from skillet will be uneven. If using flat skillet, cook tofu until golden brown on both sides. Remove grilled tofu from skillet. Add remaining 1 tablespoon oil to skillet and sear remaining tofu pieces on both sides. Serve grilled tofu pieces plain or with Mushroom Sauce, if desired. Allow 2 pieces per serving. Leftover tofu can be refrigerated up to 5 days. Then reheated in a skillet. Makes 8 servings.

Variations

Instead of pan-grilling, tofu pieces can be dusted with potato starch or cornstarch, then deep-fried at 350F (175C) until golden. Serve with Mustard-Miso Sauce, page 156, or Spicy Mustard, page 148.

Leftover grilled Monk's Tofu Loaf can be sliced and stir-fried with vegetables or meats, or added to soups.

How to Make Monk's Tofu Loaf

1/Stir sautéed vegetables into tofu mixture. Pour into foil-lined pan. Cover and steam 20 minutes or until set.

2/Cut cooled tofu into 1-inch strips. In a heavy skillet, fry tofu on both sides until golden.

Chilled Summer Tofu

Hiya Yakko

One of Japan's favorite ways to beat the summer heat.

Dipping Sauce, page 104
Condiments, page 104
2 (14- to 16-oz.) pkgs. very fresh silken
  or regular Japanese-style tofu,
  rinsed, patted dry
Cold water
Crushed ice or small ice cubes

4 small piles Pickled Pink-Ginger Slices,
  page 153
4 Prepared-Japanese-Horseradish Leaves,
  page 154, or mound of Prepared
  Japanese Horseradish
Lemon wedges

Prepare Dipping Sauce and Condiments; set aside. Cut 2 tofu blocks crosswise in 1/2 to make 4 blocks. Place each piece in an attractive glass serving dish. Place a small amount of cold water and crushed ice or small ice cubes around base of each piece of tofu. Arrange a small pile of Pickled Pink-Ginger Slices on top of each tofu piece. Add a Prepared-Japanese-Horseradish Leaf or a small mound of Prepared Japanese Horseradish to corner of each tofu piece. Serve tofu with small individual bowls of Dipping Sauce, Condiments and lemon wedges. Each diner can mix the desired Condiments into their Dipping Sauce, then dip a bite of tofu into Dipping-Sauce mixture before eating. Makes 4 servings.

Silken Strawberry Tofu

Ichigo Dofu

Celebrate Hina Matsuri *or Girls' Day on March 3rd with a rainbow of fruit-flavored tofu.*

1 (0.25-oz.) stick white agar-agar (kanten)	2 tablespoons fresh lemon juice
1 cup water	1/8 teaspoon salt
About 2 cups strawberries, hulled	1/2 teaspoon vanilla extract
1/2 lb. silken Japanese-style tofu, rinsed, patted dry	1/2 cup sugar
	8 or 9 strawberries for garnish, if desired

Tear agar-agar stick into 4 pieces. Place agar-agar and water in a medium saucepan. Press agar-agar pieces into water several seconds to soften. Shred pieces with your fingers. Soak 30 minutes. In a blender or food processor fitted with a steel blade, puree about 2 cups strawberries. Scrape into a small bowl. Measure 1 cup puree; reserve extra puree. Add 1 cup strawberry puree back to blender or food-processor bowl. Add tofu; process until mixture is smooth. Add lemon juice, salt and vanilla. Process until blended; scrape into a medium bowl. Simmer agar-agar and water over very low heat until dissolved, 10 to 12 minutes. Stir once or twice while simmering. When dissolved, add sugar; simmer 2 minutes longer. Remove from heat. Strain hot agar-agar into strawberry-tofu puree through a fine strainer. Scrape agar-agar from bottom of strainer into bowl. Quickly stir to blend. Rinse an 8-inch-square pan with cold water. *Quickly* pour mixture into damp pan. Mixture will set almost instantly at room temperature or can be refrigerated until serving time. Cut delicate tofu custard into 8 or 9 squares or flower shapes. Put 1 piece on each serving dish. Garnish each serving with a strawberry. Serve with reserved strawberry puree, if desired. Makes 8 or 9 servings.

Variations

Silken Kiwifruit Tofu (Kiwi Dofu): Substitute 1 cup kiwifruit puree for strawberry puree. Garnish with fresh mint leaves, if desired.

Silken Peach Tofu (Momo Dofu): Substitute 1 cup peach puree for strawberry puree. Substitute 1/2 teaspoon almond extract for vanilla extract. Garnish with fresh peach leaves, if desired.

For a Girls' Day celebration, prepare 3 flavors of fruit tofu. Cut into equal-sized diamond shapes. Arrange a piece of each flavor on each small serving dish. Three colors and the diamond shape are traditional for this happy occasion.

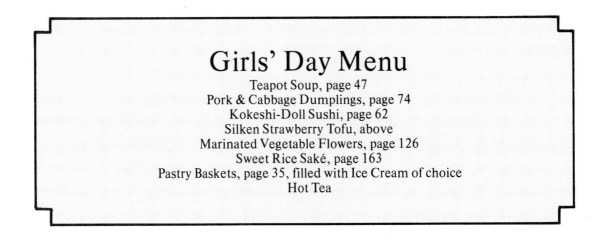

Girls' Day Menu

Teapot Soup, page 47
Pork & Cabbage Dumplings, page 74
Kokeshi-Doll Sushi, page 62
Silken Strawberry Tofu, above
Marinated Vegetable Flowers, page 126
Sweet Rice Saké, page 163
Pastry Baskets, page 35, filled with Ice Cream of choice
Hot Tea

How to Make Silken Strawberry Tofu

1/Strain hot agar-agar into strawberry-tofu puree through a fine strainer.

2/Quickly pour mixture into dampened pan. Let set at room temperature or in refrigerator. To serve, cut into shape of choice.

Mixed Fried Tofu & Vegetables

Tofu Champura

If you omit the ham, you won't miss the meat in this protein-packed Okinawan specialty.

1 (16- to 20-oz.) pkg. firm Chinese-style
   tofu, rinsed, patted dry
1/4 cup vegetable oil
2 teaspoons soy sauce
1 heaping cup 1-inch pieces green cabbage
1 medium carrot, shredded
2 garlic cloves, minced
1 heaping cup fresh bean sprouts,
   rinsed, drained

1/3 cup baked-ham strips, if desired
1 scant teaspoon dashi-no-moto powder
2 teaspoons soy sauce
1/4 teaspoon salt
1/4 cup Japanese chives (nira) or
   regular chives, minced

Place tofu between double layers of clean kitchen towels or several layers of paper towels. Drain 15 minutes. Cut tofu into 1-inch cubes; pat dry. In an 11- or 12-inch non-stick skillet, heat 2 tablespoons oil over medium-high heat 30 seconds. Add tofu cubes; sauté until golden brown on all sides. Sprinkle 2 teaspoons soy sauce over tofu; mix well. Remove tofu from skillet; set aside. Wipe moisture from skillet. Add remaining 2 tablespoons oil; heat over high heat 30 seconds. Add cabbage, carrot and garlic; stir-fry 2 minutes. Add bean sprouts and ham strips, if desired; stir-fry 1 to 2 minutes longer. Return sautéed tofu to skillet. Sprinkle with dashi powder, 2 teaspoons soy sauce and salt; mix well. Stir in chives. Remove tofu and vegetables to a serving platter. Makes 4 to 5 small servings.

Peanut Tofu

Jimami Dofu

Jimami *means earth-bean. This version was adapted from a popular Okinawan snack.*

1 (0.25-oz.) stick white agar-agar
  (kanten)
2 cups water
1 cup unsalted cocktail peanuts
1 (14- to 16-oz.) pkg. Japanese-style tofu,
  rinsed, patted dry

1 tablespoon light-brown sugar
1/4 teaspoon salt
Dipping Sauce, see below
Condiments, see below

Dipping Sauce:
2/3 cup soy sauce
1/3 cup water

1/4 teaspoon dashi-no-moto powder

Condiments:
1/2 cup dried-bonito thread shavings
1/3 cup grated daikon radish
2 tablespoons grated fresh gingerroot
6 green onions, minced

1 tablespoon Prepared Japanese Horseradish,
  page 154
1/4 cup unsalted cocktail peanuts,
  finely chopped

Tear agar-agar stick into 4 pieces. Place agar-agar and water in a medium saucepan. Press agar-agar pieces into water several seconds to soften. Shred pieces with your fingers. Soak 30 minutes. In a blender or food processor fitted with a steel blade, chop 1 cup peanuts until finely ground. Add tofu to peanuts; process until as smooth as possible. Blend in sugar and salt; set aside. Simmer agar-agar and water over very low heat until dissolved, 10 to 12 minutes. Stir once or twice while simmering. When dissolved, remove pan from heat. Scrape tofu-peanut mixture into agar-agar; blend with a whisk. Strain mixture into a medium bowl through a fine strainer. Scrape mixture from bottom of strainer into bowl. Quickly stir to blend. Rinse an 8-inch-square pan with cold water. *Quickly* pour tofu-peanut mixture into damp pan. Mixture will set almost instantly at room temperature or can be refrigerated until serving time. In a small bowl, combine Dipping-Sauce ingredients. Prepare Condiments. Cut firm tofu into 8 or 9 squares. Place 1 square on each serving dish. Invite diners to season tofu with small amounts of Dipping Sauce mixed with the desired Condiments. Makes 8 or 9 servings.

Sugar & Spice Okara

Ama Okara

Sprinkle this high-protein soybean mixture over hot cereals or muffin batters.

3 cups fresh soybean pulp (okara),
  leftover from making Tofu, page 102
3/4 cup packed light-brown sugar

1/2 teaspoon ground cinnamon or nutmeg
1/8 teaspoon salt
1 teaspoon vanilla extract

Preheat oven to 325F (165C). Spread soybean pulp in a 15'' x 10'' jelly-roll pan. Dry in oven 25 to 30 minutes, stirring occasionally. Place dried pulp in a medium bowl. Add brown sugar, cinnamon or nutmeg, salt and vanilla. Mix together with your hands. Refrigerate in an airtight container up to 2 weeks or freeze several months. Makes about 3 cups.

Deep-Fried Foods (Agemono)

The Japanese excel at deep-frying. No other cuisine can consistently match the high-quality of the crisp grease-free fried foods of Japan. Deep-frying was introduced through European influences and the Japanese have refined and elevated the cooking method into an art.

Tempura, an example of batter frying (koromo-age), is so popular that small tempura shops thrive all over Japan. Piping-hot pieces of batter-coated seafood and vegetables are removed from the hot oil and passed directly over the counter to the customer for immediate consumption. The high quality never varies, but the coating on the foods can range from snowy white to golden yellow, depending on the area of the country and the chef's preference. The tempura chef has mastered his art so

skillfully that he can fry a batter-coated frozen ice-cream ball and serve it before it begins to melt.

Firm-textured foods are sometimes fried without a coating (su-age) so their shapes and natural colors are retained. Other foods are lightly coated with a starch before frying (kara-age). Kuzu starch, potato starch or cornstarch are the favored coatings. *Matsuba-age* indicates that foods have been dipped in egg, then coated with pieces of green-tea soba for frying. This gives the appearance of a covering of green pine needles. *Harusame-age* is a similar technique, except the foods are coated with pieces of snipped dried bean-thread noodles (harusame). When deep-fried, the harusame noodles puff up and form a lacy flower-like coating on the foods.

Japanese cooking requires the use of top-quality oil for deep-frying. The oil must be light enough to prevent the fried foods from becoming excessively oily and neutral in taste to allow the natural flavors of the foods to shine through. Peanut oil, corn oil and safflower oil are good choices. Never use butter or olive oil. Many chefs combine several oils to produce their own special blend. Sesame oil is often added as a perfume. Interestingly, the highly flavored sesame oil was used exclusively as a lamp oil during the Nara period (A.D. 710-784).

Japanese cooks rely on instinct and familiar signs to gauge oil temperature to prevent over-browned uncooked foods or cooked foods with soggy exteriors. It may be helpful for the inexperienced cook to regulate oil temperatures with a deep-fat-frying thermometer. Some chefs dip a pair of wooden cooking chopsticks in the oil; bubbling activity around the ends of the chopsticks indicates that the oil has reached about 360F (180C). You can test the oil by frying a small cube of bread or a small amount of batter. If the oil is in the 350F (175C) range, the bread will sink to the bottom of the pan then bob back to the top after a few seconds. If the oil isn't hot enough, the bread will sink to the bottom and stay there. If it is too hot, the bread will stay on top and brown instantly. Never add food to hot oil by standing away from the pan and tossing it in. This causes the oil to splash which is extremely dangerous. The oil will behave if you lower the pieces of food to the oil level and slip them in or slide them in from the side. Greaseless fried foods are a result of maintaining the correct oil temperature. Do not lower the temperature by overcrowding the pan with pieces of food. Skim the oil with a fine mesh strainer several times while frying to remove pieces of batter. Do not overheat the oil; it will cause rapid deterioration and allow the food to absorb excess oil.

If the oil is still light-colored after frying, you can recycle it for future use. Clean the oil by skimming the surface, then filter it first through a fine-meshed strainer and then through several layers of cheesecloth into a large container. Store the oil in a cool dark place to prevent rancidity. You can fry a piece of peeled fresh ginger-root in the recycled oil to neutralize any odors which might cling to foods during future fryings. A combination of used oil and new oil will produce a golden-colored batter on fried foods. Discard the oil after one or two uses, especially if it begins to darken. At this point oil begins to break down structurally and develops a low smoking point. Fried foods cooked in such oil will be of poor quality with a strong odor.

The pot you use for deep-frying should be sturdy with a wide surface and deep enough to hold 2 to 3 inches of oil comfortably, depending on the thickness of the foods to be fried. A small Chinese flat-bottomed iron wok will work fine for deep-frying. Its swift heat conduction will produce quick and even browning. The wok requires less oil for deep-frying because of its unique bowl shape.

Batter-Fried Foods

Tempura was once considered *namban ryori,* or "the cooking of southern barbarians." The "barbarians" were Spanish and Portuguese missionaries who came to southern Japan in the 16th century. Fish fried in sesame oil was the earliest type of tempura taught to the Japanese. By the 19th century, tempura was being sold by street vendors on almost every corner of Edo (old Tokyo). Throughout the years, tempura has evolved into the light and lacy battered food we associate with Japanese cooking today.

One of the secrets of frying tempura lies in a good batter, or *koromo* meaning *clothing.* For tempura, the "clothing" should be as transparent as a woman's veil. The batter must be made at the final moment before cooking. Use ice-cold water to make the batter. The temperature contrast of the hot oil and icy batter is important. Hot oil seals the batter immediately. The resulting steam inside helps to cook the food quickly. Undermix the batter to keep the tempura light and lacy. Tiny lumps of unmixed flour puff up in hot oil.

Pass steaming bowls of miso soup to guests as you begin to fry the first batch. Good tempura waits for no one. Serve it hot and crisp as it comes from the hot oil. For each place setting, provide a pair of chopsticks and a small basket or plate lined with a folded piece of absorbent paper. Use napkins or special coated sheets of paper sometimes available in Oriental markets. Hot steamed rice and a side dish of pickled vegetables complete the menu. Serve warm saké, hot green tea or cold beer to drink.

How to Make Pork Rolls with Plum Paste

1/Spread plum paste over pork. Place a nori strip over plum paste. Roll up pork slice; secure with wooden picks. Roll in flour, then dip in beaten egg. Press roll into panko, covering all sides.

2/In hot oil, fry pork rolls 3 to 4 minutes or until brown and crisp. Turn several times for even browning. Serve warm or at room temperature with Spicy Mustard, if desired.

Pork Rolls with Plum Paste

Ume Buta Make

Each pork roll can be cut into four or five pieces and served with wooden picks for appetizers.

1/4 cup soy sauce	**1/2 cup all-purpose flour**
2 tablespoons mirin	**About 2 cups panko (coarse dry**
2 tablespoons sugar	**bread crumbs)**
1 lb. shabu-shabu pork (pork butt	**2 (8" x 7-1/2") sheets nori,**
sliced 1/8 inch thick)	**cut in 16 (4" x 1-3/4") strips**
12 to 14 small pickled plums	**About 4 cups peanut oil or**
(umeboshi), halved, pitted	**vegetable oil for deep-frying**
1 large egg, slightly beaten	**Spicy Mustard, page 148, if desired**

In a shallow pan, mix soy sauce, mirin and sugar until sugar dissolves. Marinate pork slices in soy-sauce mixture 10 minutes. In a small dish, use a fork to mash pickled plums into a paste. Place egg, flour and panko in separate shallow pans. Remove 1 slice pork from marinade; shake off excess liquid. Place pork on a flat surface. Carefully spread about 1/2 teaspoon plum paste over pork. Place a nori strip over plum paste. Roll up pork slice, beginning at shortest side; secure with wooden picks. Roll in flour, then dip in beaten egg. Press coated pork roll into panko, covering all sides; set aside. Repeat with remaining pork slices. In a wok or shallow heavy saucepan, heat oil to 350F (175C) or until a 1-inch cube of bread turns golden brown in 65 seconds. Fry pork rolls, 3 or 4 at a time, 3 to 4 minutes or until brown and crisp. Turn several times for even browning. Drain pork rolls on a wire rack. If necessary, check cooking time by cutting open 1 roll. Pork should not be pink inside. Remove wooden picks. Cut rolls diagonally in 1/2. Serve warm or at room temperature with Spicy Mustard, if desired. Makes about 28 pieces or 5 or 6 servings.

Lacy Batter-Fried Foods   Photo on cover.

Tempura

Seafood and vegetables are encased in a feather-light coating.

Tempura Ingredients, see below
Dipping Sauce, see below
Condiments, see below
About 5-1/2 cups peanut oil or
    vegetable oil for deep-frying
1/2 cup sesame oil, if desired

Tempura Batter, see below
All-purpose flour
5 to 6 cups hot Steamed Rice, page 139
1 teaspoon roasted-soybean powder
    (kinako powder),
    or dash of ground cinnamon

Tempura Ingredients:
1 lb. Fan-Shaped Shrimp, page 122
1/2 lb. fish fillets, cut in 1-inch pieces
1 lb. bay scallops or sea scallops
    halved across the grain
6 large fresh shiitake mushrooms,
    tops scored in a star-fluted pattern,
    page 29
6 small Japanese-Eggplant Fans, page 32
1 medium carrot, cut in 1/4-inch
    diagonal slices

2 small onions, cut in 1/2,
    sliced 1/3 inch thick (secure
    half rings in each slice with
    a wooden pick)
1 large green or red bell pepper,
    cut in 6 strips
12 fresh small string beans,
    ends trimmed
6 large fresh strawberries
2 small bananas

Dipping Sauce:
1/3 cup light (thin) soy sauce
1-1/2 cups Instant Sea-Vegetable &
    Fish Stock, page 45

1/4 cup mirin

Condiments:
1/2 cup grated daikon radish
Red-Maple Radish, page 155

1 lemon, cut in wedges
1 tablespoon grated fresh gingerroot

Tempura Batter:
1 cup tempura-ko or cake flour
1/4 cup potato starch or cornstarch
1/2 teaspoon baking powder
1 large egg white

About 1-1/4 cups ice-cold sparkling water
    or tap water
Additional flour, if necessary

Prepare Tempura Ingredients, Dipping Sauce and Condiments; set aside. At the table, heat peanut oil or vegetable oil and sesame oil, if used, in a tempura-nabe or electric wok to 360F (180C) or until a 1-inch cube of bread turns golden brown in 60 seconds. Prepare Tempura Batter at the last minute, as needed. Coat 4 or 5 shrimp with flour, then dip into batter. Lower coated shrimp into hot oil, holding tails above oil a few seconds to set shrimp and prevent curling. Fry 2 to 3 minutes or until crisp. Continue coating, dipping and frying a few pieces of shrimp, fish and vegetables at a time. Cooking times will vary slightly with each ingredient. Dip mushrooms and eggplant fans into batter on 1 side only. This will help retain their natural appearance. Drain cooked Tempura on a wire rack. Instruct diners to mix Condiments of their choice into their own bowls of Dipping Sauce. Tempura should be dipped into sauce and Condiment mixture. Serve with hot Steamed Rice. Stir roasted-soybean powder or cinnamon into remaining batter after seafood and vegetables are fried. If necessary, prepare 1/2 recipe more of batter. Cut bananas into 1-inch pieces. Dip strawberries and banana pieces in batter; fry until crisp. Makes 6 servings.

Tempura Ingredients:

Prepare ingredients. Pat dry with paper towel until no moisture remains. Arrange foods attractively on 1 or 2 serving platters. If foods are prepared ahead of time, cover and refrigerate up to 2 hours. It is best to cut onions at the last minute. Store strawberries separately. Cut bananas at the last minute.

Dipping Sauce:

In a medium saucepan, heat ingredients over low heat until warm. Provide 1/3 cup sauce for each diner in a small bowl. Makes about 2 cups.

Condiments:

Prepare Condiments; place in separate tiny glass or pottery dishes. Guests can help themselves at the table.

Tempura Batter:

In a medium bowl, combine tempura-ko or cake flour, potato starch or cornstarch, and baking powder. In a small bowl, use a pair of chopsticks to mix egg white and 1 cup water. Pour into dry ingredients. Stir several times with chopsticks, leaving batter lumpy and undermixed. Set bowl of batter in a larger pan of water filled with ice. If batter becomes too smooth, sprinkle in some extra flour. Stir once or twice. Add extra water depending on how thick or thin you desire fried coating on foods. Experiment to find consistency you like best. Makes about 2-1/4 cups.

Deep-Fried Ginger Oysters   Photo on page 107.

Kaki No Shoga Age

Oysters are served dozens of ways at the famous floating oyster-boat restaurants in Hiroshima.

2 recipes Spicy Dipping Sauce, page 120
24 fresh oysters, shucked,
   shells reserved
2 teaspoons grated fresh gingerroot
2 tablespoons saké
1/2 cup potato starch or cornstarch
2 or 3 dashes ground sansho pepper
2 eggs, slightly beaten
1/3 cup milk
2 cups panko (coarse dry bread crumbs)

About 6 cups peanut oil or
   vegetable oil for deep-frying
Scalloped Lemon Slices, page 23,
   from 2 large lemons
1-1/2 to 2 cups thinly shredded
   green cabbage
1 medium carrot, shredded
2 large tomatoes, cut in wedges
Watercress or parsley

Prepare Spicy Dipping Sauce; set aside. Place oysters in a medium bowl. Add gingerroot and saké; marinate 10 minutes. In a shallow pan, mix potato starch or cornstarch and sansho pepper. In another shallow pan, blend eggs and milk. Place panko in another shallow pan. In a wok or shallow heavy saucepan, heat oil to 365F (185C) or until a 1-inch cube of bread turns golden brown in 50 seconds. Drain oysters. Roll 3 or 4 oysters in potato starch or cornstarch, then dip in egg mixture. Press oysters in panko until completely coated. Fry in hot oil 3 to 4 minutes or until golden brown and crisp. Turn several times for even browning. Drain on paper towels. Repeat with remaining oysters. Arrange fried oysters on reserved half shells. Arrange around edge of 2 large platters, 12 to a platter, placing Scalloped Lemon Slices between each oyster shell. Pile 1/2 of cabbage in center of each platter. Place shredded carrot on top of cabbage. Overlap tomato wedges around base of cabbage in a flower design. Garnish platter with watercress or parsley. Serve fried oysters with Spicy Dipping Sauce. Makes 5 or 6 servings.

Autumn-Leaf Tempura

Photo on page 121.

Aki No Ha Tempura

An exquisite vegetarian tempura, reminiscent of the elegant cuisine of old Kyoto.

Tempura Ingredients, see below
Dipping Sauce, page 116
Condiments, page 116
2 recipes Lemon-Ginger Sauce, opposite
6 small Lemon Cups, page 23, if desired
About 4 cups peanut oil or
    vegetable oil for deep-frying

1/4 cup sesame oil, if desired
Tempura Batter, page 116, more as needed
All-purpose flour
4 to 5 cups hot Chestnut &
    Sweet-Potato Rice, page 142

Tempura Ingredients:

1 cup cooked spaghetti squash
    (from 3/4 lb. raw squash),
    chopped into short lengths
18 fresh shiso leaves
1 (20-oz.) pkg. firm Chinese-style tofu,
    rinsed, patted dry
1 (1-lb.) yam, peeled
18 ginkgo nuts (ginnan), fresh-shelled or
    canned, drained

12 Scalloped Lotus-Root Flowers,
    page 32
4 or 5 drops red or yellow food coloring,
    if desired
2 (8" x 7-1/2") sheets nori,
    cut in 12 (4" x 2-1/2") pieces
1 firm ripe Japanese persimmon,
    cut in slices

Prepare Tempura Ingredients, Dipping Sauce and Condiments; set aside. Prepare Lemon-Ginger Sauce; keep warm. If desired, serve in Lemon Cups. At the table, heat peanut oil or vegetable oil and sesame oil, if used, in a tempura-nabe or electric wok to 360F (180C) or until a 1-inch cube of bread turns golden brown in 60 seconds. Prepare Tempura Batter at the last minute, as needed. Pour 1/3 of batter into bowl of squash; mix with chopsticks. Spread 1 tablespoon squash mixture over underside of each shiso leaf. Dip squash-coated leaf into remaining batter. Fry in hot oil 25 seconds or until batter is crisp. Continue dipping and frying remaining foods. To help batter adhere to foods, coat them lightly with flour. This is especially helpful for yam, ginkgo nuts, Scalloped Lotus-Root Flowers and persimmon slices. Cooking times will vary depending on each ingredient. Drain cooked Tempura on a wire rack. Instruct diners to dip Tempura into small bowls of Lemon-Ginger Sauce or Dipping Sauce mixed with the desired Condiments. Serve with hot Chestnut & Sweet-Potato Rice. Makes 6 servings.

Tempura Ingredients:

Place cooked squash in a small bowl. Rinse shiso leaves; pat completely dry. Slice tofu horizontally into 1/4-inch-thick slices. Lay slices between double layers of clean kitchen towels or several layers of paper towels. Place 1 to 2 pounds of weight on top to press out excess liquid and firm tofu for frying. Press 15 minutes. Cut into 2-1/2-inch scalloped flower shapes with metal cookie cutters. Or, cut into 1-inch pieces. Cut yam into 1/8-inch-thick slices. Cut into leaf shapes with a metal cutter, or a small knife. To increase leaf size, cut larger yam slices by slicing on the diagonal. Put yam leaves into a small bowl of cool water. If desired, yam can be left in slices. Skewer ginkgo nuts on 6 wooden picks, 3 nuts per pick. Put 1/2 of Scalloped Lotus-Root Flowers into a separate small bowl of water. Add red or yellow coloring to tint them an autumn color. Leave remaining Scalloped Lotus-Root Flowers white. Using scissors, cut a stack of nori pieces into oval leaf shapes. At serving time, drain yam leaves and Scalloped Lotus-Root Flowers. Pat dry on paper towels. Arrange vegetables, nori leaf shapes and persimmon slices attractively on a serving platter.

How to Make Autumn-Leaf Tempura

1/Pour egg-white mixture into dry ingredients. Stir several times with chopsticks, leaving batter lumpy and undermixed.

2/Pour 1/3 of batter into bowl of squash; mix with chopsticks. Spread 1 tablespoon squash mixture over underside of each shiso leaf. Dip into remaining batter. Fry in hot oil 25 seconds or until crisp.

Lemon-Ginger Sauce

This delicate amber-colored sauce is delicious with fried shrimp or fried zucchini.

3/4 cup chicken stock
3 tablespoons fresh lemon juice
1/4 cup sugar
2 teaspoons light (thin) soy sauce
1/4 teaspoon grated fresh gingerroot

1 tablespoon mirin
2 teaspoons cornstarch
1/8 teaspoon sesame oil
Pinch of salt, if desired

In a small saucepan, combine chicken stock, lemon juice, sugar, soy sauce, gingerroot and mirin. In a small bowl, dissolve cornstarch in a small amount of chicken-stock mixture. Stir into mixture in saucepan. Cook over medium-high heat, stirring constantly, until thickened. Strain sauce into a small bowl through a fine strainer. Stir in sesame oil and salt, if desired. Makes about 3/4 cup.

Deep-Fried Pork with Spicy Dipping Sauce

Tonkatsu

A terrific dish for your first attempt at Japanese cooking.

Spicy Dipping Sauce, see below
1 lb. pork tenderloin or pork loin,
   sliced 1/2 inch thick
Salt and ground pepper to taste
1/2 cup all-purpose flour
1 egg, slightly beaten
2 tablespoons milk

1 cup panko (coarse dry bread crumbs),
   more if needed
About 6 cups peanut oil or
   vegetable oil for deep-frying
1/2 medium, green or red cabbage,
   or 1/2 of each
Tomato wedges

Spicy Dipping Sauce:
1/2 cup ketchup
2 tablespoons soy sauce
1 tablespoon sugar
1 tablespoon mirin

1-1/2 teaspoons Worcestershire sauce
1/2 teaspoon minced fresh gingerroot
1 garlic clove, minced

Prepare Spicy Dipping Sauce; set aside. Lightly pound pork slices until slightly flattened. Sprinkle with salt and pepper. Coat lightly with flour. In a shallow pan, combine egg and milk. Place panko in a shallow pan. Dip pork slices in egg mixture, then coat both sides of pork slices with panko; set aside on a platter. In a wok or shallow heavy saucepan, heat oil to 360F (180C) or until a 1-inch cube of bread turns golden brown in 60 seconds. Fry, 2 or 3 slices at a time, 6 to 8 minutes or until golden brown and done inside. Larger pork-loin slices could need a slightly longer frying time. Turn once or twice for even browning. Drain pork on paper towels. Skim oil occasionally to remove pieces of fried coating. When pork slices have all been fried, keep warm in a 150F (65C) oven while slicing cabbage. Cut piece of cabbage in 1/2 vertically. Slice each piece into thin shreds. Place some sliced cabbage on each serving plate. Slice each cooked pork piece into 1/2-inch strips, keeping pieces in original shape. Place a sliced pork piece on top of each portion of sliced cabbage, arranging pork in its original shape, as if it had not been sliced. Serve with Spicy Dipping Sauce and tomato wedges. Makes 4 servings.

Spicy Dipping Sauce:
In a small bowl, combine all ingredients; mix well. Cover and let stand 30 minutes for flavors to develop. Makes 3/4 cup.

Variation

Cabbage can be stir-fried with 2 tablespoons oil in a large skillet over high heat 1 minute. Salt lightly before serving.

Cherry blossoms, yes
They're beautiful . . .
But tonight
Don't miss the moon!   *So'in*

Autumn Supper for Moon Viewing (tsukumi), clockwise starting at top left: Bubbling Tofu Hot Pot, page 104; Autumn-Leaf Tempura, page 118; Red-Maple Radish, page 155; Almond Pine Cone, page 166; and Chestnut & Sweet-Potato Rice, page 142.

Fish-Cake Tempura

Tsuke-age

Leftover fish cake can be added to soups, noodle dishes or stews.

1/2 lb. fresh fish fillets, skinned	**1 (2-inch) piece burdock root (gobo),**
(halibut, flounder, scrod, haddock	**if desired**
or shark)	**1/2 medium carrot, shredded**
1 tablespoon saké	**1 green onion, minced**
1/2 cup sugar	**About 4 cups peanut oil or**
1 cup water	**vegetable oil for deep-frying**
1 cup cornstarch	**Soy sauce to taste**
1 large egg	**Prepared Japanese Horseradish,**
1 tablespoon salt	**page 154, to taste**

Cut fish into 1-inch pieces. In a blender or food processor fitted with a steel blade, grind fish to a paste. Add saké, sugar, water, cornstarch, egg and salt. Process ingredients until smooth. If used, scrape and rinse burdock root. Shred burdock. Swish shreds in a small bowl containing cool water and 1 tablespoon vinegar. Drain burdock; add to fish paste with carrot and green onion. Process ingredients 5 seconds or until blended. Scrape fish paste into a medium bowl. Cover and refrigerate 30 minutes. In a wok or shallow heavy saucepan, heat oil to 350F (175C) or until a 1-inch cube of bread turns golden brown in 65 seconds. Spread 1/3 cup fish paste on a 2-1/2- inch-wide wooden rice paddle or spatula; smooth paste to fit shape of paddle. Fish cake should be about 3/4 inch thick. Hold paddle to edge of hot oil. Using a knife, scrape fish cake off paddle upside down into hot oil. Form 2 or 3 more cakes. Fry batch slowly 15 to 18 minutes or until fish cakes are puffy and golden brown. Drain on paper towels. Fish cakes deflate upon cooling. Do not cook fish cakes at too high a temperature or they will brown too quickly and remain uncooked in center. Repeat with remaining fish paste. Fish cakes will have a slightly chewy consistency. Serve warm or cold with a mixture of soy sauce and Prepared Japanese Horseradish. Makes 7 fish cakes.

Note: Fish paste made from frozen fish will be much wetter than paste made using fresh fish. If you use frozen fish, increase the amount of cornstarch to get a paste which can be spread on the rice paddle. Fish cakes made with frozen fish taste as delicious as those made with fresh fish.

Fan-Shaped Shrimp   Photo on cover.

Ebi Sensu

Serve shrimp deep-fried, or poached with mounds of Sweet Vinegared Rice, page 58.

1 lb. large shrimp,	**3 tablespoons saké**
not peeled (16 to 18)	**1 teaspoon fresh gingerroot juice, page 8**

Peel shrimp, leaving tails intact. Cut lengthwise down bellies of shrimp, about 3/4 of the way through; do not cut into tail sections. Carefully remove any large veins. Turn shrimp over on a flat surface, cut-sides down. Lightly pound backs of shrimp 2 or 3 times to flatten slightly. Place shrimp in a shallow dish. Add saké and gingerroot juice. Cover and refrigerate at least 1 hour or up to 12 hours; drain well. Makes 1 pound shrimp.

How to Make Fish-Cake Tempura

1/Spread 1/3 cup fish paste on a wooden rice paddle; smooth paste to fit shape of paddle. Fish cake should be about 3/4 inch thick.

2/Hold paddle to edge of hot oil. Using a knife, scrape fish cake off paddle upside down into hot oil. Fry each batch slowly 15 to 18 minutes or until cakes are puffy and golden brown.

Serving Saké

Saké is served on all important occasions in Japan, including holidays, festivals and at wedding ceremonies. Except in summertime when it is traditionally served cold, saké is always warmed before serving. To warm saké, pour it into a small pottery or porcelain bottle called a *tokkuri*. Place the bottle in a pan of hot water over low heat; heat saké to 100F to 110F (40C to 45C). In the wintertime, saké can be heated to a slightly warmer temperature. Warming saké mellows it and releases its delicate bouquet. Never allow saké to boil, or the fragrance and bouquet will be destroyed. Pour warm saké into tiny cups called *sakazuki*.

Individual servings of cold saké come in a small cedar measuring box (masu) with a small amount of salt placed near one corner. The saké and salt should be downed quickly. The salt brings out the sweetness of the saké.

Japanese etiquette decrees that no one ever fills his or her own saké cup but instead each person holds their cup in their hands while the saké is poured by a companion or serving person. The act of receiving or pouring saké is called receiving or performing *o'shaku*. If you are offered more saké while your cup is still full, the polite thing to do is to take a sip from your cup and present it for filling. If you do not wish any more, hold your fingers, palm down, over your cup or if it is empty, turn the cup upside down.

Saké is always served as an accompaniment to foods and is never served alone. It is especially enjoyed with fresh chilled raw fish (sashimi) and other appetizing snacks. Some people feel that without several rounds of saké, many delicious meals in Japan might never be completed! Next time you drink saké, either in a restaurant or at home, put everyone in the right mood by toasting them in the traditional manner with the word *"Kamai!"*

Dressed Foods & Vinegared Salads (Aemono & Sunomono)

The Western concept of salad does not exist in traditional Japanese cuisine. Japanese-style salads are miniature arrangements composed from a variety of fresh fish, shellfish, vegetables, fruits and other ingredients. Dried fruits, especially persimmons and apricots, are excellent additions. Japanese-style salads taste as delicious as they look; flavor is never sacrificed for beauty.

Salads can be divided into two categories. *Aemono* is made up of mixed ingredients coated with a mild-tasting slightly thickened dressing. *Sunomono* consists of mixed ingredients tossed with a thin tangy dressing.

The thin dressing for sunomono is made with a base ingredient of rice vinegar, carefully blended with a variety of complimentary seasonings. Soy sauce, lemon juice, sea-vegetable and fish stock (dashi), mirin, grated ginger-root or daikon radish, sugar, sesame seeds and mustard are optional flavor boosters. The mild rice vinegar enhances the flavors of the foods and helps to keep them fresh-tasting. Vinegar and sugar with a dash of salt or soy sauce make a simple and popular dressing combination for sunomono. Sugar enriches the flavor of the rice vinegar and softens the acidity. A small amount of prepared sea-vegetable and fish stock can add depth to the dressing and round out the flavors.

Dressings for aemono are generally thickened with a base ingredient of miso, ground sesame seeds, creamed tofu, thickened cooked egg yolk, soybean pulp (okara) or steamed fermented soybeans (natto). Vinegar is added as a flavoring agent along with any of the desired flavoring ingredients used in making dressing for sunomono.

Fresh fish, shellfish and chicken for the salad can be poached, steamed or grilled in preparation. Raw vegetables often benefit from a short salting period or from quick blanching in boiling water or sea-vegetable and fish stock to intensify bright colors and natural flavors. Blanching softens the vegetable fibers making them more easily digestible. After blanching, plunge vegetables into an iced-water bath for quick chilling. This action stops the cooking process, insuring the vegetables will stay crisp and fresh-tasting. Drain and dry the vegetables well. If possible, chill them before blending with the dressing.

Western-style green tossed salads are also popular throughout Japan. They are especially noteworthy because they often resemble small sculpted flower gardens within a bowl. Vegetables carved into flowers, and sometimes pieces of fresh fruit, are arranged upon nests of finely shredded lettuce and cabbage.

How to Make Spinach Logs

1/Lay spinach bundle along edge of a bamboo sushi mat. Roll up spinach inside mat; press gently to set log shape.

2/Remove mat. Cut spinach into pieces to serve. Sprinkle each log with dressing and sesame seeds.

Spinach Logs

Horenso No O-shi-tashi

For added flavor, sprinkle the top of each log with a tiny amount of dried-bonito thread shavings.

**1/2 recipe Vinegar-Lemon Dressing,
   page 126**
2 (1/2-lb.) bunches fresh spinach

**2 teaspoons Dry-Roasted Sesame Seeds,
   page 150**

Prepare Vinegar-Lemon Dressing; set aside. Remove ties binding bunches of spinach; set aside ties. Carefully rinse each spinach leaf under cool running water. Trim roots from stem end; retain stems. Gather spinach leaves back into original bunch. Use ties or kitchen string to bind spinach stems together. In a medium saucepan, bring about 6 cups water and 1 teaspoon salt to a boil over high heat. Holding spinach by stems, lower it into boiling water. Release stems. Blanch spinach about 1 minute or until wilted and bright green. Rinse spinach with cool water. Gently squeeze out excess water. Remove ties. Lay spinach bundle along edge of a bamboo sushi mat. Roll up spinach, using bamboo mat underneath to help form the roll. To help set shape, wrap mat around spinach and gently press mat. Remove mat. Cut spinach into 1-1/4- to 1-1/2-inch pieces. Place each spinach log, cut-side up, on a small serving dish. Sprinkle with a small amount of dressing and Dry-Roasted Sesame Seeds. Makes 6 servings.

Variation

Nori Spinach Roll (Nori To Horenso Make): Prepare spinach roll as above. Do not cut roll in pieces. Sprinkle a small amount of soy sauce over roll; pat off excess liquid. Place a sheet of Toasted Nori, page 59, on a bamboo sushi mat. Cover it with a sheet of Egg Pancake, page 80, trimmed to size of nori. Place spinach log on edge of nori and egg. Roll them using mat as a guide. Press gently to set roll shape. Unroll; cut into 6 (1-1/4- to 1-1/2-inch) pieces.

Marinated Vegetable Flowers

Yasai Sunomono

Vary the vegetable shapes by cutting them into matchstick strips or shreds.

Vinegar-Lemon Dressing, see below
1/2 European-style cucumber or
  1 small regular cucumber,
  rinsed, dried

2 or 3 small unpeeled turnips, thinly sliced
1 large carrot, thinly sliced
2 teaspoons black Dry-Roasted Sesame
  Seeds, page 150

Vinegar-Lemon Dressing:
1/2 cup sugar
1/2 cup rice vinegar
1/2 teaspoon sesame oil

1/2 teaspoon salt
Freshly grated peel of 1 small lemon
Dash of hot-pepper sauce, if desired

Prepare Vinegar-Lemon Dressing; set aside. Cut off and discard ends from cucumber. Cut cucumber in 1/2 lengthwise. Using a small spoon, scrape out seeds. Cut cucumber halves crosswise into 1/4-inch-thick pieces. Place in a medium bowl. Using a medium, metal, flower-shaped cutter, cut flower shapes from turnip slices. Place in bowl with cucumber pieces. Blanch carrot slices 1 minute in boiling water; drain. Place in iced water to chill; drain. Using a small cutter, cut carrot slices into flower shapes. Add to vegetables in bowl. Add Vinegar-Lemon Dressing; toss to mix well. Cover and refrigerate at least 30 minutes or up to 2 hours. Using a slotted spoon, place vegetables in small serving dishes. Sprinkle with Dry-Roasted Sesame Seeds. Makes 6 to 8 servings.

Vinegar-Lemon Dressing:
In a small bowl, combine all ingredients. Stir well to dissolve sugar. Makes about 3/4 cup.

Persimmon & Daikon Salad   Photo on page 106.

Kaki Daikon Namasu

If persimmons are not in season, prepare this favorite New Year's dish with shredded carrot.

1 firm ripe Japanese persimmon or
  1 medium carrot
1/2 lb. daikon radish
1/2 teaspoon freshly grated lemon peel
2 tablespoons sugar

2 tablespoons rice vinegar
1/2 teaspoon salt
1 teaspoon saké
Freshly shredded lemon peel, if desired

Peel and shred persimmon or carrot. Place in a medium bowl. Peel and shred daikon. Gently squeeze excess liquid from shredded daikon. Add to persimmon or carrot. In a small bowl, combine grated lemon peel, sugar, vinegar, salt and saké; stir to dissolve sugar. Add to persimmon or carrot mixture; mix well. Cover and refrigerate 30 minutes or until chilled. Using a slotted spoon, lightly press scoops of mixture against side of bowl to remove excess liquid. Spoon into small serving dishes. Garnish with shredded lemon peel, if desired. Makes 6 servings.

Variation

Vary the flavor by adding 3 to 4 tablespoons slivered dried apricots or dried persimmons.

How to Make a Turnip-Rose Sunomono

1/Using a Benriner cutter, cut peeled turnip into paper-thin slices. Blanch slices. Place slices in vinegar mixture; refrigerate.

2/Mold softened turnip slices around turnip cone to resemble a rose in full bloom. Gently bend back tops of slices to resemble rose petals. Garnish with shiso leaves or rose leaves.

Turnip-Rose Sunomono

Bara Sunomono

Invite your guests to pluck the petals from this delicious edible vegetable flower, using their chopsticks.

1 (1/2-lb.) well-shaped round turnip
2 tablespoons rice vinegar
2 tablespoons fresh lemon juice
1/4 cup sugar

1/2 teaspoon salt
Fresh shiso leaves or
 fresh rose leaves, if desired

Peel turnip, keeping shape as rounded as possible. Using a Benriner cutter, or large sharp chef's knife, cut into paper-thin slices, about 1/16 inch thick. Blanch turnip slices 30 seconds in boiling water; drain. Rinse in cool water; drain again. Place turnip slices in a small bowl with vinegar, lemon juice, sugar and salt. Cover and refrigerate at least 30 minutes or up to 6 hours. Slices will become very soft and flexible. At serving time, drain turnip slices. Make a cut on 1 slice from center to edge. Overlap cut edges tightly, forming a cone-shape. Mold 5 or 6 turnip slices around turnip cone. Set this portion of flower upright or on its side on a small serving dish. Mold remaining turnip slices around it to resemble a rose in full bloom. Gently bend back tops of slices to resemble rose petals. Garnish with shiso leaves or rose leaves, if desired. Serve immediately. Makes 1 or 2 roses.

Variation

Turnip-Rose Table Decoration: Slice turnip into thin slices. Soak in a briny salt-water solution 1 hour. Slices will soften. Form rose as instructed above. Secure petals with 5/8-inch carpenters' brads (finishing nails or **U**-shaped pins). Fold back tops of slices to resemble rose petals. Drop rose into iced water; leave several hours to ''bloom.'' Add fresh rose leaves for garnish. Use for table decorations or flower arrangements; these roses are **not** edible.

Scallop Blossoms with Raspberry-Sesame Sauce

Hana Kai-ba-shira To Rasu-beri No Goma Aye

If you can find flowering herbs, use them to form the miniature herb wreaths.

1 qt. water
2 (1/4-inch-thick) slices peeled
   fresh gingerroot, smashed
1/4 cup saké
1 sprig thyme, rosemary or parsley
1 lb. sea scallops

Raspberry-Sesame Sauce, see below
4 fresh raspberries
2 or 3 sprigs thyme, rosemary or parsley
Black lumpfish caviar,
   black sesame seeds or poppy seeds

Raspberry-Sesame Sauce:
2 tablespoons raspberry vinegar
1/4 cup almond oil or corn oil
2 teaspoons sugar
1/8 teaspoon salt

1 teaspoon Dry-Roasted Sesame Seeds,
   page 150
1 teaspoon dairy sour cream
2 or 3 drops sesame oil

In a 2-quart saucepan, combine 1 quart water, gingerroot, saké and 1 sprig thyme, rosemary or parsley. Bring to a boil over high heat. Reduce heat so liquid barely simmers. Add scallops; poach 2 to 3 minutes or until firm and opaque. Do not overcook. Remove scallops from liquid; cool. Cover and refrigerate until chilled. Prepare Raspberry-Sesame Sauce; set aside. Slice scallops into 3 or 4 thin slices. To make 4 blossoms, select 20 of the most attractive scallop slices. Arrange 5 slices on each serving plate in a flower shape. Cut remaining scallop slices into julienne strips. Make a small mound of scallop strips in center of each blossom. Top each blossom with a raspberry. Form tiny wreaths around base of each raspberry using tiny sprigs of fresh herbs. Place a cluster of caviar, black sesame seeds or poppy seeds in center of each petal. Serve Scallop Blossoms with Raspberry-Sesame Sauce. Makes 4 servings.

Raspberry-Sesame Sauce:
In a small bowl, combine all ingredients using a small whisk. Use immediately or refrigerate until needed. Whisk again before using. Makes scant 1/2 cup.

Variations
If fresh raspberries are not available, substitute well-drained, unsweetened, thawed, frozen raspberries. Or, use any other kind of small berry.

Scallop Blossoms with Raspberry-Sesame Sauce

Sweet & Sour Mandarin Shrimp

Ebi Amazu

Why not try chunks of crabmeat or lobster, or strips of fresh blanched squid in this flavorful salad?

1/2 lb. small shrimp, cooked, peeled
4 small white onions
3 celery stalks
2 Japanese cucumbers or 1 European-style
   cucumber, rinsed, dried
Sweet & Sour Sauce, see below

1 mandarin orange, peeled, segmented, or
   1 (11-oz.) can mandarin-orange
   segments, drained
1 tablespoon Dry-Roasted Sesame Seeds,
   page 150

Sweet & Sour Sauce:
1/2 cup chicken stock
3 tablespoons sugar
2 tablespoons light (thin) soy sauce,
   or regular soy sauce and
    1/4 teaspoon salt

5 tablespoons rice vinegar
1/4 teaspoon salt
1 teaspoon sesame oil
1/2 cup pineapple juice
2 tablespoons cornstarch

Cover and refrigerate shrimp until needed. Slice onions paper thin. Soak sliced onions in iced water 15 minutes to crisp; drain well. Place in a medium bowl. Cut celery stalks in 1/2 lengthwise. Cut strips into 1/4-inch-thick diagonal slices. Add celery to onion. Cut off and discard ends from cucumbers. Cut cucumbers in 1/2 lengthwise. If using European-style cucumber, scrape out seeds using a small spoon. Cut halves diagonally into 1/4-inch-thick pieces. Add cucumber to onion and celery. Cover and refrigerate until needed. Prepare Sweet & Sour Sauce. At serving time, combine shrimp, vegetable mixture and Sweet & Sour Sauce. Cut each mandarin-orange segment into 2 or 3 pieces. Add to shrimp mixture. Serve salad on a serving platter or small serving dishes. Sprinkle with Dry-Roasted Sesame Seeds. Salad can be completely assembled 2 hours before serving time. Keep refrigerated. Makes 6 to 8 servings.

Sweet & Sour Sauce:
In a small saucepan, combine chicken stock, sugar, soy sauce, vinegar, salt and sesame oil. Heat over medium-high heat. In a small bowl, blend pineapple juice and cornstarch. When sauce mixture comes to a boil, stir in cornstarch mixture. Stir constantly until sauce has thickened. Remove from heat; cool to room temperature. Pour into a small bowl; cover and refrigerate until needed. Makes about 1-1/2 cups.

Variation
Omit shrimp. Substitute 3 chicken-breast halves, poached in 1 quart simmering water 20 minutes with 3 (1/4-inch-thick) slices peeled fresh gingerroot. Remove and discard skin and bones from chicken; cut meat into thin strips. Strain poaching liquid. Use 1/2 cup for chicken stock called for in Sweet & Sour Sauce.

To substitute a regular cucumber for a Japanese or European-style cucumber, cut off ends of cucumber then cut in 1/2 lengthwise. Scrape out seeds with a small spoon. Cut halves again lengthwise. It may be necessary to cut extra-large strips lengthwise once again. Cut thin strips crosswise into the desired thickness.

How to Make String Beans with Sesame-Miso Dressing

1/Grind sesame seeds in a grinding bowl until a paste forms. Add remaining sauce ingredients; mix well.

2/Gently mix Sesame-Miso Dressing and cooked beans. Sprinkle with sesame seeds.

String Beans with Sesame-Miso Dressing

Saya-Ingen Goma Aye

Dressing is equally delicious over other cooked vegetables including broccoli and zucchini.

1 lb. fresh small string beans, ends trimmed
Sesame-Miso Dressing, see below

**1 tablespoon Dry-Roasted Sesame Seeds,
page 150**

Sesame-Miso Dressing:
**2 tablespoons Dry-Roasted Sesame Seeds,
  page 150**
3 tablespoons white or yellow miso
1 tablespoon sugar
2 tablespoons mirin

1 teaspoon fresh lemon juice
1/2 teaspoon light (thin) soy sauce
**1/2 teaspoon freshly grated orange
  or lemon peel, if desired.**

Steam beans 12 to 15 minutes or until crisp-tender. Or, cook beans in boiling salted water 3 to 5 minutes or until crisp-tender. Drain steamed or boiled beans; plunge into iced water to cool 10 minutes. Drain again; pat dry on clean kitchen towels. To French-cut beans, fit a food processor with slicing blade. Trim beans to fit feed tube horizontally. With lid in place, stack beans in feed tube. Activate machine; push beans through feed tube with food pusher. Or, beans can be cut diagonally into 2-inch lengths. Prepare Sesame-Miso Dressing. Gently mix with cut beans. Divide beans among small serving dishes. Sprinkle with Dry-Roasted Sesame Seeds. Makes 6 servings.

Sesame-Miso Dressing:
Grind Dry-Roasted Sesame Seeds in a grinding bowl until a paste forms. Add remaining ingredients; mix well. Use immediately or refrigerate until needed. Makes about 1/2 cup.

Noodles & Rice (Menrui & Gohan)

Noodles are the fast food of Japan. They are inexpensive, filling and delicious. They are eaten for lunch or a quick snack. The Japanese have always had a passion for noodles. The history of noodles began when they were introduced from the eighth century Tang Dynasty of China by Buddhist priests. The two primary types of noodles are made from brownish buckwheat flour and white wheat flour. Yellow ramen is a type of modified wheat noodle introduced into Japan from China sometime in the Meiji era (1868-1912).

Buckwheat was first cultivated and made into a type of dumpling as an emergency food substitute for rice. High in protein and vitamins, its growth is especially suited to cold weather. This partly explains its popularity in Tokyo and the northern areas of Japan. Buckwheat was mixed with wheat flour, boiling water, egg and sticky mountain yam (yamo-imo) to make noodles (soba) in the Edo period (1603-1868). *Soba* is a symbol of good fortune and longevity. On December 31st at midnight, people welcome in the New Year and wish for good luck by eating special New Year's noodles (toshikoshi soba). Soba is the customary gift given by new neighbors when they move into a neighborhood.

Soba can be served in many ways. Cold cooked noodles sprinkled with nori strips are often served on individual flat bamboo baskets. Noodles are dipped into a cup of Savory Noodle Dipping Sauce and then eaten. Soba can also be served in a bowl of Savory Noodle Broth to which other ingredients, such as cooked duck, chicken, tempura, fried tofu or rice cakes, have been added.

A forerunner of the thick white wheat noodle (udon) was made in the Nara period (A.D. 710-784). Unlike the modern noodle, it resembled a round dumpling. *Udon* is favored in the south of Japan. Its shape can vary through flat, round, wide or thick. Udon is usually eaten in a bowl of Savory Noodle Broth and can be embellished with many of the same ingredients as soba. Sometimes udon is served hot, covered with a tasty sauce.

Precooked instant ramen is sold in small individual packages and cups. Its appeal lies in the fact that it can be prepared in about 3 minutes, a boon for the working person. Each package includes a packet of instant soup mix and additional dried ingredients. Ramen is also called *Chinese noodles (chukamen)*. Use it fresh or dried as soup noodles or salad noodles. Yaki soba is a similar yellow noodle used for stir-frying. Fresh (nama) *hiyashi chuka* noodles, a kind of instant noodles, should be quickly cooked, rinsed in cold water and topped with the accompanying sauce in the package of *tare*—a flavoring mixture of vinegar and sesame oil. All three kinds of noodles can be used interchangeably in recipes.

Other popular noodles include thin white wheat noodles (hiyamugi), thinner white wheat noodles (somen), flat white wheat noodles (kishimen) and dried bean-thread noodles (harusame). Refer to the glossary, page 8, for further information.

Noodles are eaten with gusto in Japan. Proper etiquette dictates that noodles should be eaten with a slurping sound. I am afraid that noodles might not taste quite as good for some people if they had to eat them in silence. For them, it would be like omitting the final and most important seasoning ingredient of all! Soba, udon, ramen and kishimen are available packaged fresh and dried in Oriental markets and some supermarkets. Somen, hiyamugi and harusame are only available dried.

Cooking Noodles

To cook noodles, bring a large pot of unsalted water to a boil over high heat. Slowly add noodles. Stir several times to prevent sticking. Begin testing noodles after 2 to 3 minutes. White wheat noodles (somen) will cook in 2 to 3 minutes, fresh ramen in 2 to 3 minutes, fresh buckwheat noodles (soba) in 3 to 4 minutes and fresh, thick, white, wheat noodles (udon) in 8 to 10 minutes. Fresh yellow noodles (yaki-soba) should only be blanched for 1 minute, because they will be heated again during stir-frying. Dried noodles will take longer than fresh noodles. Dried, thick, white, wheat noodles (udon) will require the longest cooking time of all, 10 to 12 minutes.

Noodles should be slightly al dente. Do not let them overcook. The Japanese refer to overcooked noodles as ''stretched'' noodles because they have lost their firmness. Have cold water on hand to pour into the boiling pot if you think the noodles are in danger of being overcooked. Drain noodles and rinse immediately in cold water. If they are to be served hot in certain dishes, dip into hot water to warm before use.

A favorite method of cooking noodles is called *sashimizu* which means *to add water while cooking*. A cup of cold water is added each time the water comes to a boil. This is repeated 3 or 4 times for buckwheat noodles and thick white wheat noodles and 2 or 3 times for thin white wheat noodles. It is believed that noodles will cook more evenly with this method.

Savory Noodle Dipping Sauce

Tsuke-Jiru

A flavorful dipping sauce for cold buckwheat or other noodles.

**3 cups Sea-Vegetable & Fish Stock
   or Instant Sea-Vegetable & Fish
   Stock, page 45
3/4 cup soy sauce**

**3 tablespoons sugar
1/4 cup mirin
Rinsed cooked noodles of choice**

In a medium saucepan, combine stock, soy sauce and sugar over medium heat. Simmer 2 to 3 minutes or until sugar has dissolved. Remove from heat. Stir in mirin. Cool sauce to room temperature. Refrigerate until serving time. To serve, pour 1/2 cup chilled sauce into each serving bowl. Dip each bite of cold noodles into sauce before eating. Refrigerate leftover sauce 2 to 3 days. Makes 4 cups.

Mixed Fried Noodles

Somen Champura

Noodles become a tasty stir-fried dish in this Chinese-influenced Okinawan recipe.

2 (3-oz.) bundles white wheat noodles
  (somen)
1/4 cup vegetable oil
1 small onion, halved, thinly sliced
1 small carrot, shredded
1 garlic clove, minced
1 teaspoon minced fresh gingerroot
2 to 3 oz. thinly sliced boiled ham,
  cut in 1-1/2" x 1/2" strips

3 small hollow fish rolls (chikuwa)
  cut in 1/4-inch rings
8 to 10 edible pea pods, blanched,
  julienned
1 teaspoon dashi-no-moto powder
1 to 2 tablespoons soy sauce
1/2 teaspoon salt
4 green onions, sliced

In a medium saucepan, combine 1 quart water and 2 teaspoons salt. Bring to a boil; add noodles. When water returns to a rapid boil, pour noodles into a fine strainer. Rinse with cool running water; drain thoroughly. In a wok or medium skillet, heat oil over medium-high heat. Add onion, carrot, garlic and gingerroot; stir-fry 30 seconds. Add ham and fish rolls; stir-fry 30 seconds. Add pea pods; stir-fry 30 seconds longer. Add drained noodles to wok or skillet. Toss with vegetable mixture. Sprinkle in dashi powder, soy sauce, salt and green onions; mix well. Scoop noodle mixture onto a warmed serving dish. Makes 4 servings.

Fox Noodles

Kitsune Udon

At the Inari Shrine in Kyoto, hundreds of stone foxes stand guard wearing colorful bibs.

2 recipes Seasoned Fried Tofu Pouches,
  page 136, using 6 pouches
1 Spinach Log, page 125, using
  1/2 lb. fresh spinach, omit dressing
2 pieces Fish-Cake Tempura, page 122, or
  4 slices steamed pinwheel fish loaf
  (narutomaki)

1/2 recipe Savory Noodle Broth,
  page 137
3/4 lb. dried white wheat noodles (udon)
1 teaspoon sesame oil, if desired
1 bunch small green onions, thinly sliced

Prepare Seasoned Fried Tofu Pouches. Cut pouches in 1/2 diagonally making triangles. Prepare Spinach Log; cut into 1-1/2-inch pieces. Slice Fish-Cake Tempura into thin strips. Prepare Savory Noodle Broth; keep warm over low heat. In a large saucepan, bring 3 quarts water to a boil. Slip noodles into boiling water, stirring once or twice. When water returns to a rapid boil, cook noodles 10 to 12 minutes or until tender. Test a noodle for tenderness. If noodles are becoming too tender, add 2 cups cold water to slow down cooking process. Drain noodles; mix in sesame oil, if desired. Divide noodles among 4 deep bowls. Add 3 triangles tofu pouches, 1 piece Spinach Log and a few strips of fish cake or a slice of steamed pinwheel fish loaf to each bowl. Pour about 1 cup hot broth over each bowl of noodle mixture. Garnish each serving with green onions. Makes 4 servings.

Chilled Noodles with Peanut-Miso Sauce

Hiyashi Chuka No Peanut-Miso Aye

A colorful mosaic of noodles and vegetables with a spicy Chinese-influenced sauce.

Peanut-Miso Sauce, see below
1/4 cup dried hijiki
2 or 3 Seasoned Fried Tofu Pouches,
  see below
3/4 to 1 lb. fresh ramen noodles or
  1/2 lb. spaghettini, cooked,
  rinsed in cold water, drained
1 tablespoon sesame oil
1/4 cup fresh coriander (cilantro) leaves

1/4 lb. edible pea pods, blanched,
  cut sen-giri, page 18
1 carrot, blanched, cut sen-giri
1 small red bell pepper,
  cut sen-giri
1 bunch green onions, slivered
1 pkg. radish sprouts (kaiwari daikon),
  if desired

Peanut-Miso Sauce:
2 tablespoons unsalted cocktail peanuts
1 (1/8-inch-thick) slice peeled fresh gingerroot
2 tablespoons red miso
2 tablespoons mirin
2 tablespoons sugar

2 dashes ground sansho pepper
2 tablespoons rice vinegar
2 teaspoons soy sauce
1 cup corn oil
Red-pepper sauce to taste, if desired

Seasoned Fried Tofu Pouches:
2 or 3 fried tofu pouches (abura-age)
3/4 cup water
1/2 teaspoon dashi-no-moto powder

1 tablespoon sugar
2 teaspoons light (thin) soy sauce
2 teaspoons mirin

Prepare Peanut-Miso Sauce; set aside. Place hijiki in a small bowl. Add warm water to cover. Soak 1 hour. In a fine strainer, rinse hijiki under cool running water. Cut into 1-inch lengths. Prepare Seasoned Fried Tofu Pouches. Keep all prepared ingredients in separate piles. Place cooked noodles in a medium bowl. Add sesame oil to noodles; toss until coated. Add coriander leaves; toss until mixed. Pile noodle mixture in center of a large serving dish. Arrange vegetables and sliced tofu pouches in separate piles around noodles. Serve with Peanut-Miso Sauce. Diners mix their own bowl of noodles, vegetables and sauce. Makes 6 servings.

Peanut-Miso Sauce: Photo on page 75.
In a blender or food processor fitted with a steel blade, grind peanuts and gingerroot to a paste. Add miso, mirin, sugar, pepper, vinegar and soy sauce; process until blended. With machine running, pour corn oil through feed tube in a steady stream. As soon as oil is incorporated, stop processing; sauce should not be as thick as mayonnaise. Add red-pepper sauce, if desired. Use immediately or refrigerate until needed. If not used immediately, whisk before serving. Makes about 2 cups.

Seasoned Fried Tofu Pouches:
Blanch tofu pouches 2 minutes in boiling water to remove excess oil. Cover with a drop-lid while blanching. Or, press them under water several times with a fork. Drain; cool slightly. Squeeze out excess liquid. In a small saucepan, combine 3/4 cup water, dashi powder, sugar, soy sauce and mirin over medium-high heat until simmering. Add tofu pouches; cook 8 to 10 minutes, turning them several times. Most of seasoning liquid will evaporate. Cool; squeeze dry if too moist. Cut open on 3 sides. Unfold tofu pouches and slice into 2- to 3-inch julienne strips.

How to Make Chilled Noodles with Peanut-Miso Sauce

1/Arrange prepared ingredients in separate piles. Add sesame oil to cooked noodles; toss until coated.

2/Pile noodle mixture on a large serving dish. Arrange vegetables and tofu pouches in separate piles around noodles. Serve with Peanut-Miso Sauce.

Savory Noodle Broth

Kake-Jiru

Serve this tasty broth over cooked noodles.

7 cups Sea-Vegetable & Fish Stock,
 page 45, or Chicken Stock with
 Ginger, page 50
About 1 teaspoon salt
1/3 cup soy sauce

2 teaspoons sugar
2 tablespoons mirin
Few drops of concentrated soup
 flavoring (memmi), if desired
Rinsed cooked noodles of choice

In a large saucepan, combine stock, salt, soy sauce, sugar and mirin. Heat until hot but not boiling; remove from heat. Stir in concentrated soup flavoring, if desired. To serve, pour 1 cup broth over noodles in each serving bowl. Makes 2 quarts.

Rice

Raw rice (kome) is the staple food crop of Japan. It is cooked and eaten three times a day. It is regarded with such reverence that the name for cooked rice—gohan—also refers to a complete meal. Rice was introduced into Japan from China. In ancient days, Japan's economy was based upon its rice production. The wealth of the feudal lord (daimyo) was determined by the yield of his rice acreage. Land taxes were often paid in rice. Even the samurai were paid wages of rice.

The Japanese prefer the Japonica-type rice. The short polished white grains contain a high percentage of amylopectin, a starch substance which causes the cooked grains to become soft and moist. This type of rice is perfect for eating with chopsticks. Another type of rice, mochi gome, has fat chalky-white round grains and becomes even stickier and more cohesive during cooking. It is used to make rice cakes, dumplings and sweet rice wine.

Cooked rice is considered the primary dish at each meal. All other dishes are considered side dishes (okazu), and are served to stimulate the appetite for eating rice. In Japan, rice and side dishes are eaten alternately, one bite at a time. Saké, a rice-based alcoholic beverage, and cooked rice are felt to be interchangeable during a meal. Saké and cooked rice are rarely consumed together. The saké will be drunk with side dishes. If rice has been served, it will be eaten at the end of the meal.

Rice is considered a ceremonial food during festivals. Mochi-tsuki or rice-cake making, is conducted each year to produce soft white elastic rice cakes for the New Year's celebrations. They are displayed at religious ceremonies and offered with prayers for good luck in the New Year. The photo on pages 106 and 107 shows the traditional stack of rice cakes (kagami mochi) which has been set in an alcove (tokonoma) as an offering to a deity. An orange has been placed on top to symbolize continuity between generations and the fern underneath stands for growing prosperity. A strip of dried kelp, placed between the rice cakes, conveys joy. Rice cakes are also an important part of New Year's Soup with Grilled Rice Cakes, page 48, a special soup served during the first meal on New Year's Day. Considered a source of strength and vitality, rice cakes are eaten to insure that one will possess these qualities in the New Year. Short-grain sweet glutinous rice (mochi gome) is used for making Steamed Red Beans & Rice. This special-occasion dish is always served on Boys' Day (May 5th) and on Shichi-Go-San, a holiday celebrating the growth of children seven, five and three years old. Daikokuten, the god of wealth, is always depicted smiling and sitting on top of plump straw sacks of rice.

From the early days, rice has been prepared in the same respectful way. Careful rinsing will remove any starchy coating and produce cooked rice with a clean pure taste.

The seed of all song
Is the farmer's
Busy hum
As he plants his rice   *Basho*

Cooking Rice

It is difficult to suggest an exact amount of water for cooking rice. The moisture content in rice varies depending on factors such as time of harvest, humidity, age of the rice and even the method of cooking. New rice (shinmae) requires less water than older rice. Rice for making sushi requires less water to produce a characteristic chewy firm-textured rice. Cook rice in a solid flat-bottomed pot with a tight-fitting lid. Use the appropriate size of pot to prevent undercooked, burnt or mushy rice. For example, a medium 2-quart saucepan is ideal for cooking 2 cups raw rice. In Japan, the automatic rice cooker has simplified life considerably. The important daily job of preparing cooked rice has been entrusted to this marvelous machine. It produces perfect rice every time. After the rice is cooked, a thermostatic control turns the heat unit off. Some models will keep the rice warm for several hours.

Steamed Rice

Gohan

If you prefer softer rice, add an additional 1/4 cup water.

2 cups short-grain rice
2-1/2 cups bottled spring water or
tap water

Place rice in a large bowl in the sink. Add a large amount of cool water. Swish your hand around in water. Pour off milky water or reserve it for cooking vegetables. Add fresh water. Gently rub rice grains between your hands to remove any powdery coating. Pour off milky water. Inspect rice for any foreign material such as gravel or rice hulls. Continue washing rice in this manner until rice water is clear. This will take 3 to 5 minutes. Drain rice in a strainer. In a 2-quart saucepan, combine rice and 2-1/2 cups bottled spring water or tap water. Soak rice 30 minutes. Bring water and rice to a boil; continue boiling 30 seconds. Reduce heat to low. Cover saucepan with a tight-fitting lid. Simmer rice 15 minutes. Turn off heat. Let stand, covered and undisturbed, 10 to 15 minutes. Carefully break up steamed rice with a dampened wooden rice paddle or spatula. Remove rice as needed to a serving bowl. Keep remaining rice covered in saucepan until needed. Makes about 6-1/2 cups.

Variation

An alternative method for cooking rice is to rinse and drain it well then set aside in a strainer 1 to 2 hours. Omit soaking time. Cook drained rice in measured amount of water following directions above.

Note: For 1 cup rinsed uncooked rice, use 1-1/2 cups water. Cooking smaller amounts of rice is not recommended.

Tree Oyster-Mushroom Rice

Shimeji Gohan

Serve with Sukiyaki Beef Rolls, page 95.

1/2 recipe Steamed Rice, above, with
variation noted below
1-1/4 cups water
1 tablespoon loose-leaf jasmine tea
1/2 lb. tree oyster mushrooms
1 tablespoon vegetable oil

2 green onions, minced
1 teaspoon light (thin) soy sauce
1/4 teaspoon salt
1 tablespoon Dry-Roasted Sesame Seeds,
page 150

Wash and drain rice; set aside. In a 2-quart saucepan, bring 1-1/4 cups water to a boil. Remove from heat; add tea. Let stand 1 minute for a delicate infusion. Strain and discard tea leaves. Return tea water to saucepan. Cool, then add rice. Soak 30 minutes. Cook rice following directions above; keep warm. Quickly rinse clumps of mushrooms under cool running water. Drain well; pat dry on paper towels. Separate mushrooms. In a large skillet, heat vegetable oil over high heat. After 30 seconds, add mushrooms and green onions; stir-fry 1 to 2 minutes. Remove from heat. Stir in soy sauce and salt. Stir mushroom mixture into warm rice. Serve in small bowls. Sprinkle with Dry-Roasted Sesame Seeds. Makes 3 to 4 servings.

Variation

Other types of mushrooms can be substituted.

Hidden-Treasure Rice Balls

Onigiri

In Japan, the popular rice ball is often filled with pickled plums and sprinkled with sesame seeds and salt.

Fillings, see below	**Toppings, see below**
Coatings, see below	**Hot Steamed Rice, page 139**
Wrappers, see below	

Fillings:

Pickled plums (umeboshi)
Lemon-Miso Broiled Fish, page 73, flaked
Mixed Sweet Vegetable Pickles,
    page 156, chopped
Sweet Simmered Mushrooms, page 93,
    chopped

Pickled Pink-Ginger Slices, page 153
Salt-Pickled Vegetables with Raisins,
    page 150, chopped

Coatings:

Dry-Roasted Sesame Seeds, page 150
1/4 cup white Dry-Roasted Sesame Seeds
    mixed with 1 to 2 teaspoons sea salt

Fresh parsley, finely chopped

Wrappers:

Toasted Nori sheets, page 59, or
    toasted pink bonito sheets (katsuo
    maki), cut in 3-1/2-inch
    circles or 1/2-inch strips
Fresh shiso leaves

Egg Pancake, page 80, cut in strips
Pickled mustard-cabbage leaves
Salt-pickled Napa-cabbage leaves
Smoked-salmon strips
Ham strips

Toppings:

Lumpfish caviar
Salmon-roe caviar (ikura)
Smelt eggs
Finely chopped pickled vegetables,
    any kind

Sweetened pink or green dried-
    fish flakes (denbu)
Sieved hard-cooked egg yolk

Prepare desired Fillings, Coatings, Wrappers and Toppings; set aside. Prepare Steamed Rice. In a small bowl, combine 1/2 cup water and 1/2 teaspoon salt for moistening your hands. With damp hands, gather up about 1/3 cup rice. Firmly but gently press it into a ball. Push a hole in the center. Add a small amount of desired Filling; close opening. Sprinkle filled ball with 1 of the Coatings, if desired. Or, enclose rice ball in 1 of the Wrappers. For a fancier version, set a filled rice ball on a circle of toasted nori or toasted bonito. Press circle around bottom of rice ball. With a small pair of scissors, snip a cross or an **X** in center of a second circle. Place circle over top of rice ball; press around top. Rice ball should be completely enclosed. Peel back snipped corners; add 1 of the Toppings.

Note: Size of rice balls can be increased to any desired dimension. In a Robata-Yaki restaurant in Japan, I was fascinated to see a giant onigiri rice ball wrapped in several sheets of nori. The onigiri completely filled a large plate. I have often wondered at the vast treasures hidden inside.

How to Make Hidden-Treasure Rice Balls

1/With damp hands, gather up about 1/3 cup rice. Firmly but gently press it into a ball. Push a hole in the center. Add a small amount of desired Filling; close opening.

2/Fill and decorate rice balls with a selection of prepared ingredients.

Savory Rice Stew   Photo on page 149.

Zosui

A popular Japanese stew which utilizes leftover rice.

2 medium, dried shiitake mushrooms
1 cup warm water
4 cups Chicken Stock with Ginger,
   page 50
1 tablespoon soy sauce
3 cups cooled Steamed Rice, page 139
1 chicken-breast half, skinned, boned
2 tablespoons shredded carrot
1/3 cup tiny cooked shrimp or crabmeat
1/4 cup chopped pickled mustard greens

3 green onions, minced
About 1 teaspoon salt
2 teaspoons saké
1 tablespoon mirin
1 large egg, slightly beaten
6 tablespoons Cabbage & Shiso Pickle, page
   151, 1 or 2 minced fresh shiso leaves
   or several watercress sprigs
2 tablespoons shredded red pickled
   ginger (beni shoga)

Place mushrooms in a small bowl; add warm water to cover. Soak 30 minutes or until needed. Squeeze mushrooms dry. Cut off and discard tough stems. Mince mushrooms; set aside. Place chicken stock and soy sauce in a large saucepan. Bring to a boil. Rinse cooked rice in a fine strainer to remove excess starch. Add rice to boiling stock mixture. Reduce heat; simmer 5 minutes. Dice chicken into 1/4-inch cubes. Add chicken to rice mixture; simmer 2 to 3 minutes. Stir in carrot, shrimp or crabmeat, mustard greens, green onions and minced mushrooms; simmer 1 minute. Add salt, saké and mirin; stir until blended. Remove pan from heat. Drizzle in egg, stirring mixture with a pair of chopsticks in a circular motion. Ladle hot stew into individual bowls. Garnish each serving with 1 tablespoon Cabbage & Shiso Pickle, some minced shiso leaf or a watercress sprig. Add 1 teaspoon pickled ginger to each serving. Makes 6 servings.

Box-Lunch Rice   Photo on cover.

Moso Gohan

Steamed Rice can be mixed with many ingredients and molded into shapes to decorate box lunches.

Hot Steamed Rice, page 139   **Additional ingredients, suggested below**

Prepare Steamed Rice. In a small bowl, combine 1/2 cup water and 1/2 teaspoon salt for moistening your hands. Combine rice with desired ingredients as suggested below. With damp hands, pack rice mixture into molds. Unmold and decorate for serving.

Camellia-Flower Rice: For each camellia, shape 1/3 cup cooked rice into a ball. Flatten ball slightly. Add a small amount of sieved hard-cooked egg yolk to center. Garnish with a camellia leaf. Makes about 18 rice camellias.

Fancy Rice Molds: Sprinkle some sweetened pink dried-fish flakes (denbu), or 6 sugar-sweetened, sieved, hard-cooked jumbo egg yolks into bottoms of about 12 flower-shaped molds. Add about 1/2 cup rice. Unmold; add chopped egg white to make flower centers. Garnish with fresh flower leaves. Makes about 12 molds.

Mushroom-Rice Mold: Lightly oil small custard cups. Arrange 2 or 3 blanched tree oyster mushrooms in a pattern in bottom of each cup. Carefully press about 1/3 cup cooked rice into each cup. Unmold; mushrooms will be on top. Makes about 18 molds.

Chestnut & Sweet-Potato Rice   Photo on page 121.

Kuri Gohan

If you don't have time to prepare fresh chestnuts, purchase chestnuts in syrup from the Oriental market.

2 cups short-grain rice,
   well-rinsed, page 139
2-1/2 cups water
2 medium, dried shiitake mushrooms
1/2 lb. fresh chestnuts
1 medium sweet potato or yam, peeled, diced

1 teaspoon salt
2 tablespoons light (thin) soy sauce
2 tablespoons mirin
1 tablespoon Dry-Roasted Sesame Seeds,
   page 150
Radish sprouts (kaiwari daikon), if desired

In a 3-quart saucepan, combine rinsed rice and water; soak 30 minutes. Place mushrooms in a small bowl; add warm water to cover. Soak 30 minutes or until needed. Squeeze mushrooms dry. Cut off and discard tough stems. Dice mushrooms. Using a small sharp knife, make a slit in flat side of each chestnut. Place chestnuts in a medium saucepan; add water to cover. Bring to a boil. Reduce heat to low; simmer 8 to 10 minutes. Turn off heat. Remove 1 chestnut from hot water; peel off shell and inner skin. Repeat with remaining chestnuts, 1 at a time. If necessary, simmer chestnuts a few minutes longer if skins do not come off easily. You can also try rubbing skins off with a clean kitchen towel. Cut chestnuts into quarters. Add diced mushrooms, chestnut quarters, diced sweet potato or yam, salt, soy sauce and mirin to saucepan with rice; stir. Bring to a boil. Reduce heat to low. Cover saucepan with a tight-fitting lid. Simmer 15 minutes. Remove from heat. Let stand, covered and undisturbed, 10 minutes. Carefully break up rice mixture with a dampened wooden rice paddle or spatula. Spoon rice mixture into serving bowls. Sprinkle with Dry-Roasted Sesame Seeds and radish sprouts, if desired. Makes 3 to 4 servings.

Steamed Red Beans & Rice   Photo on page 107.

Seikihan

This festive pink rice dish is served on special occasions throughout the year.

1/2 cup red beans (azuki), well-rinsed
About 3-1/2 cups water
3 cups sweet glutinous rice (mochi gome),
**   well-rinsed, drained, page 145**
1 (7-oz.) jar sweet chestnuts in syrup,
**   if desired, drained, halved**

1 tablespoon black Dry-Roasted Sesame
**   Seeds, page 150, mixed with**
**   1 teaspoon sea salt**
Fresh edible leaf, such as shiso or
**   watercress, if desired**

In a medium saucepan, combine beans and 3-1/2 cups water; bring to a boil. Reduce heat to low; simmer 45 minutes to 1 hour or until beans are soft but not completely cooked. Cool to room temperature. Drain bean liquid into a medium bowl. Place cooked beans in a small bowl with a few teaspoons water; cover and refrigerate overnight. Add rice to bean liquid. If necessary, add enough water to cover rice; soak overnight. Drain rice, reserving soaking liquid. In a wok or deep pot, bring about 4 cups water to a boil. Spread a piece of dampened unbleached muslin or several layers of cheesecloth over a steamer tray. Combine rice and beans; spread evenly over dampened cloth. With your finger, poke holes in rice mixture. Sprinkle with some of reserved soaking liquid. Cover tray; place over boiling water. Steam 45 minutes or until beans are tender; do not overcook beans or they will split. Sprinkle additional soaking liquid over mixture every 15 minutes. During last 10 minutes of cooking time, add sweet chestnuts, if desired. Spoon rice mixture into a lacquer serving box or other serving dish. Sprinkle 1 to 2 teaspoons sesame-salt mixture over top. Garnish with fresh edible leaf, if desired. Pass remaining sesame-salt mixture in a small bowl. Makes 6 to 8 servings.

Tri-Colored Autumn Rice Balls

Sanshoku Ohagi

A traditional autumn tea snack, sweet rice balls can be served with hot tea throughout the year.

Sesame Sugar, page 164,
**   using black sesame seeds**
Warm Sweet Glutinous Rice, page 145
1 cup Sweetened Red-Bean Paste, page 166,
**   or canned bean paste, chilled**

1/2 cup Sugar & Spice Okara, page 112,
**   or 1/2 cup lightly sweetened**
**   roasted-soybean powder (kinako)**

Prepare Sesame Sugar; set aside. Prepare Sweet Glutinous Rice. Dampen your hands with water. Divide warm rice into 12 equal portions. Shape 4 portions into balls. Wet a clean dish towel; squeeze dry. Place 2-1/2 tablespoons bean paste on damp towel; pat into a 4-inch circle. Place 1 rice ball in center of bean-paste circle. Use towel to mold bean paste around rice ball. When rice is covered, mold mixture into an oval shape; set aside. Repeat using some of remaining bean paste and 3 rice balls. Flatten remaining 8 rice portions. Form remaining bean paste into 8 balls, using about 2 teaspoons for each ball. Place 1 in center of each piece of flattened rice. Shape rice around bean paste. Mold filled rice balls into oval shapes. Roll 4 ovals in Sesame Sugar. Roll remaining 4 balls in Sugar & Spice Okara or roasted-soybean powder. Serve on a lacquer tray. Allow 2 balls per serving. Makes 6 servings.

Sweet Glutinous-Rice Cakes

Omochi

If fresh rice cakes are not available, try making your own.

1 cup sweet glutinous-rice flour (mochiko)	**1/2 cup water**
1/4 teaspoon salt	**Potato starch or cornstarch**
1 tablespoon sugar	

In a medium bowl, stir together rice flour, salt and sugar. Stir in 1/2 cup water to form a soft dough. Lightly knead about 30 seconds. In a wok or deep pot, bring about 4 cups water to a boil. Spread a piece of dampened unbleached muslin or several layers of cheesecloth over a steamer tray. Spread dough evenly over dampened cloth, about 1/2 inch thick. Cover tray; place over boiling water. Steam 20 minutes. Remove steamer tray from pan. Lift out cloth with dough. Pull cloth away from dough letting dough fall onto a flat surface dusted with potato starch or cornstarch. Cool dough 1 to 2 minutes. While still hot, knead 1 minute or until smooth and shiny. Roll glutinous dough into an 8-inch-long sausage-shaped roll. Cut into 8 equal pieces. Dust with potato starch or cornstarch as needed to prevent sticking. Form tops of pieces into smooth round shapes. They will flatten on the bottom when placed on a flat surface. Serve rice cakes the same day while fresh, if possible. Rice cakes can be well-wrapped and refrigerated up to 2 days or frozen for several months. Makes 8 rice cakes.

Variations

Grilled Rice Cakes: Place completed rice cakes on a baking sheet; broil in the oven several minutes until puffy and golden on both sides, turning frequently.

Deep-Fried Rice Cakes: Cut leftover rice cakes into small pieces. Heat vegetable oil to 360F (180C) or until a 1-inch cube of bread turns golden brown in 60 seconds. Deep-fry rice-cake pieces until crisp. Serve with soy sauce as a snack or add to soups.

Boiled Rice Cakes: Simmer leftover hard rice cakes in soups or other hot liquids 1 minute to soften.

Pan-Fried Rice Cakes: Place completed rice cakes in a small skillet over medium-low heat. Turn rice cakes frequently until golden brown on both sides. Serve with soy sauce as a snack or add to soups.

Boys' Day Rice Cakes (Azuke Mochi): Prepare dough. Divide into 8 equal-sized pieces; flatten into circles. In center of each circle, place 1 tablespoon Sweetened Red-Bean Paste, page 166. Shape dough around filling into oval balls. Increase steaming time to 25 minutes. Cool. Wrap each piece in commercially prepared oak leaf or other non-poisonous leaf for serving.

Thin Sweet Rice Cakes (Gyuhi Mochi): Substitute 1 cup unrefined sweet glutinous-rice flour (shiratamako) for 1 cup sweet glutinous-rice flour in recipe. Increase sugar to 1/4 cup. Mix 3 to 4 drops red or green food coloring with water used in dough. Steam dough as directed above. Roll steamed dough into a sheet no thicker than 1/2 inch. Cut into 1/2-inch squares. Serve as a sweet snack or over ice cream or mixed with pieces of fruit. Regular sweet glutinous-rice flour can also be used in this recipe.

Fermented-Soybean-Stuffed Rice Cakes (Natto Mochi): Prepare dough. Steam as directed above. Divide into 12 equal-sized pieces. Flatten each piece into a thin circle. Place 1 teaspoon fermented sticky soybeans (natto) in center of each circle. Fold dough circle in 1/2. Wrap each piece in a fresh shiso leaf.

How to Make Sweet Glutinous-Rice Cakes

1/Spread dough evenly over dampened cloth in steamer. Cover and steam 20 minutes.

2/Roll kneaded dough into a long sausage-shaped roll. Cut into 8 pieces. Form tops of pieces into smooth round shapes.

Sweet Glutinous Rice

Mochi Gome

Oval grains of pearly rice cook into a delicious sticky rice, excellent for rice cakes and dumplings.

1-1/2 cups sweet glutinous rice   **Water**
    (mochi gome)

Place rice in a medium bowl. Wash thoroughly in cool water, rubbing grains gently between your hands. Pour off milky water; add fresh water. Continue washing rice in this manner until rice water is clear. Drain rice and return to bowl; add 3 cups water. Soak rice at least 6 hours or as long as overnight. Drain well. Spread out rice evenly in a round, 10-inch, shallow, heatproof pan. Add 1/3 cup water. In a wok or deep pot, bring about 4 cups water to a boil over medium-high heat. Place pan of rice on a steamer tray. Cover and place over boiling water. Steam rice 30 minutes. If rice is not tender, sprinkle with 2 or 3 tablespoons additional water and steam 5 minutes longer. When tender, remove pan of rice from steamer tray. Makes about 4-1/2 cups.

Pickles & Condiments
(Tsukemono & Yakumi)

The art of pickling (tsukemono), began as a vital method of food preservation in Japan. For centuries, pickling was a common household activity throughout Japan although pickling agents and foods for pickling would vary from region to region. Referred to as *konomono* or *fragrant things,* pickled fruits and vegetables are an indispensable part of the Japanese diet. They are often served as accompaniment to saké and tea. Most people enjoy eating them daily with rice and green tea at the end of a meal. Sometimes the entire meal might consist of rice, pickles, a bowl of steaming hot miso soup and of course tea. It might be difficult to convince you of the merit of such a simple meal unless you are already familiar with the incredible range and depth of flavors of Japanese pickles. Just try the Mixed Sweet Vegetable Pickles and see what I mean. This chewy sweet-sour dried pickle can be used as an ingredient in many dishes, as well as being featured as a tasty side dish.

Pickles are especially appreciated in remote mountain villages where much of the arable land is terraced and suitable only for rice growing. In the cold winter months when the country folk are knee-deep in snow, pickled autumn vegetables are a means of extending the season

and adding rich variety to the diet. Pickled vegetables serve as a much-needed source of vitamins and minerals.

Throughout Japan, the preference has been for quick pickling so the taste of each seasonal vegetable can be enjoyed. It is said in Japan that "to eat tsukemono is to fully enjoy the changing seasons." The salty taste, the crisp natural textures and the characteristic flavor and aroma of fermentation are the qualities of pickles the Japanese most enjoy.

There are several important methods of preparing pickles. They are salt pickling (shio-zuke), miso pickling (miso-zuke), rice-bran pickling (nuka-zuke) and fermented-rice pickling (kasu-zuke). The fermented rice (saké lees) used in the last method is a by-product of making saké. *Su-zuke* is pickling with vinegar and *karashi-zuke* involves combining vegetables with soy sauce, mustard, sugar and vinegar.

Korean-style pickles are becoming popular in Japan. Typically, sliced or whole miniature fermented vegetables are tinged with ground hot red peppers. The simplest form of pickle is prepared by salting vegetables, fruits or flowers, then putting them under pressure until their liquids are extracted. The resulting liquid is a briny solution which acts as a preserving agent for the vegetables. The Japanese have invented the *tsukemono-ki,* photo on page 151, a plastic jar with a built-in press especially for salt-pickling. It is available in some Oriental markets.

Items suitable for pickling are not restricted to vegetables. Salted cherry blossoms can be added to rice, mixed with other pickled vegetables or used for making tea. The tart salt-pickled plum (umeboshi) is the treasured pickled fruit of Japan. In a simple rice dish sometimes found in the popular box lunch, a single red pickled plum is placed in the center of a box of plain cooked rice. Known as the "rising-sun box lunch" (hino-maru bento), it is a tiny replica of the Japanese flag.

Many vegetables are salted or sun-dried then layered in a pickle bed. Rice-bran mash, miso paste, saké lees and steamed rice innoculated with koji mold are the major types of bed. The reaction of the enzymes causes a lactic-acid fermentation which gives this type of pickle its special taste and crunchiness. The addition of salt prevents the growth of harmful toxin-producing bacteria. *Nuka-zuke* is a quick form of pickling in dry rice bran and salt.

Commercially pickled daikon radish (takuan) is an example of a pickle made using this process. The bright-yellow color forms naturally as a result of the pickling process which can take up to one year.

Be sure to sample the many varieties of Japanese pickles found in Oriental markets in your area. Department stores and markets in Japan are famous for their attractive displays of open barrels and crocks filled with colorful and unusual pickles. Regional specialties are often favored as housewarming gifts and purchased as souvenirs for friends.

Condiments (yakumi), like pickles, add variety and seasoning to a meal. But unlike pickles, condiments are never eaten for their individual taste alone. Yakumi are the condiments and seasonings which add a touch of spice to the simple flavors of the foods of Japan. Prepared Japanese Horseradish is one of the most famous condiments and is the traditional accompaniment to sushi. Seven-Spice Mixture adds zest to noodle dishes and Mustard-Miso Sauce would make a tasty dip for fresh raw vegetables.

Seven-Spice Mixture

Shichimi Togarashi

Keep this spicy blend on hand to add zest to many foods, especially in one-pot cookery.

1-1/2 tablespoons freshly grated
  mandarin-orange peel
1/2 teaspoon dried sansho-pepper pods
1 oz. (1/2 cup) dried, whole, red chili
  peppers, about 1-1/2 inches long
1 teaspoon Dry-Roasted Sesame Seeds,
  page 150

1 teaspoon dry-roasted flax seeds or
  hemp seeds
1 teaspoon dry-roasted poppy seeds
1/4 teaspoon powdered sea-vegetable
  mixture (aonoriko)

Preheat oven to 200F (95C). Spread grated orange peel over the bottom of a pie plate. Dry peel in oven 30 minutes. Place sansho-pepper pods in a grinding bowl, mortar or small electric coffee mill; grind to a powder. Break open red peppers; remove and discard most of seeds. In grinding bowl, mortar or small electric coffee mill, grind peppers to a powder. Combine ground sansho pepper, ground red peppers, dried orange peel and Dry-Roasted Sesame Seeds in grinding bowl, mortar or another sturdy bowl. Pound 4 or 5 times to bruise seeds and blend mixture. Add flax seeds or hemp seeds, poppy seeds and powdered sea-vegetable mixture. Blend mixture using pestle or equivalent; do not continue crushing seeds. Spoon spice mixture into a small jar. With a paper towel, loosen any remaining mixture left in ridges of grinding bowl and add to jar. Tightly cover jar; store in a cool place 4 to 6 weeks. Makes 1/4 cup.

Variations

If mandarin-orange peel is not available, experiment with other types of fresh orange peel.

Oven-dried shiso leaves can be substituted for powdered sea-vegetable mixture. Add dried shiso to ground sansho; grind until powdered. Dry your own shiso leaves or purchase them in Oriental markets.

Quick Radish Pickles

Daikon Zuke

Try this easy recipe if you have not made Japanese pickles before.

**1-1/2 to 1-3/4 lbs. daikon radish,
   peeled, halved lengthwise**
Generous 1/4 cup sea salt
Pickling Syrup, see below

**1 (4-inch) square good-quality dried
   kelp (dashi konbu), wiped**
**1 to 2 small, dried, whole, hot,
   red peppers**

Pickling Syrup:
1 cup water
1/2 cup rice vinegar
1-1/4 cups sugar

1 teaspoon salt
Yellow food coloring, if desired

Slice daikon to desired thickness using a large sharp knife or in a food processor fitted with the slicing blade. Place sliced daikon in a large bowl. Add salt; mix well. Press down daikon in bowl. Place an appropriate-sized plate on top of daikon. Place a 3-pound weight on top; gradually increase weight to 5 pounds as vegetables shrink, releasing their liquid. Press daikon overnight. Pour off liquid. If desired, quickly rinse daikon to remove excess salt. Squeeze out as much liquid as possible from daikon. Place daikon in a 1-quart sterilized jar. Prepare Pickling Syrup. Pour hot syrup over daikon in jar or cool syrup before adding to jar. Add kelp and red peppers. Cover jar with a tight-fitting lid; refrigerate up to 3 months. Pickles can be eaten within 3 to 4 days; flavor will improve daily. Makes about 1 pint.

Pickling Syrup:

In a medium saucepan, combine all ingredients over medium-high heat. Boil 1 to 2 minutes or until sugar is dissolved, stirring constantly. Makes about 2 cups.

Variation

Oriental markets often sell a blend of red peppers and kelp strips (konbu iri togarashi) for pickling. Substitute 1 tablespoon of this mixture for kelp square and red peppers in recipe.

Spicy Mustard

Karashi

Traditionally, mustard ripens to full flavor in the bottom of an upside-down bowl.

2 tablespoons Japanese mustard powder
1 tablespoon saké
1 teaspoon mirin

2 teaspoons saké or water
1/2 teaspoon soy sauce

In a small bowl, combine mustard powder and 1 tablespoon saké. Turn bowl upside-down 10 minutes. Stir in remaining ingredients. Serve immediately. Use in small amounts. Makes about 1/8 cup.

Savory Rice Stew, page 141. Pickles clockwise from top: Quick Radish Pickles, above; Salt-Pickled Vegetables with Raisins, page 150; Mixed Sweet Vegetable Pickles, page 156.

Salt-Pickled Vegetables with Raisins   Photo on page 149.

Yasai No Ama Zuke

Raisins add a natural sweetness to these crunchy pickled vegetables.

1 Japanese cucumber or
   1/2 regular cucumber
1/2 medium carrot, cut in thin strips
1/2 lb. Napa cabbage,
   cut lengthwise in strips
1/2 red or green bell pepper,
   cut in 3 strips
1 medium Japanese eggplant, halved
   lengthwise to within 1 inch of stem

2 tablespoons sea salt
1/4 cup raisins
1 (1/4-inch-thick) slice peeled fresh
   gingerroot, smashed
Peel of 1/2 lemon, cut in thin strips
1 small, dried, whole, hot, red pepper,
   if desired
Soy sauce, if desired

Cut off and discard ends from cucumber. Cut cucumber in 1/2 lengthwise. If using 1/2 regular cucumber, scrape out seeds with a small spoon. Peel off narrow strips of skin lengthwise down cucumber pieces. Rinse cucumber, carrot, cabbage, bell pepper and eggplant; shake dry. Sprinkle with salt; rub into cut surfaces. In a Japanese screw-top pickling jar, layer salted vegetables, raisins, gingerroot and lemon peel; tighten lid. Press mixture 24 to 48 hours; do not refrigerate. Tighten lid once or twice as vegetables shrink, releasing their liquid. After pressing, remove vegetables from jar; reserve liquid. Pack vegetables into a sterilized 1-quart jar. Add reserved pressing liquid. Add hot red pepper for spiciness, if desired. Tightly cover jar; refrigerate up to 2 weeks. To serve pickled vegetables, remove only as much as needed for 1 meal. Rinse pickles; cut into thin slices or strips. Arrange a few pieces of each vegetable on small serving dishes. Add a few drops of soy sauce, if desired. Makes 6 to 8 servings.

Variation

If a Japanese screw-top pickling jar is not available, layer vegetables in a crock or glass bowl. Place an appropriate-sized plate on top of vegetables. Place a 3-pound weight on top; gradually increase weight to 5 pounds. Press vegetables 24 to 48 hours. Continue as directed above.

Dry-Roasted Sesame Seeds

Yaki Goma

Crushed roasted sesame seeds lend a marvelous nutty flavor to foods.

Hulled white or black sesame seeds

Place sesame seeds in a small heavy skillet over medium-high heat. Stir seeds constantly until white seeds begin to turn golden brown and black seeds are fragrant. When seeds begin to pop in skillet, they are almost ready. Watch carefully at this point or they will burn. Be especially careful when toasting black sesame seeds. Color is not a good indication of properly toasted seeds. Burned seeds must be discarded. Place toasted seeds in a grinding bowl or mortar, crush lightly to release fragrant oils. Do not over-crush and destroy texture. Use immediately or store in a tightly covered jar in a cool place. It is best to roast sesame seeds as you need them for maximum freshness and flavor.

How to Make Salt-Pickled Vegetables with Raisins

1/In a screw-top pickling jar, layer salted vegetables, raisins, gingerroot and lemon peel.

2/Tighten lid of jar. Press vegetable mixture 24 to 48 hours. Tighten pressing lid as vegetables shrink and release their liquid.

Cabbage & Shiso Pickle

Kya-bet-su No Shiba Zuke

Minty shiso leaves are easy to grow and would make an excellent addition to your herb garden.

1 medium head green cabbage
2 pkgs. fresh shiso leaves
  (about 18 leaves), rinsed, dried
1 teaspoon salt

1/2 teaspoon freshly grated lemon peel
About 1 tablespoon Dry-Roasted Sesame
  Seeds, opposite

Cut off core end from cabbage. Separate leaves. Select 6 to 8 attractive outer leaves. Refrigerate remaining cabbage for another use. Blanch cabbage leaves, 3 at a time, 1 minute in boiling salted water. In a medium bowl, rinse blanched leaves in cool water. Drain well; pat dry. Trim off any tough parts from cabbage leaves. Cut off stems from shiso leaves. In a 9'' x 5'' loaf pan, place a layer of 2 or 3 cabbage leaves. Sprinkle with 1/4 teaspoon salt. Cover cabbage with a layer of shiso leaves. Add another layer of cabbage leaves; sprinkle with 1/4 teaspoon salt. Make a final layer of shiso leaves. Place remaining cabbage leaves on top. Sprinkle with 1/2 teaspoon salt. Place a piece of plastic wrap on top; press layers firmly together. Place a 2- to 3-pound weight on top. Two filled salt boxes make excellent weights. Press at room temperature at least 1 hour, or up to 4 hours. Remove wilted cabbage and shiso from pan to a cutting board; pat dry. Using a large sharp knife, cut cabbage and shiso in 1/2 lengthwise. Cut crosswise into matchstick shreds. In a medium bowl, toss shreds lightly with lemon peel. Place a small pile of cabbage mixture on each serving dish. Sprinkle with about 1/4 teaspoon Dry-Roasted Sesame Seeds. Refrigerate leftover pickle in an airtight container. Makes 6 to 8 servings.

Lemon-Miso Pickles

Lemon-Miso Zuke

Scalloped Lotus-Root Flowers, page 32, or scraped burdock root can be pickled in this lemony pickle bed.

Lemon-Miso Pickling Bed, see below
1 European-style cucumber, 2 Japanese
  cucumbers or 1 seeded
  regular cucumber
2 medium Japanese eggplants,
  halved lengthwise to within 1 inch
  of stem, or 1 small regular
  eggplant, cut in large strips

1 large carrot, thinly sliced
  diagonally
1/2 red bell pepper, cut in strips
2 or 3 slices peeled lotus root
1 generous tablespoon salt
Soy sauce, if desired

Lemon-Miso Pickling Bed:
1 cup sweet white or yellow miso
1 cup torn bread pieces, preferably
  homemade without preservatives
1 cup sugar
2 tablespoons saké
1/4 cup sea salt

Peel of 1 lemon, cut in thin strips
2 dried, whole, hot, red peppers
1 (3-inch) piece dried kelp (konbu), wiped
3 (1/8-inch-thick) slices peeled
  fresh gingerroot, smashed

Prepare Lemon-Miso Pickling Bed. Cover and store in a cool place or refrigerate until vegetables have been pressed. Cut off and discard ends from cucumber. Cut cucumber in 1/2 lengthwise. Using a small spoon, scrape out seeds, if necessary. Cut cucumber halves crosswise into 2 pieces. Peel off narrow strips of skin lengthwise down cucumber pieces. Rinse cucumber, eggplants, carrot, bell pepper and lotus root; shake dry. Sprinkle with salt; rub into cut surfaces. In a Japanese screw-top pickling jar or see Variation, page 150, layer salted vegetables; tighten lid. Press mixture overnight in a cool place. Tighten lid once or twice as vegetables shrink, releasing their liquid. Pour off liquid when pressing is complete. Remove vegetables from jar; pat dry with a clean kitchen towel. Completely bury vegetables in pickling bed. Be sure mixture is spread between vegetable layers. Cover tightly and refrigerate. Vegetables can be eaten the next day, but are even better after 48 hours. Pickling process can continue several days, depending on desired saltiness and taste. Experiment to find the taste you like best. To serve, scrape pickling bed from vegetables back into crock or bowl. Rinse vegetables under cool running water; pat dry. Cut into thin slices. Serve in small serving dishes with 1 or 2 drops soy sauce, if desired. Stir Lemon-Miso Pickling Bed every 2 days. When it becomes too low or watery, mix in another 1/2 batch fresh miso mixture. Continue adding more salted vegetables to bed after removing pickled vegetables. Properly cared for, pickling bed will keep many weeks. Flavor of pickles will improve as bed matures. Makes 8 to 10 servings.

Lemon-Miso Pickling Bed:
In a medium bowl, combine all ingredients; stir well. Scrape mixture into a medium crock, glass jar or bowl, or a plastic container with a tight-fitting lid. Mixture can be doubled for larger quantities of vegetables. Makes 2 cups.

Variation

Sweet Miso-Beer Pickles: Combine 1 cup sweet white miso, 1 cup sugar, 1 cup rice vinegar, 1/2 cup sea salt and 1/2 cup beer. Add 1 (2-inch) square wiped dried kelp (konbu) and 1 tablespoon dried, hot, red-pepper flakes. Prepare salted pressed vegetables and pickle them in pickling bed as directed above.

How to Make Lemon-Miso Pickles

1/Prepare vegetables. Rub salt into cut surfaces. Layer salted vegetables in a pickling jar; tighten lid. Press mixture overnight.

2/ Remove pressed vegetables from jar; pat dry. Completely bury vegetables in Lemon-Miso Pickling Bed. Cover tightly and refrigerate.

Pickled Pink-Ginger Slices

Amazu Shoga

Paper-thin slices of tender young gingerroot turn pink when marinated in vinegar.

1/3 lb. fresh young gingerroot, large pieces, preferably with pinkish skin, scraped

1/3 cup rice vinegar
1/4 cup sugar
1/4 teaspoon salt

Using a sharp knife or a Benriner cutter, shave gingerroot into paper-thin slices. In a small airtight container, combine vinegar, sugar and salt. Blanch gingerroot slices 30 seconds in boiling water. Drain gingerroot; cool. If desired, reserve ginger blanching liquid for other cooking uses. Add cooled ginger to vinegar mixture; mix well. Store marinating ginger in the refrigerator. Pickled ginger can be eaten after 24 hours of marinating. It will keep several weeks. Serve with sushi and other rice or noodle dishes. Save flavorful ginger marinade to add to salads, pickles or sauces. Makes about 1/2 cup.

Variation

One or 2 fresh shiso leaves whole or in julienne strips, can be added to pickle.

Pickled Winter Cabbage

Hakusai No Kim Chee

Originally from Korea, Pickled Winter Cabbage can be found in almost every market in Japan.

1 large head Napa cabbage
1/4 cup salt
Seasoning Mixture, see below
6 green onions, shredded

1 lb. daikon radish, cut sen-gri, page 18
1 large carrot, cut sen-giri
1 pear-apple, shredded, if desired

Seasoning Mixture:

3 garlic cloves, minced
1 tablespoon minced fresh gingerroot
1 tablespoon Korean, dried, hot,
  red-pepper threads (shile kochu)
3 to 5 tablespoons Korean, ground,
  hot, red peppers (kochu)

1 small onion, halved, cut in strips
2 tablespoons sugar
2 tablespoons Dry-Roasted Sesame Seeds,
  page 150
1 tablespoon salted shrimp paste,
  if desired

Cut cabbage in 1/2 lengthwise; sprinkle with salt. With your hands, rub salt in between cabbage layers, especially near core. Place cabbage in a large bowl; add water to cover. Soak cabbage several hours or overnight. When cabbage wilts, it is ready to be pickled. Rinse in cool running water; drain well. In a small bowl, combine all ingredients for Seasoning Mixture. In a large bowl, place cabbage, green onions, daikon, carrot and pear-apple, if desired. With your hands, rub seasoning over cabbage halves and between layers. Fold cabbage halves into 2 neat bundles. Place in a metal kim-chee pot with a tight-fitting lid, or a large glass jar with a lid. Pour any liquid from bowl over cabbage. Cover tightly and refrigerate several hours or overnight before serving. Flavor of pickled cabbage continues to mature each day. Some connoisseurs enjoy the strong, slightly sour flavor of cabbage which develops after 1 to 2 weeks. To serve, slice bundles and arrange on a serving platter in their original shape or coarsely chop. Makes 10 to 12 servings.

Prepared Japanese Horseradish

Wasabi

This fiery condiment is a traditional accompaniment to sushi and Fresh Chilled Raw Fish, page 54.

1 tablespoon Japanese horseradish powder
1/2 teaspoon rice vinegar

3 teaspoons water

Place horseradish powder in a small dish. Add remaining ingredients; blend until a thick paste. Turn bowl upside-down 10 minutes for flavors to develop. Horseradish paste should be thick enough to be molded in a small cone shape. Use sparingly. Makes 1 tablespoon.

Variation

Prepared-Japanese-Horseradish Leaves: Photo on page 55.
Prepare horseradish paste. Press into a sheet, about 1/4 inch thick. Using a tiny leaf-shaped cutter or a small knife, cut out leaf shapes. Lift leaves onto serving plates with a small narrow spatula.

Note: Prepared horseradish can also be purchased in tubes. Squeeze out the amount needed.

How to Make Pickled Winter Cabbage

1/Rub Seasoning Mixture over wilted cabbage and between layers. Fold cabbage halves into 2 neat bundles. Place in a metal kim-chee pot or large glass jar. Cover tightly and refrigerate.

2/To serve, slice bundles and arrange in their original shape on serving dishes.

Red-Maple Radish   Photo on page 121.

Momiji-Oroshi

This spicy hot condiment is an excellent accompaniment to Chicken Hot Pot, page 99.

1 (3- to 4-inch) piece daikon radish, peeled
3 to 4 dried red chili peppers

1/2 teaspoon grated fresh gingerroot, if desired

Using a chopstick, push 3 or 4 holes through piece of daikon. Push a chili pepper into each hole. Wrap whole daikon tightly or use a fine grater to grate daikon in a circular motion; refrigerate whole or grated daikon 1 to 2 days. At serving time, grate daikon, if necessary, using a fine grater. Grated daikon will be speckled with red chili-pepper flakes. Serve in individual tiny condiment dishes. Or, serve in a single dish with a mound of grated gingerroot on top. Makes 8 to 10 servings.

Variations

One teaspoon freshly grated lemon peel can be stirred into finished condiment. This is especially delicious mixed with soy sauce and served with Fresh Chilled Raw Fish, page 54.

To tame the fire in Red-Maple Radish, you can scrape out some of the seeds from chili peppers before inserting in daikon.

Mixed Sweet Vegetable Pickles   Photo on pages 37 and 149.

Sanbai-Zuke

Flavorful rehydrated vegetables are bathed in a light syrup similar to a teriyaki glaze.

1 (2-oz.) pkg. shredded dried kelp (konbu)
1 (3-oz.) pkg. dried daikon radish
   (kiriboshi daikon)
1 (2-oz.) pkg. dried-eggplant strips
1-1/2 cups soy sauce
2 cups rice vinegar
2 cups sugar

2 tablespoons mirin
3 (1/8-inch-thick) slices peeled fresh
   gingerroot, smashed
1 tablespoon Dry-Roasted Sesame Seeds,
   page 150
2 or 3 small, dried, whole, hot,
   red peppers

Place kelp, daikon and eggplant in 3 separate medium bowls. Add a large amount of water to each bowl. Swish kelp around in water several times; drain well. Rinse kelp again in fresh water; drain well. Squeeze out all water. On a cutting board, cut kelp 2 or 3 times into shorter lengths; set aside. Soak daikon 15 minutes. Swish around in water several times; drain. Rinse daikon again in fresh water; drain. Squeeze out all water. On cutting board, cut daikon 3 or 4 times into shorter lengths; set aside. Soak eggplant 30 minutes; drain. Rinse again in fresh water; drain. Rinse again or until water is almost clear. Squeeze out all water. On cutting board, chop eggplant into small pieces, about 1/2 inch square; set aside. In a large saucepan, combine soy sauce, vinegar, sugar, mirin and gingerroot. Bring to a boil over medium-high heat. Stir to dissolve sugar. Boil 5 minutes. Add kelp, daikon and eggplant; mix well. Cook 5 minutes. Pour vegetables and liquid into a large colander set in a large bowl. Press out liquid. Set colander of vegetables in another bowl. Pour liquid back into saucepan. Boil over medium-high heat 5 minutes. Add vegetables to hot sauce; mix well. Drain mixture again through colander into a large bowl. Press out liquid. Boil liquid 5 minutes. Add vegetables to hot mixture for the final time. Bring to a boil. Strain vegetables; cool. Stir in Dry-Roasted Sesame Seeds. Pour liquid into a small saucepan. Add hot red peppers. Boil over medium-high heat until reduced to 1 cup. If desired, strain syrup to remove peppers. Cool syrup to room temperature. Pack cooled vegetables into a 1-1/2-quart sterilized jar. Add cooled syrup. Cover and refrigerate. Pickled vegetables can be eaten immediately or refrigerated several months. Recipe can be halved. Makes 1-1/2 quarts.

Mustard-Miso Sauce

Karashi Miso

A tasty sauce for fried tofu or grilled chicken or fish.

2 tablespoons Dry-Roasted Sesame Seeds,
   page 150
1/2 cup Dijon-style mustard
1/2 teaspoon sesame oil
1 teaspoon soy sauce

1 teaspoon mirin
1 teaspoon sugar
1 tablespoon mellow white miso
Hot red-pepper sauce to taste

In a grinding bowl or blender, grind Dry-Roasted Sesame Seeds until powdery. Add remaining ingredients; thoroughly grind together. Makes about 1/2 cup.

Variation

Mustard-Miso Cream Sauce: Fold 1/3 cup whipped cream into finished sauce. Makes 3/4 cup.

Desserts & Confectionery
(Okashi)

Okashi, or confectionery, was introduced into Japan around the eighth century. At this time, rice flour was molded into fruit-shapes, dipped into hot water, dried and then deep-fried. Before then, the word *okashi* referred to fresh fruits, dried fruits and other naturally sweet foods. When sugar became widely available in the 16th century, sweet cakes and steamed buns filled with sweetened red-bean paste became popular. Most traditional sweets were made with sweet rice, rice flour or sweet rice cakes (mochi). Tokyo became known for its tasty substantial style of sweets. A more refined type of confectionery developed around the court of Kyoto.

When tea became popular, tea cakes called *wagashi* were served to balance and enhance the astringent taste of green tea used during the tea ceremony. The famous tea cakes of Kyoto (kyo-gashi) are miniature works of art shaped with features to resemble natural seasonal objects. They are shaped like flowers, birds, leaves and even vegetables. Moist sweets are known as *namagashi* and include Cherry-Blossom Rice Cakes and Red-Bean Jelly with Macadamia Nuts. Dry sweets called *higashi* in-

clude a variety of rice crackers and colorful molded-sugar candies. You can duplicate the candies by molding slightly dampened tinted sugar in small plastic or rubber candy molds and then letting them dry. Select molds shaped like flowers, butterflies, leaves, snowflakes and other seasonal objects. Japanese tea sweets are often representative of seasons of the year. Cherry-Blossom Rice Cakes herald the coming of spring and budding cherry trees.

The Portugese and Dutch introduced many Western-style cakes and candies into Japan including the *castilla,* a rich tender spongecake. The original version has been adapted with different flavorings and cooking methods into one of Japan's most popular sweets. My own variation of the original cake can be tasted and enjoyed in the Steamed Chestnut-Ginger Cakes. The Japanese have a great sweet tooth for Western-style sweets. Hundreds of top-quality sweets made with rich cream and pure butter are available in markets, bakeries and French-style pastry shops throughout the country. The success of these shops is partly because home ovens are not common in Japan. In traditional Japanese-fashion, bakery sweets are served between meals with tea, rather than as a sweet course at the end of a meal. Western-style snacks and traditional Japanese sweets are popular at *osanji,* the "honorable three o'clock afternoon snack break." Fresh seasonal fruits are generally served after a meal, if anything at all. Plump grapes, mandarin oranges (mikan), crisp pear-apples (nashi), juicy apples, melons, plump strawberries and persimmons are among the most popular seasonal offerings. Expensive tropical fruits, such as papaya, mango and bananas, are regularly shipped in.

Although green tea is the traditional beverage with sweets, soft drinks are quite popular and are grouped into three categories; carbonated soft drinks, fruit-juice drinks and fermented-soybean-milk and fermented-regular-milk drinks. A popular lemon drink called *Ramune* was one of the original bottled drinks in Japan. It comes in an amusing glass soft-drink bottle which has a glass ball trapped inside the neck. A traditional tea-house beverage is Sweet Rice Saké which I first tasted at a 300-year-old Kyoto tea house. Low in alcoholic content, its rich creamy taste is a favorite with children and adults. Young girls delight in serving it with colorful rice crackers during the Peach Fête, or Girls' Day Doll Festival. It can be chilled in the summertime for a refreshing drink.

Strawberries in Snow   Photo on page 107.

Awayuki-kan

A spectacular molded gelatin dessert which reminds us of the wintertime strawberries and snow in Japan.

2 (1/4-oz.) envelopes unflavored gelatin	Pinch of salt
1/2 cup cool water	3 large egg whites, room temperature
2 cups water	1 tablespoon sugar
1-1/4 cups sugar	2-1/2 cups fresh strawberries
1/4 cup fresh lemon juice	Custard Sauce, see below

Custard Sauce:

3 egg yolks	Pinch of salt
1-1/2 cups milk	1 teaspoon potato starch or cornstarch
3 tablespoons sugar	1/2 teaspoon vanilla extract

Lightly oil a 5- to 6-cup ring mold. In a small bowl, soften gelatin in 1/2 cup water. In a medium saucepan, heat 2 cups water and 1-1/4 cups sugar over medium heat. Stir in softened gelatin. When sugar and gelatin are dissolved, remove pan from heat. Stir in lemon juice and salt. Pour gelatin mixture into a medium bowl set in a larger bowl of water with ice cubes. Refrigerate gelatin mixture until slightly thickened; stir occasionally. When gelatin begins to thicken, remove bowl from iced water. In a medium bowl, beat egg whites until foamy. Sprinkle in 1 tablespoon sugar; continue beating until egg whites are stiff but not dry. Slowly pour thickened gelatin mixture into beaten egg whites, beating constantly on low speed. Beat several seconds or until gelatin and egg-white mixture are completely combined. Place 8 small strawberries around bottom of oiled mold, if desired. Slowly pour gelatin mixture into mold; refrigerate until set. Prepare Custard Sauce. To unmold dessert, dip bottom of mold quickly in and out of warm water once or twice. Place serving dish upside-down on top of mold. Invert dish and mold; gelatin mold should fall out. Fill center with remaining strawberries. Serve with Custard Sauce. Makes 6 to 8 servings.

Custard Sauce:

Place egg yolks in top of a double boiler. Beat with a small whisk. Whisk in milk, sugar, salt and potato starch or cornstarch. Place over simmering water. Do not allow water to touch bottom of container holding egg-yolk mixture. Cook, stirring constantly, until mixture thickens slightly and coats a spoon. Stir in vanilla. Cool to room temperature. Cover and refrigerate until serving time. Makes about 1-3/4 cups.

Cherry-Blossom Rice Cake, page 160.

Cherry-Blossom Rice Cakes   Photo on page 159.

Sakura Mochi

This springtime confection is an example of pure Japanese artistry.

3 drops red food coloring
1-1/4 cups sweet glutinous rice (mochi gome),
   well-rinsed, soaked, drained,
   page 145, with changes noted below
3 tablespoons water
1/2 teaspoon almond extract

1/8 teaspoon salt
3 tablespoons sugar
3/4 cup Sweetened Red-Bean Paste,
   page 166, or canned sweetened
   red-bean paste
8 Marzipan Cherry Leaves, see below.

Marzipan Cherry Leaves:
2 (7-oz.) rolls marzipan,
   broken in small pieces
Tiny amount of leaf-green paste food
   coloring or 2 to 3 drops green
   food coloring

1/4 teaspoon almond extract
About 1 tablespoon powdered sugar,
   if necessary

Add food coloring to soaking water for rice. Add only 3 tablespoons water to rice for steaming. When cooked, rice should be tender yet firm enough to withstand a second steaming. Stir almond extract, salt and sugar into cooked rice. Pound rice with a grinding stick (surikogi), a cleaver handle or the end of a rolling pin 30 to 45 seconds. Rice will begin to stick together. Do not overpound or rice will become a glutinous mass with no texture. Moisten your hands with water each time you touch rice mixture. Divide rice into 8 equal portions. Flatten 1 portion. Place 1 heaping tablespoon bean paste in center. Mold rice around bean paste into an oval shape. Pinch opening closed. Continue flattening and filling remaining portions of rice mixture. Place filled rice cakes, 1/2 inch apart, in a shallow heatproof pan. In a wok or deep pot, bring about 4 cups water to a boil over medium-high heat. Place pan of rice cakes on a steamer tray; cover tray. Place over boiling water. Reduce heat to medium-high; steam 10 to 12 minutes or until slightly puffy. Cool completely. Prepare Marzipan Cherry Leaves. Fold 1 leaf around each steamed rice cake with stem and veins on the outside. Serve with hot green tea. Texture of rice cake is best when served the same day. Store in a cool place but not the refrigerator. Makes 8 servings.

Marzipan Cherry Leaves:
Place marzipan pieces in a small bowl. Add food coloring and almond extract. Knead until coloring and extract are blended in. If marzipan is sticky, knead in 2 to 3 teaspoons powdered sugar. Divide marzipan in 1/2. On a sheet of foil, roll out 1/2 of colored marzipan 1/8 inch thick. On a piece of cardboard, draw an oval leaf-shaped pattern with a stem. Pattern should measure 5-1/2 inches long and 3 inches wide. Cut out pattern. Cover with foil. Lay pattern on marzipan sheet. Cut out a leaf using a 1-1/2-inch-wide fluted pastry-cutting wheel. Ridged edge of pastry wheel will cut a zig-zag pattern similar to edge of a cherry leaf. With a blunt-edged knife, mark a stem the length of leaf. Or, roll a tiny rope of marzipan for stem. Moisten 1 side and press it down length of leaf. Press vein marks on leaf, angling them on each side of stem. Make 3 more leaves from sheet of marzipan. Roll out remaining marzipan. Make 4 more leaves. Makes 8 leaves.

Variations
If you can obtain salted, preserved, Japanese cherry leaves, rinse them in hot water to remove excess salt. A slight saltiness will linger and provide an excellent contrast to the sweet rice and bean paste. Wrap each filled unsteamed rice cake in a cherry leaf. Steam wrapped rice cakes as directed above. Serve immediately or store in an airtight container at room temperature. Delicious cherry leaf can be eaten with the rice-cake filling.

How to Make Cherry-Blossom Rice Cakes

1/Flatten 1 portion rice. Place 1 heaping tablespoon bean paste in center. Mold rice around bean paste into an oval shape. Pinch opening closed. Steam filled rice cakes 10 to 12 minutes.

2/Roll out marzipan 1/8 inch thick. Use leaf pattern and a fluted pastry-cutting wheel to cut out marzipan leaves. Roll a tiny rope of marzipan for stem. Mark veins with a blunt-edged knife.

Steamed Chestnut-Ginger Spongecakes

Kuri Castilla

For tasty variations, substitute minced dried persimmons, dates or apricots for ginger.

1 (7-oz.) jar sweet chestnuts in syrup, drained	1 teaspoon baking powder
1/2 cup unsalted butter, room temperature	1/3 teaspoon salt
1/2 cup packed light-brown sugar	1 teaspoon vanilla extract
2 large eggs, separated	3 tablespoons minced crystallized ginger
1/2 cup cake flour	4 sweet chestnuts in syrup, if desired, halved

Grease 7 or 8 fluted (1/2-cup) tartlet pans, brioche pans or miniature cake pans. In a blender or food processor fitted with a steel blade, process chestnuts until smooth. You will have about 1/3 cup paste. In a large bowl, blend butter, sugar, egg yolks and chestnut paste until smooth. In a small bowl, combine flour, baking powder and salt. Stir into chestnut mixture with vanilla. In a wok or deep pot, bring about 4 cups water to a boil. In a small bowl, beat egg whites until stiff but not dry; fold into chestnut mixture. Stir in ginger. Spoon 1/4 cup batter into each greased pan. Place in a heatproof dish on a steamer tray; cover. Place over boiling water. Reduce heat to medium; steam 20 minutes or until a wooden pick inserted in center comes out clean. Turn off heat and remove cakes. Cool 5 minutes. Gently loosen cakes from edges of pans. Turn out on a tray. Decorate each cake top with a sweet-chestnut half, if desired. Makes 7 or 8 cakes.

Variation

Batter can be steamed in a round or square 8-inch pan. Steam 20 minutes or until cake tests done.

Sweet Peanut Rice Cakes

Rakkasei No Mochi

If you find plain rice cakes too bland, try my peanut-flavored version and the variations noted below.

1 cup sweet glutinous-rice flour (mochiko)
1/4 teaspoon salt
1/4 cup packed light-brown sugar
1/3 cup cocktail peanuts
1/2 cup water

Potato starch or cornstarch
Orange-blossom honey or unsulfered
  molasses
1/2 cup roasted-soybean powder (kinako),
  if desired

In a medium bowl, stir together rice flour, salt and brown sugar. In a blender or food processor fitted with a steel blade, grind peanuts until they form a paste. Add water; process until blended, scraping sides of container once or twice. Pour peanut mixture into rice-flour mixture. Stir to form a soft dough. Lightly knead dough about 30 seconds. In a wok or deep pot, bring about 4 cups water to a boil. Spread a piece of dampened unbleached muslin or several layers of cheese-cloth over a steamer tray. Spread dough evenly over dampened cloth, about 1/2 inch thick. Cover tray; place over boiling water. Steam 20 minutes. Remove steamer tray from pan. Lift out cloth with dough. Pull cloth away from dough letting dough fall onto a flat surface dusted with potato starch or cornstarch. Cool dough 1 to 2 minutes. While still hot, knead 1 minute or until smooth and shiny. Roll glutinous dough into an 8-inch-long sausage-shaped roll. Cut into 8 equal pieces. Dust with potato starch or cornstarch as needed to prevent sticking. Form tops of pieces into smooth round shapes. They will flatten on the bottom when placed on a flat surface. Drizzle rice cakes with honey or molasses until coated. Roll in roasted-soybean powder, if desired. Serve the same day while fresh. Place 1 piece of rice cake on each small serving plate. Serve with hot green tea. Makes 8 rice cakes.

Variations

Coconut Rice Cakes: Omit cocktail peanuts. Substitute 1/2 cup rich coconut milk for 1/2 cup water. Substitute granulated sugar for light-brown sugar. Prepare rice cakes as directed above. Roll warm rice cakes in 1 cup shredded coconut, if desired.
Stuffed Rice Cakes: Prepare Peanut- or Coconut-Rice-Cake dough as directed above. Divide into 8 equal pieces; flatten into circles. In center of each circle, place 1 tablespoon Sesame-Peanut Sugar, below. Shape dough around filling into balls. Increase steaming time to 25 minutes. Cool. Coat rice cakes with honey or molasses. Roll in roasted-soybean powder.

Sesame-Peanut Sugar

Goma Rakkasei Zato

Stir some into Sweet Rice Saké, opposite, or use as a filling for Stuffed Rice Cakes, above.

1/3 cup cocktail peanuts, toasted,
  finely chopped
2 tablespoons Dry-Roasted Sesame Seeds,
  page 150

1 tablespoon shredded coconut, chopped
1 tablespoon sugar

In a small bowl, combine all ingredients. Makes about 1/2 cup.

Sweet Rice Saké

Amazaké

This tea-house specialty is delicious sipped as tea, or can be used as a sweetener in place of honey.

Amazaké Base, see below
About 1 cup water
1/8 teaspoon salt

1 teaspoon finely grated fresh gingerroot
1/4 cup saké or brandy, if desired

Amazaké Base:
1/2 cup short-grain rice
1-1/2 cups water

1 cup granular rice koji starter

Prepare Amazaké Base. In a medium saucepan, stir Amazaké Base and water over medium-high heat. Amount of water can be varied to adjust consistency to personal taste. Add salt and gingerroot. When mixture is hot, stir in saké or brandy, if desired. Serve hot in small teacups. Makes 8 to 10 servings.

Amazaké Base:
Place rice in a small bowl. Wash thoroughly in cool water, rubbing grains gently between your hands. Pour off milky water; add fresh water. Continue washing rice in this manner until rice water is clear. Drain rice. Place rice and 1-1/2 cups water in a small saucepan over high heat. When water boils, immediately reduce heat to lowest setting. Cover with a tight-fitting lid. Cook rice slowly 1 hour, stirring once or twice to prevent burning. Long slow cooking of the rice is essential to break down grains in preparation for fermentation. When rice is soft, cool to 140F (60C). Sterilize a 1-quart wide-mouth jar or heatproof glass bowl in boiling water. Add cooked rice; stir in rice koji. Cover tightly with a lid or plastic wrap. Place in an oven with temperature setting at warm or 140F (60C). Do not allow temperature to rise above 150F (65C). It is difficult to maintain this temperature but turning the oven on and off several times may help. Incubate mixture 10 to 12 hours; do not disturb. After this time Amazaké Base will have a rich distinctive taste and will be very sweet. Consistency will be like rice porridge or soft oatmeal. After incubation period, boil Amazaké Base in a medium saucepan 1 minute; cool. Pour into an airtight container. Refrigerate until needed to prepare Sweet Rice Saké. Base can be stored in refrigerator several days. Makes 2 cups.

Variations

Strawberry Amazaké: Stir 1/2 cup chopped fresh strawberries into Sweet Rice Saké.
Almond Amazaké: Substitute almond-flavored liqueur for saké. Stir 1/4 cup finely chopped toasted almonds into Sweet Rice Saké.
Mandarin-Orange Amazaké: Substitute orange-flavored liqueur for saké. Stir 1/2 cup chopped fresh or canned, drained, mandarin-orange segments into Sweet Rice Saké.

For a smooth-textured beverage, puree Amazaké Base in a blender or food processor fitted with a steel blade.

Rose Snow with Custard Sauce

Bara Awayuki-kan

This delicate, rose-flavored dessert will enchant your guests.

Custard Sauce, page 158	**1/8 teaspoon salt**
1 (0.25-oz.) stick white agar-agar (kanten)	**1/4 teaspoon rose or almond extract**
1-1/2 cups water	**2 or 3 drops red food coloring**
1/2 cup sugar	**1 large egg white, room temperature**
1 cup milk	**1 tablespoon sugar**

Prepare Custard Sauce. Tear agar-agar into 4 pieces. Place agar-agar and water in a small saucepan. Press agar-agar pieces into water several seconds to soften. Shred pieces with your fingers. Soak 30 minutes. Simmer agar-agar and water over very low heat until dissolved, about 10 minutes. Stir once or twice while simmering. When dissolved, stir in 1/2 cup sugar, milk and salt; simmer 2 minutes. Remove from heat. Strain hot mixture into a medium bowl through a fine strainer. Scrape agar-agar mixture from bottom of strainer into bowl. Stir in rose or almond extract and food coloring. Cool mixture to 110F (45C) which is just before it begins to set. While mixture is cooling, beat egg white in a medium bowl until foamy. Sprinkle in 1 tablespoon sugar; continue beating egg white until stiff but not dry. Pour warm agar-agar mixture slowly into beaten egg-white mixture. Beat constantly on low speed. When combined, rinse a 6-1/2" x 4-1/2" nagashi-bako; 8-inch-square pan; round, 8-inch pan; or 3-cup mold with cold water. Tap out excess liquid. *Quickly* pour mixture into prepared pan. Mixture will set almost instantly at room temperature or can be refrigerated until serving time. When set, use large cutters to cut mixture into flower or heart shapes. Or, mixture can also be cut into squares. Spoon Custard Sauce into each serving dish. Set a flower, heart or square on top of sauce in each dish. Makes 6 to 9 servings.

Variations
Crème de Menthe Snow: Substitute 2 or 3 drops crème de menthe extract and 1 or 2 drops green food coloring for rose or almond extract and red food coloring.
Plum-Wine Snow: Substitute 1 cup plum wine for milk. Substitute 1/2 teaspoon vanilla extract for rose or almond extract.

Rose Snow can be poured into a 3-cup heart-shaped mold for a Valentine's Day surprise dessert.

Note: If agar-agar mixture is hotter than 110F (45C) when it is added to egg-white mixture, dessert will separate into 2 layers when set. This can make an attractive variation.

Sesame Sugar

Goma Zato

For a sweet touch, sprinkle rice balls with Sesame Sugar.

1/4 cup black or white Dry-Roasted Sesame Seeds, page 150	**1 tablespoon sugar**

Prepare Dry-Roasted Sesame Seeds. Place warm seeds in a grinding bowl or mortar with sugar. Using a pestle or equivalent, lightly crush them together. Seeds should be lightly bruised, but not completely crushed. Cool; store in a small jar. Makes about 1/3 cup.

Rose Snow with Custard Sauce

Sweetened Red-Bean Paste

Koshi An

Homemade bean paste traditionally requires a lot of effort; try this simplified version.

12 oz. dried small red beans (azuke),
  well-rinsed
Water
About 1/4 cup mirin

1-1/2 cups sugar
1/8 cup millet jelly (mizu-ame) or
  light corn syrup, if desired
1/4 teaspoon salt

Place beans in a medium bowl; add plenty of water to cover. Soak overnight; drain well. In a large saucepan, combine soaked beans and 1 quart fresh water. Bring to a boil; drain beans. Pour another quart fresh water over beans. Bring to a boil; drain beans. Add 2 quarts fresh water to beans. Bring to a boil. Reduce heat to medium-low; simmer beans, uncovered, 3 to 4 hours. As water evaporates during cooking, add more as needed. Continue cooking beans until tender and water is almost evaporated. Watch beans carefully to prevent burning. In a blender or food processor fitted with a steel blade, process beans until smooth, adding up to 1/4 cup mirin, if necessary, to help beans become smooth. Scrape sides of container 2 or 3 times while processing. Scrape bean mixture into a medium saucepan; set over low heat. Add 1/2 cup sugar. Stir constantly with a wooden rice paddle or spatula, using a back and forth motion. When sugar is blended, add remaining 1/2 cup sugar; stir in. Using a large rubber spatula, press paste through a fine strainer into a medium bowl. Wipe spatula often; scrape paste from bottom of strainer into bowl. Discard bean skins left in strainer. Return paste to saucepan over low heat. Add 1/4 cup sugar, stirring back and forth. When blended, stir in remaining 1/4 cup sugar. Stir in millet jelly or light corn syrup for gloss, if desired. Cook mixture over very low heat 20 to 30 minutes, stirring often. To help prevent burning, you can shield pan from direct heat by using a metal heat diffuser. Stir in salt. Paste should be thick and fudgy. Cool to room temperature; refrigerate in an airtight container or freeze in small batches several months. Paste will thicken slightly as it chills. Makes about 3 cups.

Variation

Chunky Sweetened Red-Bean Paste (Tsubushi An): Cook beans as directed above until tender and dry. Do not puree. Omit mirin. Stir in sugar, syrup or jelly, and salt. Cook over low heat up to 30 minutes, stirring constantly with a wooden rice paddle or spatula in a back and forth motion. Beans will break down and thicken naturally. A large amount of beans should be left whole for texture. Cool; refrigerate in an airtight container.

Almond Pine Cones   Photo on page 121.

Matsukasa Aamondo

Decorate each pine cone with a sprig or two of real pine needles on the serving plates.

2 cups Sweetened Red-Bean Paste, above,
  or canned sweetened red-bean paste,
  chilled, or 2 (7-oz.) pkgs. marzipan

Thinly sliced blanched or
  unblanched almonds, lightly toasted

Form chilled bean paste or marzipan into 1-1/2-inch oval shapes using about 1 tablespoon for each oval. Ovals should be slightly pointed at 1 end and rounded at the opposite end. Press pointed ends of almond slices into bean-paste or marzipan ovals slightly at an angle; cover completely. Store at room temperature. Serve with tea or as a sweet snack. Makes 14 to 16 pine cones.

How to Make Sweet-Bean-Paste-Filled Pancakes

1/Form 1 tablespoon bean paste into a ball. Place on center of a warm pancake. Top with another pancake, attractive-side up.

2/Gently press centers and edges of pancakes together.

Sweet-Bean-Paste-Filled Pancakes

Dora-yaki

In Tokyo, I enjoyed this sweet snack right from the push carts of the street vendors.

1 cup all-purpose flour
1/4 cup sugar
1/2 teaspoon baking soda
1/2 teaspoon baking powder
2 large eggs

1 teaspoon honey
1 teaspoon soy sauce
1/2 cup plus 1 tablespoon water
3/4 cup Sweetened Red-Bean Paste, opposite,
    or canned sweetened red-bean paste

Stir flour in container. Lightly spoon flour into a 1-cup measure. Level top with a knife. Sift flour, sugar, baking soda and baking powder into a medium bowl. In a small bowl, blend eggs, honey, soy sauce and water. Stir egg mixture into flour mixture; blend just until smooth. Mixture should be thick, but thin enough to pour from a spoon. Heat a griddle or flat skillet over medium-high heat. Wipe griddle once with a lightly oiled paper towel. Pour 1 generous measuring tablespoon batter in a steady stream on griddle or skillet. Pancake should spread to 3 inches in diameter. If not, add water to batter, 1 teaspoon at a time, to thin batter to correct consistency. Cook pancake 1 minute or until bubbles form on top. With a spatula, turn pancake over. Cooked side of pancake should be medium-brown all over. Cook second side 30 seconds or until set. Repeat with remaining batter. To fill pancakes, lay 1/2 of total number of warm pancakes on a flat surface, attractive-sides down. Form 1 tablespoon bean paste into a ball. Place on center of a pancake. Top with another pancake, attractive-side up. Gently press center and edges together. Repeat with remaining bean paste and warm pancakes. If bean paste is too soft to form into a ball, spread 1 tablespoon evenly over bottom pancake. Makes 22 pancakes, 11 when filled.

Kiwifruit-Tofu Ice Cream

Kiwi Dofu Aisu Kurimu

Kiwifruit and tofu combine to create a nutritious ice cream loaded with flavor.

1 lb. kiwifruit, peeled, (about 5 kiwifruit)
1 (8- to 10-oz.) pkg. silken or
   regular Japanese-style tofu,
   rinsed, patted dry
1/2 cup whipping cream
1-1/2 to 2 cups corn syrup

1/2 cup fresh orange juice
1/8 teaspoon salt
1/2 teaspoon vanilla extract
1/4 teaspoon almond extract
1 tablespoon fresh lemon juice
3 or 4 drops green food coloring

Cut kiwifruit into small cubes. Place in a blender or food processor fitted with a steel blade; process until smooth. Add tofu; process until blended. Add whipping cream, corn syrup, orange juice, salt, vanilla, almond extract and lemon juice; process until blended. Add coloring; process again. Depending on size of blender or food processor, mixture may have to be processed in 2 batches. Refrigerate mixture until chilled. Freeze in an ice-cream freezer according to manufacturer's directions or follow directions, opposite. When frozen, serve immediately or store canister of ice cream in the freezer. To store, remove dasher from canister. Put lid back into place. Cover lid with foil. If necessary, scoop ice cream from canister and pack into airtight containers for freezing. Makes about 2 quarts.

Strawberry-Tofu Sherbet

Ichigo Dofu No Sha-be-to

For a richer version, try Strawberry-Tofu Ice Cream, below.

2 cups fresh strawberries, hulled
1 (14- to 16-oz.) pkg. silken or
   regular Japanese-style tofu,
   rinsed, patted dry
1 cup corn syrup

1/2 cup fresh orange juice
2 tablespoons fresh lemon juice
1/8 teaspoon salt
1 teaspoon vanilla extract
1 teaspoon freshly grated orange peel

Puree strawberries and tofu in a blender or food processor fitted with a steel blade. Add remaining ingredients; process until blended. Depending on size of blender or food processor, mixture may have to be processed in 2 batches. Refrigerate mixture until chilled. Freeze in an ice-cream freezer according to manufacturer's directions or follow directions, opposite. When frozen, serve immediately or store canister of sherbet in the freezer. To store, remove dasher from canister. Put lid back into place. Cover lid with foil. If necessary, scoop sherbet from canister and pack into airtight containers for freezing. Makes about 1-1/2 quarts.

Variation
Strawberry-Tofu Ice Cream: In a small bowl, soften 1 (1/4-ounce) envelope unflavored gelatin in orange juice. Set bowl in a large saucepan of hot water over low heat. Heat gelatin mixture until dissolved; cool. Add to strawberries and tofu in blender or food processor. Add remaining ingredients and 1/2 cup whipping cream; process until blended. Continue as directed above. Makes about 1-1/2 quarts.

Red-Bean Jelly with Macadamia Nuts   Photo on page 107.

Macadamia Yokan

Lily Hataye's easy modern version of a traditional Japanese sweet.

2 (0.25-oz.) sticks red agar-agar (kanten)
1-1/2 cups water
1 cup sugar
2 cups Sweetened Red-Bean Paste,
   page 166, or 1 (18-oz.) can sweetened
   red-bean paste

1 cup macadamia nuts, chopped
1/4 teaspoon salt
1 teaspoon amaretto liqueur or
   1/4 teaspoon almond extract

Tear each agar-agar stick into 4 pieces. Place agar-agar and water in a medium saucepan. Press agar-agar pieces into water several seconds to soften. Shred pieces with your fingers. Soak 30 minutes. Simmer agar-agar and water over very low heat until dissolved, about 10 minutes. Stir once or twice while simmering. Stir in sugar. Cook until mixture comes to a boil. Add bean paste. Stir mixture until blended. Cook over very low heat 30 minutes or until mixture is thick and fudgy, stirring frequently to prevent burning. When thick, remove mixture from heat. Stir in nuts, salt, amaretto or almond extract. Rinse a 6-1/2'' x 4-1/2'' nagashi-bako; 8-inch-square pan; or round, 8-inch pan with cold water. Tap out excess liquid. *Quickly* pour nut mixture into prepared pan. Jelly will set almost instantly at room temperature or can be refrigerated until serving time. To serve, cut into rectangles or other shapes. Makes 12 servings.

Variations

Red-Bean Jelly with Walnuts: Substitute 1 cup chopped walnuts for macadamia nuts.
Red-Bean Jelly with Peanuts: Substitute 1 cup chopped cocktail peanuts for macadamia nuts.
Red-Bean Jelly with Almonds: Substitute 1 cup chopped almonds for macadamia nuts.

Making Ice Cream in the Freezer

If you do not have an ice-cream maker, ice cream and sherbet can be frozen successfully in metal pans or in empty ice-cube trays in the freezer. Set the freezer setting to the lowest temperature. Freeze prepared mixture until slushy. Scrape it away from the sides of the pan. Stir well to break up ice crystals. Freeze again until firm. Turn into a large bowl. Beat with an electric mixer 1 minute to incorporate air to lighten the mixture. Or, beat in a food processor fitted with a steel blade. Refreeze until firm. Serve as soon as possible. Ice crystals continue to form quickly, causing the texture of the frozen dessert to deteriorate.

Plum-Wine Jelly   Photo on page 107.

Umeshu Kanten

Fresh poached plums and Japanese plum wine are gelled into a refreshing summertime confection.

1 cup water	**Pinch of salt**
1 (0.25-oz.) stick white agar-agar (kanten)	**2 to 3 dashes ground cinnamon**
1/2 cup water	**1/2 cup Japanese plum wine**
1/2 cup sugar	**1/4 cup sugar**
1 lb. ripe red or purple plums,	
** pitted, quartered**	

Pour 1 cup water into a small saucepan. Tear agar-agar into 4 pieces. Press into water several seconds to soften. Shred agar-agar with your fingers. Soak 30 minutes. In a medium saucepan, bring 1/2 cup water and 1/2 cup sugar to a boil over medium-high heat. Stir to dissolve sugar. Add plum pieces; reduce heat to low. Cover pan; cook 10 to 12 minutes. Strain plum syrup into a medium bowl. Place plum pulp in a blender or food processor fitted with a steel blade; process until smooth. Add puree to bowl with plum syrup. Stir in salt, cinnamon and plum wine. Simmer agar-agar and water over very low heat until dissolved, about 10 minutes. Stir once or twice while simmering. Stir in 1/4 cup sugar; simmer 2 minutes. Remove from heat. Using a fine strainer, strain hot mixture into plum mixture. Scrape agar-agar mixture from bottom of strainer into bowl. Quickly stir mixture. Rinse an 8-inch-square or round, 8-inch pan with water; tap out excess liquid. *Quickly* pour plum mixture into prepared pan. Mixture will set almost instantly at room temperature or can be refrigerated until serving time. When set, cut into plum-blossom shapes using Japanese, 1-1/2-inch, metal, flower-shaped cutters. Or, cut into 32 (2'' x 1'') rectangular pieces. Allow 2 pieces per serving. Makes 10 to 16 servings.

Variation

Plum-Sauce Dip: Poach and puree plums as directed above. Combine with reserved plum syrup, salt, cinnamon and 1/4 cup plum wine. Refrigerate until chilled. Serve as a dipping sauce. Makes about 2 cups.

Agar-Agar

   Brittle agar-agar sticks (kanten) are sold in pairs. The color may be white, red or green. Package weights can vary an ounce or two, depending on the manufacturer. Recipes in this book were tested with packages weighing 0.5 ounces or 14 grams, each stick weighing 0.25 ounces or 7 grams. If you are using packages of less weight (quite commonly 0.4 ounces or 11 grams), adjust the amount of agar-agar in the recipe. For the 0.4-ounce package, you should use 1 stick and 2-1/4 inches of another for each package called for.

   Melted agar-agar must be blended into foods while it is still hot or warm. It gels at around 105-110F (40-45C), without refrigeration. Tiny bits of congealed agar-agar form quickly throughout the food being gelled. If the food is poured from pan to pan or stirred during this time, the gelling process will be interrupted. The consistency of the molded food will not be smooth and it will not set properly. Foods stiffened with agar-agar do not melt easily and are not rubbery like those made with regular gelatin.

   One-half stick of agar-agar is equal to about 1 envelope regular gelatin, however, substitutions are not recommended because gelatin will give a rubbery result.

How to Make Plum-Wine Jelly

1/Pour 1 cup water into a small saucepan. Tear agar-agar stick into 4 pieces. Press into water several seconds to soften. Shred agar-agar with your fingers. Soak 30 minutes.

2/To serve, cut jelly into plum-blossom shapes using 1-1/2-inch, metal, flower-shaped cutters.

Pineapple-Yam Jelly   Photo on page 107.

Imo Yokan

A soft jelly with fresh pineapple; impossible with gelatin because enzymes in pineapple prevent setting.

1 cup fresh orange juice
1 (0.25-oz.) stick white agar-agar (kanten)
1-1/2 lbs. yams or sweet potatoes,
   peeled, cubed

1 cup chopped fresh pineapple, drained
1/2 teaspoon vanilla extract
1/2 cup sugar
1/8 teaspoon salt

Pour orange juice into a small saucepan. Tear agar-agar into 4 pieces. Press into orange juice several seconds to soften. Shred pieces with your fingers. Soak 30 minutes. Place yams or sweet potatoes in a medium saucepan; add water to cover. Cook over medium-high heat until tender; drain well. Puree yams or sweet potatoes in a blender or food processor fitted with a steel blade. Add pineapple and vanilla; blend quickly to combine ingredients; set aside. Simmer agar-agar and orange juice over very low heat until dissolved, about 10 minutes. Stir once or twice while simmering. When agar-agar is dissolved, add sugar and salt; simmer 2 minutes. Remove from heat. Strain hot mixture into a medium bowl through a fine strainer. Scrape agar-agar mixture from bottom of strainer into bowl. Quickly stir in pineapple mixture. Rinse a 6-1/2'' x 4-1/2'' nagashi-bako; 8-inch-square pan; or round, 8-inch pan with cold water. Tap out excess liquid. *Quickly* pour mixture into prepared pan. Jelly will set almost instantly at room temperature or can be refrigerated until serving time. To serve, cut into rectangles or other shapes. Makes 9 to 12 servings.

Index

Index

Mail-Order Sources

Japanese Foods & Equipment

Here are the addresses of some companies which specialize in Japanese foods and/or cooking equipment. Write or telephone to inquire about specific products.

Anzen Hardware & Supply
220 East 1st Street
Los Angeles, CA 90012

Anzen Japanese Foods & Imports
736 North East Union Avenue
Portland, OR 97232

Arirang House
7918 Georgia Avenue
Silver Springs, MD 20910

Asia Food Market
2000 Judah Street
San Francisco, CA 94122

Asia Market
1241 Colonial Market
Orlando, FL 32803

Asian Supermarket
2581 Piedmont Road
Atlanta, GA 30324

Erewhon
236 Washington Street
Brookline, MA 02146
1-800-222-8028
Variety of Japanese foods and cooking equipment, koji rice starter.

Far East Trading Company
2837 North Western Avenue
Chicago, IL 60618

GEM Cultures
30301 Sherwood Road
Fort Bragg, CA 95437
Calcium sulfate and nigari used in tofu making.

Ichi Corporation
7404 Trade Street
San Diego, CA 92121
(619) 695-9234
Ichi grill, page 75.

Import Shop
1775 Fort Henry Drive
Kingsport, TN 37664

International House of Foods
75 West Island Avenue
Minneapolis, MN 55401

Iwatani & Co. (U.S.A.), Inc.
60 East 42nd Street, Suite 1740
New York, NY 10165
Casset Feu grill, burner unit and gas canisters, pages 15 and 79.

Japan Food Corporation
445 Kaufman Court
San Francisco, CA 94080
(415) 873 8400
Write to the Consumer Service Supervisor for a list of supermarkets which carry Asian foods.

Joyce Chen Products
411 Waverley Oaks Road
Waltham, MA 02154
(617) 894-9020
Sushi tool kit and sushi food kit.

Katagiri Company
224 East 59th Street
New York, NY 10022

H.A. Mack, Inc.
P.O. Box 410
Boston, MA 02117
(617) 542-8255
Rice molds.

Maid of Scandinavia
3244 Raleigh Avenue
Minneapolis, MN 55416
Write for a catalog.

Mountain Ark Trading Co.
120 South East Street
Fayetteville, AR 72701
1-800-643-8909
Variety of Japanese foods and cooking equipment.

Mutual Trading Co. Inc.
P.O. Box 2919
Terminal Annex
Los Angeles, CA 90051
(213) 626-9458
Saladacco cutting box.

Pacific Mercantile Grocery
1925 Lawrence Street
Denver, CO 80202

Rafu Bussan Inc.
326 East 2nd Street
Los Angeles, CA 90012

Taylor's Herb Gardens Inc.
1535 Lone Oak Road
Vista, CA 92083
(619) 727-3485

The Learning Tree
P.O. Box 1145
Sebastopol, CA 95472
Tofu-making kit.

The Soyfoods Center
P.O. Box 234
Lafayette, CA 94549
(415) 283-2991 (attn. William Shurtleff)
Research material on tofu and miso, tofu-pressing kits available.

The Wok Shop
804 Grant Street
San Francisco, CA 94108
(415) 989-3797
Traditional Japanese rice molds, woks, steamers, sushi-making equipment.

Tokyo Foods
1005 Pierce Street
Sioux City, IA 51105

Wok Talk
420 Lexington Avenue, Suite 2626
New York, NY 10170

Yoshinoya
36 Prospect Street
Cambridge, MA 02139

Metric Chart

Comparison to Metric Measure

When You Know	Symbol	Multiply By	To Find	Symbol
teaspoons	tsp	5.0	milliliters	ml
tablespoons	tbsp	15.0	milliliters	ml
fluid ounces	fl. oz.	30.0	milliliters	ml
cups	c	0.24	liters	l
pints	pt.	0.47	liters	l
quarts	qt.	0.95	liters	l
ounces	oz.	28.0	grams	g
pounds	lb.	0.45	kilograms	kg
Fahrenheit	F	5/9 (after subtracting 32)	Celsius	C

Liquid Measure to Milliliters

1/4 teaspoon	=	1.25 milliliters
1/2 teaspoon	=	2.5 milliliters
3/4 teaspoon	=	3.75 milliliters
1 teaspoon	=	5.0 milliliters
1-1/4 teaspoons	=	6.25 milliliters
1-1/2 teaspoons	=	7.5 milliliters
1-3/4 teaspoons	=	8.75 milliliters
2 teaspoons	=	10.0 milliliters
1 tablespoon	=	15.0 milliliters
2 tablespoons	=	30.0 milliliters

Liquid Measure to Liters

1/4 cup	=	0.06 liters
1/2 cup	=	0.12 liters
3/4 cup	=	0.18 liters
1 cup	=	0.24 liters
1-1/4 cups	=	0.3 liters
1-1/2 cups	=	0.36 liters
2 cups	=	0.48 liters
2-1/2 cups	=	0.6 liters
3 cups	=	0.72 liters
3-1/2 cups	=	0.84 liters
4 cups	=	0.96 liters
4-1/2 cups	=	1.08 liters
5 cups	=	1.2 liters
5-1/2 cups	=	1.32 liters